The
Guru Papers

MASKS OF AUTHORITARIAN POWER

Joel Kramer
and
Diana Alstad

Frog, Ltd.
Berkeley, California

Other books by Joel Kramer:
The Passionate Mind

The Guru Papers: Masks of Authoritarian Power

Copyright © 1993 by Joel Kramer and Diana Alstad. All rights reserved. No portion of this book, except for brief review, may be reproduced in any form without written permission of the publisher. For information contact Frog, Ltd. c/o North Atlantic Books.

Published by
Frog, Ltd.

Frog, Ltd. books are distributed by
North Atlantic Books
P.O. Box 12327
Berkeley, California 94701

Cover and book design by Paula Morrison
Typeset by Catherine Campaigne

Printed in the United States of America by Malloy Lithographing

Library of Congress Cataloging-in-Publication Data

Kramer, Joel, 1937–
    The guru papers : masks of authoritarian power / Joel Kramer and Diana Alstad.
      p. cm.
    Includes bibliographical references and index.
    ISBN 1–883319–00–5
    1. Authoritarianism.   2. Control (Psychology)
3. Authoritarianism—Religious aspects.   4. Control (Psychology)—
Religious aspects.   5. Gurus—Psychology.   I. Alstad, Diana, 1944–.
II. Title.
BF698.35.A87K73   1993   93–18494
303.3'3—dc20   CIP

2 3 4 5 6 7 8 9 / 97 96 95 94

Dedicated to Isadore Kramer

Beneath the visible authoritarianism in politics, social structures, and personalities is a far more pervasive, covert authoritarianism. It is hidden in culture, values, and daily life. By unmasking authoritarianism in such areas as addiction, intimate relations, morality, and religion, the authors expose it as a major factor in social disintegration.

Part One examines the most extreme example of one person giving power to another, the guru/disciple relationship, because this reveals less obvious occurrences of control. "Guru" is a metaphor for anyone who manipulates others under the guise of "knowing what's best" for them, whether leaders, mothers, or lovers.

Part Two decodes the authoritarian control concealed in contemporary values and beliefs. It portrays how basic problems, both personal and global, are tied to authoritarian assumptions so embedded they are taken for granted.

The Guru Papers shows there is a worldwide battle for people's minds over basic values. At stake in these "morals wars" is our very survival as a species. When people take back the authority that has been unknowingly invested in others, this can unleash the intelligence and care needed to ensure that our history will continue.

Contents

PART 2: IDEOLOGICAL MASKS

Preface and
Map of the Book

The Guru Papers has had a strange evolution. Many of the papers in Part One on gurus were sketched some years ago (in 1984) as a dalliance. Eventually we polished them, added several more, and put them out ourselves as a booklet, mainly for friends. When the publisher offered to put it out as a book, the idea was to put it out quickly as is. But given this opportunity, we thought why not include a few more essays, and broaden the topic of authoritarianism beyond gurus.

We thus began to pull on the thread of authoritarianism, and in doing so, much of the fabric of civilization began conceptually to unravel. Historically, authoritarianism has been part of the structural weave holding social orders together. It still is interwoven and disguised in most arenas of human interaction, including religion, morality, power, institutions, the family, intimacy, and even sexual relations and personal problems, such as addiction. We found authoritarianism embedded in people's psyches, affecting much more of day-to-day existence than is generally conceived. This is because in most people's minds authoritarianism is associated with political systems such as dictatorships, rather than with worldviews, values, and the usually unconscious programming people use to maintain control over their own lives and over others. In the process of writing this book, we deepened our understanding of how authoritarianism in its varied guises has been and largely still is a primary mode of social cohesion—and also how it has now become a major factor in social disintegration.

In the four years that have gone by since the original decision to publish the booklet, what has emerged is a far more ambitious project now called *Control*, of which this book is a part. The original papers on gurus have been restructured and expanded to introduce and highlight basic themes within authoritarianism. In addition more than thirty new essays have been completed or mapped out all aiming to show authoritarianism at work in such diverse areas as addiction, parenting, love, control within intimacy and sexuality, abortion, reproduction, ecology, censorship, freedom and equality, capital punishment, animism, mysticism, Buddhism, and karma/rebirth. And still we are not done. Clearly the venture had gotten out of hand. We thus decided to put out this first book containing not only the essays on gurus (Part One), but also six chapters (Part Two) from other sections of the larger work *Control*, which show the often-disguised authoritarianism within ideologies.

The introductory chapter, *"Authority, Hierarchy, and Power,"* defines and clarifies how we use these concepts, delineating the difference between authority and authoritarian power, and between hierarchy and authoritarian hierarchy. Authority and hierarchy are inescapable constructions within any social order, however they need not be authoritarian. Though hierarchies have been (and still are) predominantly authoritarian, we maintain that the authoritarianism embedded in hierarchy, not hierarchy itself, is the source of the problems that have made many people "anti-hierarchy." This chapter sets the stage for our perspectives on authoritarian control.

"Religion, Cults, and the Spiritual Vacuum" establishes a framework geared at demonstrating that morality is breaking down worldwide because its foundations come from "renunciate" religions and worldviews that are unable to deal with technologically leveraged power. This chapter describes the nature of renunciate religions, why they must be authoritarian, and also why traditional views of the sacred need to be reexamined.

Part One, "Personal Masks," deals primarily with control and manipulation on the personal level, utilizing the relation between charismatic leaders and their followers as a stark example. Living relationships have a tangible, three-dimensional quality that makes the dynamics of authoritarianism within them the easiest to unmask. We focus on the relationship between guru and disciple because it displays the epitome of surrender to a living person, and thus clearly exhibits what it means to trust another more than oneself.

The traditional framework between guru and disciple is as absolute in authoritarian demands (total surrender and obedience) as any on the planet. By unambiguously exhibiting the mechanisms of control and surrender, it offers a quintessential example of mental authoritarianism, whose power lies in controlling minds rather than in overt physical coercion. Our intention in using this relationship as an exemplar is to show the seductions, predictable patterns, and corruptions contained in any essentially authoritarian form. Though extreme, the guru model illustrates well the workings of authoritarian power that occur less overtly in many other relationships and contexts. Its relatively simplistic structure, combined with very sophisticated justifications, displays the dynamics of authoritarianism writ large.

Although gurus are already tainted with corruption in the minds of many, this is ordinarily seen as the failing of individuals. Instead we wish to show that the abuses of power that occur in such contexts are structural rather than personal, and why this is necessarily so. The papers on gurus and cults depict in concrete terms the mechanisms, rewards, disguised collusions, and dangers of surrendering to those who position themselves as knowing what's best for others. Decoding the dynamics of manipulation can help people avoid such traps.

Part One uses the guru/disciple relationship as the primary vehicle in deciphering authoritarian power. Each chapter also contains more general observations, including how what is being described applies to other less obvious areas. *"The Seductions of Surrender"* examines the emotions that make people susceptible to authoritarian control. *"On Channeling Disembodied Authorities"* is included because many people approach channels with the same unexamined assumptions they have of gurus. Here we show that whatever the reality of the phenomenon, channeling usually operates within an authoritarian system of belief. *"Do You Create Your Own Reality?,"* a critique of a worldview espoused by many channels and New Age leaders, is a chapter from the section in *Control* that examines authoritarianism within the ideology of karma and reincarnation. *"Healing Crippled Self-Trust"* offers perspectives pertinent to anyone who has been deeply deceived.

Since authoritarian leaders promulgate ideologies that justify their power and actions, no understanding of power is complete without examining the ways ideologies are used to support it. If the power is authoritarian, the ideology will also be so. Some ideologies mask their authoritarianism, while others do not. But even those that do not, do mask the way they are utilized to support self-interest and authoritarian control.

Part Two, "Ideological Masks," highlights control by ideology. It is comprised of six chapters from other sections of *Control* aimed at revealing the usually veiled authoritarianism within worldviews and values. These chapters spell out in more depth where susceptibility to being controlled comes from, showing how these forms work, why they attract people, and their far-reaching effects. Included are arguments demonstrating why authoritarian ideologies are not only personally crippling, but are now threatening planetary survival.

"The Morals Wars" introduces Part Two by mapping out what we feel is at stake. It presents why we think the basic planetary struggle that will determine the future is between the forces of the old and the new for people's minds.

1. Fundamentalism and satanism are both examples of overt control by ideology that show the workings of authoritarianism within Western traditions. *"Fundamentalism and the Need for Certainty"* deals not only with the power and appeal of such ideologies, but with why they are difficult to revise. Included is an examination of the nature of the fundamentalist and revisionist mentalities and the problems inherent in each.

2. In *"Satanism and the Worship of the Forbidden: Why It Feels Good to Be Bad"* satanism is shown to be an example of an extreme reaction against a morality that denigrates carnality. As a mirror image of fundamentalism, it utilizes authoritarian control to promote and unleash the taboo. This chapter discusses the way the absolute concepts of good and evil have created a deep division in people, which in turn generates and magnifies the allure of the dark and forbidden. The appeal of being "bad" is explained in terms most people can relate to in themselves. This and the following chapter on addiction develop a framework that demonstrates how a dualistic morality generates conflict by implanting an inner authoritarian which people then try to escape—satanism being one avenue of escape, addiction being another.

3. *"Who is in Control? The Authoritarian Roots of Addiction"* views the dysfunctionality and core conflict within addiction as just one manifestation of having internalized authoritarian values. Deciphering the dynamics within the authoritarian psyche reveals why people are susceptible to manipulation and control, and also prone to addictions. This chapter presents a different kind of model that views addiction as an inner battle for control resulting from a divided psyche. It elucidates what control by ideology feels like internally and explains many anomalies that other theories of addiction do not. We also show that authoritarianism is embedded in the disease model (including 12-Step programs) as well as in the "responsibility" models currently challenging the disease model.

Addiction is a graphic example of how hidden authoritarianism operates in daily life, both in the programs that attempt to ameliorate it and within the designated addict. Inner authoritarianism mirrors the outer, more familiar manifestations of it. Anyone who has ever felt "out of control" can utilize our framework to determine for themselves whether there is an inner authoritarian at the root of such feelings. Understanding how one is driven by such programming can help liberate one from it. Even though many social structures largely reward divided rather than whole people, the final section gives some direction for ending the inner battle for control.

4. *"Love and Control: The Conditions Underlying Unconditional Love"* shows the insidious nature of authoritarian ideologies in the most intimate corners of life. Ideals such as unconditional love, timeless love, or pure love come from renunciate moralities that are authoritarian. Ideologies impact and often take control of emotions, distorting love with unlivable values and expectations. We show how such ideals are used by those in power (whether in intimacy or in society at large) to maintain control over others. The relation between love and power is reframed through examining such elements as boundaries, forgiveness, measuring, and self-sacrifice. The aim is to free people from limiting perspectives of love that set one up for failure.

5. *"Oneness, Enlightenment, and the Mystical Experience"* examines the ideology most Eastern spiritual teachers (and now many Western ones) use to justify and support their authority and position. The ideology of Oneness, with its derivative concept enlightenment, embodies the most sophisticated example of religious authoritarianism. This chapter demonstrates how the mystical experience of unity has been conceptualized into a covertly authoritarian worldview. A major concern of this chapter is to show hidden control within a powerful ideology that on the surface appears beyond reproach, and certainly above crass manipulation.

6. *"The Power of Abstraction: The Sacred Word and the Evolution of Morality"* investigates the fundamental link between concepts, power, and control. By broadly describing the evolution of religious and moral thought the aim is to show how concepts become mechanisms for controlling people. Every worldview contains its unique abstractions that define it. This chapter discusses the different ways words and abstractions are used to create worldviews that structure the acceptable parameters of human interaction, and how this affects society. It shows how the evolution of abstraction enabled religions to in-

crease control through creating more abstract moralities that are authoritarian. The powers unleashed by scientific abstractions are obvious, but the enduring power of religious abstractions is less apparent—especially in more secularized cultures. A viewpoint is presented that helps recognize authoritarian elements within worldviews, and lays groundwork for what a non-authoritarian framework could be like.

Though this book has a loose continuity and a rationale that builds from start to finish, it is also constructed to enable readers to follow their thread of interest by dipping into whatever parts draw them, creating their own order. So the book has been devised to be cross-referential. Through footnotes, the reader is referred to other sections of the work that add to, further support, or deepen what is being said. Each chapter can to some extent stand alone, with the references helping to fill gaps and lead to connections that are not always obvious. Since the mechanisms of control have a structural similarity, with contextual variations, basic themes are approached and examined through different lenses and angles.

This book has two kinds of references: Most footnotes refer to chapters in this volume leading to different facets of the topic. Others refer to already written chapters from yet unpublished sections of *Control* and are included for these reasons: we wish to show what is being said is worthy of more discussion, to draw connections between this book and the larger work, and to whet curiosity for future topics. All references to chapters not in this book always state they are from *Control*.

Given that we view much of the abuse of authoritarian power as essentially structural, *The Guru Papers* was never meant to be critical of specific individuals—leaders or followers. Thus we do not name names, though those familiar with some of the occurrences may be able to glean the identity of the figures involved. Although women do assume authoritarian roles, the masculine pronoun is used throughout to refer to gurus and authorities whenever such a role has been traditionally male.

In these writings the word "paradigm" usually refers to more than just a model or exemplar; its meaning is extended to incorporate the idea of a foundational element within structures. (This usage is not original with us.) Thus "paradigm shift" indicates a change in basic viewpoint—for instance, using science as the foundation for truth rather than revelation. Also, we take the liberty of either making new word constructions or using words differently, as we do the with the word "renunciate." This is done to avoid cumbersome locutions, so that "renunciate morality," for example, replaces "a morality that mandates renunciation as a necessary virtue." The meanings of such words should be self-evident.

When words such as "spiritual" or "spirituality" are in quotation marks, this indicates we think what is being called spiritual is really part of an authoritarian exercise of power. Traditional concepts of spirituality are so interwoven with authoritarian control and self-serving otherworldly projections that it is tempting to give up on the word entirely. Our indictment is not of the concept of spirituality *per se*, but rather of the ways it is used to bolster, justify, and mask authoritarian control. The most common way of accomplishing this is to construct a realm different from and superior to daily life, label it spiritual, and then create authorities who give unchallengeable directives on how to get there. We view spirituality as embedded in daily life, not separate from it; thus what is needed is to bring spirituality down to Earth. This, however, is a topic for another book.

We feel very strongly about the point of view presented in this book, in part because it has helped explain for us why things are the way they are, and also why they must change. We present our perspective as clearly, forcefully, and accurately as we know how. Consequently, some might find the tone of this book uncompromising—perhaps to the extent of wondering if it is itself authoritarian. To this we can only respond that we have spent many years examining these issues, including what others have thought. To date we have not found a more inclusive perspective, and thus have a surety and confidence in what we are saying. But confidence need not be authoritarian in itself if one is truly open to being shown wrong. The essence of ideological authoritarianism is unchallengeability, not confidence. This book presents our current viewpoint, which in our own minds is subject to revision, structural changes, and even being abandoned, should we or others find telling weaknesses.

This work presents a point of view and ideas that we want to stand or fall on their own merit. Though over the years we have examined many other viewpoints, this is not a work of research or scholarship, and it does not use references to other people to bolster its perspectives. Our major concern is clarity—namely, that anyone who cares to follow the train of thought will understand it, whether in agreement or not. The goal is to appeal as much as possible to people's firsthand experience and reasonableness. We do this to be aligned with the spirit of the book, which we hope will foster self-trust as a foundation for living.

In the eighteen years we have lived, taught, and written together, we have only been comfortable when aligned on non-trivial issues. So part of our relationship has been (and is) confronting our differences until they are resolved. This process has sometimes taken hours, sometimes years. *The Guru Papers* is a product of that engagement to the extent that we are often no longer certain who originated which thought.

Many people have helped us by reading chapters in progress and offering valuable suggestions. Family and friends have been very supportive from the start. Though the list of those involved is too large to catalog, we wish to give them our heartfelt thanks. We single out Serena Castaldi and Court Fisher for special mention, as their involvement with our writings has been exceptional. Finally, without the foresight, understanding, and patience of our publisher, Richard Grossinger, this book would not exist.

Introduction:
Why Focus on
Authoritarianism

We are not alone in being disturbed by the present course of humanity. Why, we asked ourselves, has a species that displays the kind of almost magical intelligence that can come up with the microchip thus far ostensibly proven incapable of constructing viable ways of interacting with each other and the planet as a whole? What makes us so obtuse and seemingly uncaring in these domains? The more pessimistic answers include seeing it as a victory of evil over good, or as a fatal flaw in the human makeup that renders us incapable of acting beyond limited, short-term self-interest.

Our perspective is more sanguine, offering new grounds for hope. We view the authoritarian ideologies and practices so deeply rooted in the ways things are thought about and done as what keep the world stuck in old ways of doing things that no longer work. They are a major hindrance to the necessary kind of creative problem-solving now essential to deal with the crises that threaten basic survival. Creativity comes from self-trust, which authoritarian beliefs squelch.

A friend stated what seemed upon hearing it a truism: "If you're really interested in change, then optimism is the best strategy." If one's viewpoint is mainly historical, optimism is difficult to muster, because history has not shown the human species capable of intelligently handling the power and problems created by its technological cleverness. Technology has obviously accelerated far beyond the capacity of societies to integrate it. What has not been sufficiently seen are the reasons for this gap.

In our opinion, the past does not hold the key to closing the gap because the social structures and worldviews of the past could not even imagine the current state of the world. This is why many who are searching for a way out of contemporary dilemmas are talking about the necessity of a new model or framework, which really amounts to a new worldview—what is now being called a basic "paradigm shift."

Optimism that is not to some extent grounded in the human experience risks being a mere flight of fancy that crashes to pessimism or cynicism. Consequently, many who seek new paradigms are doing so within developmental or evolutionary frameworks. This enables keeping the thread of history, while allowing for transformational possibilities. What is clearly seen here is that if a framework is truly new, it must transform the arena where human possibility plays itself out. We view ourselves aligned with this direction, as it is a place where reasonable optimism and hope are possible. The question then becomes not only what is to be the nature of this shift, but how is it to be arrived upon?

Authoritarianism lies at the root of the old paradigms worldwide. It easily remains hidden because it is often not apparent in the specific content of a given structure, institution, ethic, or worldview. Authoritarianism rather exhibits itself in the process of how these human constructions maintain power. This includes the ways control over people's minds is obtained and maintained.

Whatever form a new worldview takes, whatever its content and values, if the process of creating or maintaining it is authoritarian, it will not be really new. It will merely be the old in disguise. Whatever else a new paradigm is about, it must gain the allegiance of people through consensus, not fiat. It must be a framework open to challenge and self-correction via the experiences of living people. This means it is essential for any viable model to promote people trusting themselves sufficiently to value their own experiences, instead of accepting unexamined assumptions and values. Thus any new system of values cannot hold tradition and the past more sacred than the living present, which includes the implications for the future contained within the present.

So often ideologies, worldviews, and other systems of establishing what is considered knowledge attempt to capture minds by "proving" their content right, or more right, than others. Yet in some of the most important issues of life and death, there has not been, and perhaps cannot be, a consensus as to what constitutes either proof or rightness. The emphasis of *The Guru Papers* is to unmask and decipher authoritarianism in the ways people are trained and conditioned to construct and maintain their views of reality. Many ideologies and worldviews on the planet today are sufficiently adept at justifying themselves to hold belief. The problem with belief is that it so often stems from preference and self-interest. People can argue endlessly about which worldview has a better or truer content, without being able to marshal sufficient proof to convince non-believers. What can be shown, however, truth or falsity aside, is whether the basis for belief is authoritarian, and whether it is masking the self-interest of those who use it to maintain control.

Our focus is not on the more obvious manifestations of authoritarianism displayed in political (or other) systems that utilize physical threat and coercion as their main mechanism for control. These have been widely studied, and to our minds are but the tip of the iceberg of authoritarianism. Instead, we are interested in unmasking the more hidden and pervasive mechanisms of authoritarian control that work by being implanted in the mentalities, beliefs, emotions, and aspirations of even modern people via ideologies that breed self-mistrust. Once people do not trust themselves, they are subject to easy manipulation.

At certain pivotal points in history, the foundations of social cohesion break down because what has made them successful in the past becomes dysfunctional. We and many others view the present as such a time. Consequently, the most basic assumptions of every culture need to be examined, for in our view basic problems are tied into basic assumptions. What is basic in any social order is how control is maintained within it. No society can maintain control long term through physical coercion alone, but must promulgate values that are internalized and transmitted to the next generation.

Morality—that is, the set of values that is internalized and, to some degree at least, acted upon—is the glue holding a social order together. A morality cannot be seen as merely arbitrary, nor can it have any force in isolation. So it is always embedded in a worldview that both constructs and justifies it. To date, the socialization process has largely been authoritarian, instilling self-mistrust because it was the easiest, most efficient way of controlling people.

Historically, the worldviews of all the planet's civilizations have been authoritarian, presenting "truth," especially moral truth, as essentially unchallengeable. This aims at bringing moral certainty, which in turn justifies control. A primary function of moral certainty is that it gives one (or the group as a whole) the right to tell people what to do. It is also used as the basis of self-control. This is why certainty, particularly moral certainty, along with the social and internal controls it brings, have greater emotional appeal than the specific beliefs in which the certainty is grounded. But the beliefs are necessary to maintain certainty. Consequently, such beliefs are very resistant to change no matter the power of differing arguments and evidence. Certainty is a psychological state. When it is protected by beliefs that are unchallengeable (that is, authoritarian), both the beliefs and the controls justified by the beliefs harden in the face of change. When the changes are so great that what is needed is a shift in values and in the worldview that stands behind the values, such hardening no longer serves the well-being of the individual or society. In our view, these are such times. Now the traditional, often hidden authoritarian modes of transmitting and protecting information are leading humanity toward its own demise. We view the degree to which a culture is authoritarian as a barometer of its dysfunctionality.

All ideological authoritarianism, including its relation to power and control, has a similar structure no matter what its content. This is masked by the often pristine ideals of the content. One such universal found in all forms of authoritarian worldviews is that they all have and promote mechanisms to instill self-mistrust. There are others. A major concern of this book is to decipher the code that masks authoritarian power.

These writings do have a viewpoint that can be gleaned, often in the background, which is evolutionary and dialectical. It is evolutionary in that it sees humanity as engaged in a process forcing it to evolve in the way it relates to itself, other species, and the planet's ecosystems. Confronting its no longer viable, destructive habits is part of that engagement. Our perspective is dialectical in the sense that it sees traditional categories of opposition, such as competition/cooperation and egoism/altruism, as embedded in each other. This view is fleshed out throughout the book. It is not necessary, however, to agree with this aspect of our thought to catch our main intent, which is to show the pervasiveness, workings, and peril of authoritarian control.

The needed change cannot come from a person (or group) claiming to have special access to the truth, as this is the very mode that needs to be changed. Neither do we think the new can emerge until the limits of both old forms and old processes are seen clearly. Authoritarianism is hidden in the fabric of much that is taken for granted, often including what is held by some to be sacred. Unmasking authoritarianism in a given context does not necessarily negate the content. But it does increase the likelihood that what is involved is far more arbitrary and more a function of vested interest than meets the eye.

The world's complex cultures, no matter how seemingly diverse, have in common the utilization of authoritarian control to maintain power. Simpler tribal cultures are not exempt from such control, though it tends more to lie in the group rather than in a specific institution or person. Democracies are now struggling with not only their authoritarian elements, but with the resurgence of authoritarian factions.

It is vital to understand the dynamics, appeal, and scope of this aspect of our human heritage. Only by unlocking the bonds of authoritarianism—not merely in social structures, but in our own psyches—can humanity find the key to meeting the evolutionary challenge our authoritarian past presents us. Just as no one could have foreseen the present results of technology, there is no way to envision all the results that a true shift in basic values would bring. Authoritarianism is the element the old paradigms share, and so there is no way to know what human possibility would be without it. Forging non-authoritarian frameworks is not only the new frontier, it is where hope lies.

Authority, Hierarchy, and Power

Change has become a rallying cry worldwide. This is because the need for some kind of change is becoming increasingly self-evident. The questions are in what direction to change and how to go about it. There are those who want to change by going back to older forms that once held the world, or their world, together. Others see the necessity of something new; this is voiced by calling for a "new world order" or "basic paradigm shift." When focusing on change, the major concern is usually the shape or form of the anticipated outcome. Yet anyone involved in any creative endeavor comes to realize the original goals rarely remain the same throughout the process. This is partially because the process itself determines what kind of information is used or not used as feedback. Consequently, when reaching for something new, the way one goes about it greatly influences the outcome.

Restructuring in social spheres involves restructuring power. If the way the new order or paradigm shift is reached for is authoritarian, whatever results will be authoritarian. Any change this brings can only be in content, that is, who holds the reins of power, but not in the way power is arrived at and maintained. What makes a process authoritarian is not always obvious because it is hidden in the values, traditions, rights, and prerogatives people take for granted. This book examines the workings of authoritarian power, including its deep roots in the human psyche.

Though critical of authoritarianism, we do not suggest it is possible to eliminate authority, hierarchy, or power from human interaction. History notwithstanding, we maintain their utilization need not necessarily be authoritarian.

There are those who argue that authoritarian hierarchy is built into the species, just as dominance and submission are genetically wired into other social animals. It could also be argued that sexuality, competition, and aggression are linked in males and hard-wired in, and that the female body is biologically programmed to want to have children. One could further argue that there are (or were) good evolutionary reasons for all the above. The truth or likelihood of such arguments aside, does a biological foundation necessarily mean biological determinism? If a woman's body is genetically programmed to want to reproduce, can she not use her intelligence to circumvent biology if she deems it appropriate? If authoritarianism were found to be linked with biological mechanisms of dominance and submission, would this automatically mean human intelligence is helpless before them—even if their mode of operation were threatening human existence? Even if dominance and submission, and more basically aggression, cannot ultimately be eliminated, humans still have the option of either catering to or mitigating against their harmful consequences.

The interplay between instinct and intentional intelligence is an ongoing part of the human drama. There is currently no consensus on the nature and role of instinct within humans. All life-forms do what they can to continue to live—to the extent that it can be postulated that it is instinctual to do so. Humans largely share this trait, but on occasion go against it, and are the only animal that willfully kills itself. Does this mean people have no instinct to live, or that the human mind is capable of overriding instinct? If the mind can override instinctual behavior in a self-destructive way, cannot it also do so to be life-affirming?

Many agree that life, especially human life, is at risk. This underlies much of the impetus for change. Technological intelligence has enormously leveraged power so as to seriously threaten not only other species, but humanity, too. Our perspective is that what is preventing people from applying the same kind of stunning brilliance and inventiveness to social spheres are old social and moral frameworks that are essentially authoritarian.

Modern democracy is an attempt to curb authoritarianism in the political sphere. But if a large number of people within a democracy are deeply programmed by authoritarian beliefs and values, when crises come, as they are bound to, the solutions resorted to will be authoritarian. If such solutions are really part of the problem, then what results can only bring greater risk.

It is difficult to change or fix anything without first adequately understanding the nature of the problem. If authoritarianism is deeply rooted, and often hidden, in social structures and the human psyche, it is essential to understand how and why this is so. So often those who abhor the results of authoritarianism still try to correct the perceived inequities by authoritarian means. This not unusual tendency is exacerbated because the dynamics and collusions of power are hidden and their implications are not sufficiently seen.

Authoritarianism is interwoven in, but not identical to, authority, hierarchy, and power. This chapter sets the stage for the rest of the book by mapping out how we distinguish these overlapping, intertwined concepts that are too often lumped together.Webster's dictionary defines authoritarian as "characterized by unquestioning obedience to authority." When the word is used in reference to a political system, it involves using force to control people without there being any recourse. We broaden the meaning to include belief systems that are unchallengeable, and the idea that someone or something other than the individual necessarily knows what's best, or right, or proper for a given person. So ideologies and belief systems can be intrinsically authoritarian if there is no way to take issue with their basic suppositions.

The extent of suffering caused by Nazism ignited interest in the authoritarian personality that under certain circumstances will blindly follow orders, no matter what. Both the willingness to follow another unquestioningly, and wanting to be strictly obeyed, may be linked to a genetic program of dominance and submission common in other social animals. But whether or not there is such a genetic propensity in humans, when dominance and submission are structured into social forms and taught to children, it becomes impossible to separate out what is "natural" from what is contrived. Traditional sex roles are another example of rigid social structures greatly exaggerating, distorting, and then institutionalizing gender differences through conditioning, social pressure, and even coercion. This travesty of whatever differences there may be is then called "natural."

Not all people blindly obey. Moreover, if people are forced to obey, they will tend to force others to obey, given the opportunity. If children are taught to mistrust themselves (a prerequisite for the authoritarian personality), as adults they will have little option other than looking for someone else to trust, especially under stress. What this shows is that whatever the genetic base, much of authoritarianism is taught. Until children are raised to trust themselves, and social forms reward not punish this, there is no basis for making nature the cause of authoritarianism in arenas of power.

Mental or psychological authoritarianism comes from an inner urge to obey someone or something that is viewed as higher, more powerful, morally superior, or more knowledgeable— or to be that for someone else. These two stances are not mutually exclusive, but usually coexist in the same person and are triggered by different circumstances. Even if this propensity, like aggression, is part of being human, this does not mean that authoritarianism and the forms of coercion and aggression that support it need be catered to or accepted. Humanity's hope lies in its capacity not to accept the way its past has been played out. Much of psychological authoritarianism is masked by ideologies that make it a virtue. This is because it only works well if it is sufficiently hidden so that it appears "the way to be." Unmasking its roots and dynamics can, at the very least, give people more options in dealing with it.

Authoritarianism as a way of establishing and maintaining power has been so prevalent that it is often equated with power itself. Social hierarchies are about power and authority. Morality has involved, among other things, the justification of power. The larger work *Control,* of which this book is a part, is an attempt to decode the historical and present foundations and workings of power—but not through making power itself the villain. From our perspective, power is intrinsic to all relationships. Simply put, it is the capacity of an individual or system to influence in any way other individuals or systems. Power does not exist in isolation; it is relational. To say "x has power" is really to say "x has power in relation to y." In this view of power it would be correct to say that the sun has power to maintain life on Earth, for without it there would be none. The power to support life is real power, as is the power to destroy it. To say an automobile is powerful is to say it can do more in relation to the road than one that is less so. Beauty, wealth, physical strength, sexuality, anything that can capture or direct attention has power. Power is just there in all relationships and cannot be done away with. Trying to do away with it is just another form of exercising it.

It is legend that power corrupts; but why? What is it in the human arena that so lends itself to this? Also, those seeking power are often maligned. To say that someone is on a power trip is usually not a compliment. However, to the extent that one is interested in controlling one's own life, one is necessarily interested in power. Wanting not to be controlled or to have at least some control over what others do involves power. Censorship is a control issue, as is keeping drunk drivers off the roads. If power is everywhere, is corruption then inescapable? Here one might object that the way the word "power" is being used is too broad, and want to limit it by saying it is coercive power that corrupts. But does using coercion with a child necessarily corrupt the parent? And what constitutes psychological coercion: social pressure? generating fear? making an offer that can't be refused? seduction via filling neurotic needs? all laws and their respective punishments?

11

The corruptions of power occur when maintaining power becomes central and more important than its effect on others. And although this danger is present within any human interaction, it is when power and position are linked that the possibilities of corruption are magnified. The power that flows from position is seated in the position, and position is what hierarchy is all about. Lord Acton's famous statement on power, "Power tends to corrupt, absolute power corrupts absolutely," is taken almost as a truism. In order to have absolute power one must be at the top of a hierarchy. It is the power within a hierarchy that lends itself to the greatest abuse and corruption. So even though one may not be anti-power, it is still tempting to be anti-hierarchy. To understand why this stance is no more viable than being anti-power, hierarchy will next be examined.

The etymology of the word "hierarchy" comes from the Greek *hieros* meaning sacred, and *archos* meaning ruler. A hierarch is the high or highest priest, and from him the sacred Word was passed down to the next rank, who in turn passed it further down. The very concept of hierarchy originated in the context of religion where the sacred Word (power) flowed only downward through a pyramidal structure.[1] Once people are positioned within such a structure, their main concern becomes either maintaining their position or moving up. Rights given through birth or other mechanisms of status are the easiest and traditional ways of maintaining position. Authoritarian hierarchies are justified by an authoritarian worldview and morality. The reigning ideology establishes the rights and privileges of the different levels of a hierarchy. If the ideology is authoritarian, the workings of the hierarchy will be, too. Democracy as a political ideology influenced the workings of hierarchies under its banner, so that not all power ran only from top down.

---

[1]"The Power of Abstraction: The Sacred Word and the Evolution of Morality" describes the relation between the sacred Word and power, as well as the major stages of religious abstraction and control.

Hierarchies occur in nature on physical, biological, and social levels. The solar system, the human body, and an ant colony all have a hierarchical component. Each is organized according to different levels of power. The human body contains organs, cells, molecules, and atoms; an organ is more vital to the body's functioning than an individual cell. Other social animals also organize in often overlapping hierarchies with different structures of dominance for different spheres of activity. Even among other animals, when any position of dominance is achieved, there is noticeable reluctance to give it up. Hierarchies are natural, and in humans there may be a natural aptitude for their use. All cultures invent and use material tools. Social hierarchy, like the wheel or any tool, is a human invention. Although seemingly very different they share some important features: both enable human beings to do more; both spread on contact between cultures; once either is utilized it is never discarded; both are tools that leverage power. At the simplest level, a person who uses a wheel has tremendous advantage in the doing of countless tasks. Those not using wheels eventually come to realize this. The same is true for social hierarchy—once it enters a social system there is no turning back.[2]

As with any new tool that leverages power, those willing to utilize hierarchy will win out over those who do not, should there be any conflict or competition between the two. This is because hierarchy is a model for internal cooperation that can contain and direct large numbers of people. It is the most efficient means found to date for coordinating the specialization of tasks. The end result of this is that hierarchy not only permits a culture to use more people efficiently, but to have more people. It supports and promotes expansion and accumulation. Should there be any competition for territory, resources, etc., a culture utilizing hierarchy can absorb one that does not, while the reverse is not true.

---

[2]See "The Power of Abstraction" on the origin of social hierarchy and its link with agriculture and accumulation.

Since authoritarianism is inherently hierarchical, one can easily think that hierarchy itself is necessarily authoritarian given that authoritarian hierarchy has been and is humanity's main way of organizing people. Hierarchy as a way of organizing and leveraging power has been villainized by people of such differing theoretical persuasions as Marxists, anarchists, feminists, tribalists, and others with egalitarian tastes. This is because hierarchies impose an unequal distribution of power and authority that seems inevitably to congeal into authoritarian structures whose main task ends up being perpetuating the hierarchy itself and the self-interest of those on top—no matter what their stated purpose. We, too, have a deep distaste for authoritarian hierarchies. However, it is not possible to do away with hierarchy itself as a mechanism for organization. Any attempt to do so can only succeed by supplanting one for another. This is because the nature of power is that it never stays equally distributed, and any attempt to force equality of power itself becomes hierarchical.

Authoritarian hierarchies foster and reward what can be described as the authoritarian virtues. They help run the hierarchy smoothly by promoting the moral complacency and unconsciousness necessary to enable people to ignore how power actually operates within the hierarchy. These virtues are loyalty, duty, and obedience. We, too, value and respect loyalty—if deserved; duty—if self-generated; and even obedience—if freely contracted for along a highly defined, specific, and limited band of activity. But when loyalty, duty, and obedience are valued in themselves, they become the rationale for using others without regard for their well-being. We call this "ideological uncaringness," for protecting the ideologies that justify the hierarchy takes precedence over people. The "I was following orders" excuse exemplifies valuing obedience over consequences to people.

Hierarchy is a way of structuring power; authority is a way of exercising it; and ultimately morality is the way authority is justified. The old moral orders are authoritarian, constructing fixed, absolute rules to obey. "Thou shalt not kill" is a rule, but the willingness to kill those who break the rule (and others, too) shows that what's really important is not the rule, but protecting the authority behind the rule.[3] The way authority is maintained and protected is the key to whether the authority is authoritarian. If hierarchy cannot be done away with, then the only way to protect against the corruption of power within it is to ensure the authority that is based on position in the hierarchy is not bottom-line authoritarian. Is this possible?

Not all authority is authoritarian, and it is crucial to distinguish the difference. Authority may be vested in a position, a role, or some perceived capacity within an individual—these three are often interwoven. If one is considered an authority on health, this means the person has some degree of expertise in the field. The doctor role contains an assumption of expertise, as does the teacher role and the parent role. The role of guru or roshi has within it the assumption that the person who takes on, or is given, that role knows best (or at least better) what life is about and how to live it. Here the reason for authority is presumed special knowledge. Such authority can be more or less authoritarian depending on how it is exercised and how it is received. The guru role is structured to be authoritarian given that unquestioned obedience to the guru is made the prime virtue.[4]

On the personal level, it is not too difficult to see when authority is authoritarian. If an authority not only expects to be obeyed without question, but either punishes or refuses to deal with those who do not, that authority is authoritarian. And on the other side, if people believe they must obey without question in order to receive whatever benefits the authority has to offer, and they are correct, the relationship is authoritarian. However,

---

[3]See "Fundamentalism and the Need for Certainty" on the double standard implicit in this rule and the ways people justify breaking it.

[4]"The Attractions of Cult Hierarchy" shows how participation in an authoritarian hierarchy is an easy route to purpose, meaning, and security. See also "Recognizing Authoritarian Control" in "The Seductions of Surrender."

authority based on knowledge or even role does not necessarily have to be authoritarian. Experts can share their expertise without expecting either agreement or obedience, and roles such as teacher need not be authoritarian. People can seek guidance and yet remain the final judge for themselves.

Establishing whether the authority vested in a position on a hierarchy is authoritarian is more difficult. Because authoritarianism constructs and works through hierarchy, and because the authority within hierarchies is often structured to be unchallengeable from lower levels, hierarchy itself appears to be intrinsically authoritarian. But hierarchy can be used as a tool, and as such, constructed in different ways. The criteria of whether a given hierarchy is authoritarian can only be established by how it's used, and how power is exercised to maintain authority within it. The difference between firing people for disobedience and shooting them is not a difference of degree, but a basic difference. A contract to obey in a specified domain in exchange for money is different from obedience from which one cannot withdraw.

Building a house usually involves a hierarchy of authority. A contractor contracts out different tasks to different roles: carpenter, electrician, etc.—each with specific expertise. Each in turn may have helpers, and in a large project the helpers may have helpers. Any in the hierarchy who refuse to do what they are told to do with reference to the job may be fired. If an electrician fires a helper because he did not or could not obey, is this an authoritarian use of power? Certainly it looks like it, for it involves a "Do it or else" attitude. Yet, the very workings of hierarchy often require the different levels (positions) doing what their superiors want. An electrician's helper may disobey orders because he believes he knows better how to do his job. He may even be right insofar as his job is concerned. But the contractor may be operating under different considerations of time, money, and design. Trying to explain to every person on the job why things are being done this way instead of that is often not the best way to get the job done. Likewise, a general cannot have his orders subject to evaluation by every soldier in the field. (This would not even be in the soldier's interest as it would increase risk.) A military hierarchy cannot work well without obedience that is at least sometimes unquestioned. This is true for other hierarchies as well.

Fortunately, the problems within hierarchy are not intrinsic to the structure of hierarchy itself, but rather come out of the way power is ordered and maintained within it. The function of hierarchy is to give authority and thus power to position. If one looks only at the internal workings of a hierarchy, there is an aspect that is inherently authoritarian, in varying degrees. In saying that hierarchy does not have to be authoritarian, what is meant is that the way hierarchy itself structures power is the issue, not the way power is exercised at any particular level or moment. What this boils down to is whether a hierarchy is essentially power-driven or task-driven. In determining this and in judging whether a hierarchy is essentially authoritarian or not, one faces the following considerations:

1. What is its purpose?

2. Who decides if its purpose is being fulfilled and how is this decided?

3. How free are the members of the hierarchy to enter and leave it? That is, how much coercion is involved in getting people to belong and stay?

4. How responsive is it to change from within or without, and how open is it to internal and external feedback? This includes who determines what is even considered relevant feedback.

5. In what direction does the power flow? Does it only flow from top to bottom, or are there mechanisms within the structure of the hierarchy that give the lower rungs a say in who the higher rungs are and what they do?

Determining whether a hierarchy is basically task- or power-driven is obscured because power-driven hierarchies nearly always present themselves as performing tasks—often ones with the highest sounding ideals. The key question in determining the real nature of a hierarchy is "In whose interest is the task?" When the main task of a hierarchy is really either the perpetuation of power or the aggrandizement of those on top, it is power-driven. The Crusades had the task of converting the infidel for their own good and for the glory of God. What this task was really about was increasing the power of the church by extending its reach, and also by getting rid of troublesome nobles. The Crusades were power-driven, as were the hierarchies involved in building the Egyptian pyramids. Neither the infidels nor the Egyptian laborers were consulted about their well-being.

Hierarchy and authority are part of the human landscape. Both become authoritarian when their main task becomes maintaining power. To avoid this, care and vigilance are necessary to counter the structural, historical, and psychological habits of power. A purpose of any hierarchy is to bring order. But the real question is what is the purpose of the order it brings? The task of maintaining order is the *raison-d'être* of all power-driven hierarchies. Too often the real purpose of order is to keep power in the hands of those who have it. It is possible to construct task-driven hierarchies that mitigate against the usual tendency to be or become authoritarian. Democracy attempts to do this through mechanisms that can dislodge people from position, and by giving those below some power in determining who those above are. Other mechanisms can be structured into a hierarchy itself, or into the larger social context in which the hierarchy is embedded, to dissolve it once its task is completed or once it becomes clear that its task is not being done properly. The hierarchy that forms for building a house dissolves when the task is complete.

House building is a simple task compared to, say, taking care of people's health within a social order. Especially with tasks that never end, unless the hierarchies constructed have mechanisms to ensure they are task-driven, they will most likely become power-driven. We use the term "power-driven" when the overt or professed task of a hierarchy becomes secondary to maintaining or increasing its power. If a society wants to guard against the corruptions of power, mechanisms must be put in place and watched carefully to ensure that hierarchies remain task-driven. This is because when one's power and privileges flow from position, protecting the position easily becomes the main concern.

Humans are extraordinarily inventive, and there is no reason why this capacity could not be directed toward constructing ways to mitigate against power becoming authoritarian. All that is needed is an overall consensus that it is important to do so. The Bill of Rights in the U.S. Constitution is one such mechanism. In recent years, however, more power has been given to authorities, with far less recourse available to those on the receiving end of that power. Now what were considered basic rights are being curtailed, and people have actually voted to take their own rights away. This is occurring because the old order is unraveling, bringing violence, disorder, and fear. Out of fear, if people are conditioned not to trust themselves, they will give away what power they have to those they think can protect them. The problem is that in doing so, one is no longer protected from one's protectors. The lessons of history unequivocally show this leads to corrupt, power-driven hierarchies that care little about the well-being of people.

The world is now at a cusp, facing the need for restructuring power. If power is restructured through authoritarian means, it will lead to authoritarian ends, and not be new at all. Mechanisms are needed to change authoritarian systems so that "reforms" do not become the old systems in disguise. Technology has created a context of complexity that old authoritarian methods are incapable of dealing with effectively. This is because the way technology leverages power over people and planetary resources is too great to be left in the hands of a power elite. The challenge facing humanity is how to use hierarchy, authority, and power in ways that protect against age-old authoritarian predilections. Hierarchy and authority need not be essentially authoritarian; nor must the utilization of power guarantee corruption. But when power and authority are contained within authoritarian hierarchies, harm, exploitation, and corruption are ensured.

Part 1

Personal Masks

Religion, Cults, and the Spiritual Vacuum

The human mind is not comfortable with large areas of caprice, uncertainty, and disorder; it is continually structuring experience to make the unknown known. In the past, and still today, religions have been the vehicle that brought order and certainty to the most uncertain and arguably most important facets of life: Where does life come from and where does it go? How should I act toward others? What is really important? Can I touch into something that can move me beyond the inequities, pains, and suffering of life, as well as beyond the endless demands of the self for self-enhancement? Can I touch into something pure that can make everything okay?

Religions have been (and for many still are) the main vehicles through which the unknown was made at least to seem more known. They each offer a worldview containing explanations of the basic elements of existence, namely, how all things, including human beings, came to be (creation); what life is about (meaning, continuity, and preservation); how and why things cease to be (death and destruction). Within Hinduism, these categories are overtly portrayed as the three personas of God: Brahma the Creator, Vishnu the Preserver, and Shiva the Destroyer.

Religion and Morality

Morality is the glue that holds civilization together; and within complex accumulation cultures, religion has been the foundation or underpinning of morality, and thus of civilization itself. Since there is a need for the rules about how to treat each other to be considered not merely arbitrary, they had to be grounded in some higher authority. Historically religion, as the only purveyor of presumptive absolute truths, had the right to dictate what's right. Religions gave meaning and direction to life by positing the existence of a higher power or authority whose purpose could at least be dimly known. Morality, the abstract concept of goodness or right human action, came to be defined as being aligned with that higher purpose. Presumed divinely inspired human intermediaries, or the divine in human form (Christ), delineated what to do and how to be.[1]

Religions have thus presented themselves as the bridge to the spiritual via their formalized codes and traditions. Basically they put forth rules of acceptable behavior that temper self-centeredness. They also channel expressions of self-centeredness into areas of acceptability, legitimizing them through the concepts of "rights," and deserved privileges. So if God gives humans dominion over all other life, this gives humans the right to use what is considered "lesser." Using others without regard for their well-being is one expression of self-centeredness. Through rights, rulers could use vassals, and husbands use wives. To facilitate this, the major extant world religions all promulgate a "renunciate" morality wherein one is expected to renounce and sacrifice self-interest to a designated higher good. They all present self-centeredness in its different forms as the villain keeping people away from what religion designates as important. To be spiri-

---

[1]"The Power of Abstraction: The Sacred Word and the Evolution of Morality" shows the historical stages of the relation between religion and morality.

tual, one must surrender one's will to the will of God or to the laws of karma, which usually involves some kind of self-sacrifice.

This used to work in imposing and maintaining order and stability, if not social justice. Idealizing sacrifice and placing self-lessness at the pinnacle of virtue did to an extent temper the way people treated each other—at least within societies, if not between them. On the other hand, the seemingly benign ideal of selflessness, which includes self-sacrifice, masks the way organized religions have provided a morality that supports social and religious hierarchy by justifying the use (and abuse) of the higher over the lower. This includes tacitly and even overtly legit-imizing whatever violence the higher deems necessary to keep the lower low, and outsiders outside. Another way renunciate religions support the power structure is by viewing hardship as either deserved (original sin), or as part of a morality play whose purpose is to give lessons to learn, and to test for righteousness. This way of framing both powerlessness and abuse makes it eas-ier for people to resign themselves to their often not very pleas-ant lot. It also makes it easier to be inured to the lot of others.

Traditional religious worldviews attempt to assuage human-ity's basic fears of the unknown, of chaos, and of death. They all promise some form of continuance after the body dies, with those who do the right thing (as they define it) getting a better deal. Belief in and obedience to religion's precepts bring the kind of peace that only comes from unwavering certitude. Faith is the coin necessary for certainty, which brings the cessation of (at least conscious) doubt and fear.

Evil is explained by most Western religions as a necessity, for it alone gives the freedom of moral choice; choosing good over evil is the only way to prove one is worthy of salvation. Much of Eastern religious thought, on the other hand, views "evil" as a product of the illusion of separateness—it, too, being ultimate-ly an illusion. Here evil is considered ignorance, a lack, as op-posed to an autonomous force. The spiritual path becomes the march away from ignorance towards enlightenment. Although seemingly different, both the East and the West, religions make the cruelties and tragedies within the human drama appear a necessary part of a higher plan, with either a personal or impersonal higher intelligence firmly at the helm.

Reward and punishment, guilt, shame, and forgiveness—this is the stuff religions use for control. Since it is obvious that the virtuous do not always benefit and sinners do not always suffer, to make this system work it is necessary that the major rewards and punishments take place in an afterlife. This is how immortality (whether heaven or a better next lifetime) became the foundation of morality. Insofar as this life is made subordinate to some conception of an afterlife, sacrifice within this life not only becomes justifiable, but is a key part of any renunciate morality that controls behavior through fear of cosmic reprisal after death.

The Challenge of Science

At its core, the search for meaning is a search for a way to live, perhaps ultimately for a reason to live. In the past, meaning was always given to us by externals—by cultural or familial traditions which were themselves filtered through a religious system at the foundation of it all. If people surrendered to this socially imposed meaning, it made life simple by bringing alignment, and with it, conformity. In fact, most people had little real choice but to comply because basic survival was problematic and often impossible outside the group framework. Unchallengeable certainty became the basis for group consensus, out of which many of the conflicts and ambiguities of life were either not felt or not conscious.

Religion's unique psychological strength and appeal revolve around bringing certainty. What really matters is not so much the specific content of a religion, but how sure one is of its worldview. That is, it's not nearly as important how true or false a belief is as how certain one is of it. All religious certainty is similar in that the beliefs one is certain of coat and comfort fear. This kind of certitude brings forth a particular state of peace through giving meaning, purpose, and a shared community of believers. Then one knows what one must do, why one is here, and where one is going. And even more specifically, there is little conflict about how to raise one's children, how to treat others, who one can count on, and so on.

No wonder it is not unusual to hear people say wistfully, "I really wish I could still be a Catholic [or a Jew or Protestant] as I once was." What they're wistful for is certainty, with clear-cut rules and roles that are more relaxing and comforting than living with ambiguity. In the past people have been able to achieve some semblance of peace in this fashion, and perhaps on rare occasions, even real peace. But in this particular historical moment, for many, religions are no longer working as vehicles for certainty. It is now more difficult to believe unquestioningly in them. As soon as questioning begins, certainty leaves—and with it the kind of peace that it alone can bring. All varieties of fundamentalism must continually struggle to preserve certainty because certainty is their major lure.[2]

Science has been peeling away at the mysteries for centuries, and in doing so, has undermined the symbolisms that were constructed at an earlier time to answer the needs of a younger, simpler humanity. It has eroded the absoluteness of belief through valuing change and questioning over faith. Copernicus, Newton, and Darwin made the literal interpretation or acceptance of the Bible difficult. Einstein superseded Newton. What next? One may try to use quantum mechanics to justify the Upanishads, or the Big Bang theory to justify the creation of the universe by a transcendent God, but how long will these theories be accepted? The problem is that science can destroy myth, but it cannot create personal meaning or values. This is why many still accept the moral dictates of religions long after ceasing to believe in the worldviews that produced them. Many people who are no longer religious, including professed agnostics, send

---

[2]See "Fundamentalism and the Need for Certainty."

their children to church or Sunday school for a proper moral education. Here religious teachers are considered specialists in morality in a not dissimilar way to psychologists being considered specialists of the mind.

The nature of religions is to shroud whatever truths they may contain in symbols, myths, and mysteries, which are then purported to be the bridge or the intermediary to the truth. These symbols and rituals become culturally and personally imbued with meaning and emotion that exert a magnetic pull, even on those who no longer believe in their literalness or origin (e.g. Christmas). It is inevitable that the symbols, in time, become more important than what they symbolize, given that people's contact is largely with them.

Religious symbols, of whatever sort, are transmitted from human mind to human mind orally or through writings and images, and have a concreteness that must crystallize over time. As these symbols are always historically bound, the movement of time eventually erodes their relevance. Yet religious symbols that promulgate certainty maintain power by constructing a world-view that remains fixed. Thus they cannot express a fluidity that allows for basic change and evolution.

From our perspective, there is a dialectically shifting interplay between such dynamic universal oppositions as creation and destruction, self and other, individuation and merging, unity and division, competition and cooperation, and control and surrender. Rather than each element being autonomous, the two sides of these oppositions are embedded within, and dependent upon, each other. They are also embedded in history, displaying a unique emphasis and expression within different epochs. As time moves and epochs change, any symbol that freezes meaning becomes heavy and laden with the past. What results is a greater and greater distancing between the symbol and that which it is attempting to symbolize.

Certainty derives from conviction in a religion's symbolic structures, which not only include its myths and parables, but also its "laws" and prescribed duties. As they become more anachronistic, some people hold onto them more rigidly. Others revise and refurbish the old meanings, reinterpreting the symbols and prescriptions in an attempt to make them more credible and livable. Still others allow doubt and questioning to creep in. The culture no longer has a mental field of consensus. With each passing generation, certainty and a sense of community based on the old shared values become more difficult to maintain.

This is the beginning of breakdown. There is much talk these days of the moral decay of Western civilization. What this really means is that the hold the old system of morality had over people's actions is failing, and nothing viable has yet taken its place. When traditional viewpoints falter, a vacuum of meaning results. The erosion of religious certainty, which was the foundation and authority for morality, is creating what we consider an inevitable rend or tear in the movement of history. On one side is an increasing push toward fundamentalism, whose stance is that all current problems come from straying from the verities of old. On the other side are a spectrum of experiments, both in the "spiritual" and secular spheres, that are either reaching for something new, or reacting against the repressions within the old. Though painful and sometimes destructive, the opposition between fundamentalism and experimentalism, conformity and deviance—in short, the old and the new—is inevitable when moral systems are breaking down, as they are today.[3]

Science and technology have leveraged power in ways that create ethical problems that the old moral orders, which were constructed long before, cannot handle. Among other things, science has greatly increased the capacity to kill, use and exploit resources, pollute, centralize power, and increase both the numbers and density of population. All these are major factors in the current crisis. The question now before us is whether the intelligence that tapped into nature, creating a self-destructing juggernaut, is also capable of constructing viable systems of

---

[3]See "The Moral Wars" and "Fundamentalism."

interaction. This would not only include the ways people interact with each other, but with all planetary systems.

An ethics for survival is needed that makes what goes on in this world of paramount importance. One reason for this book is that we view the old authoritarian moralities with their renunciate values as part of the problem now leading us to the brink of extinction. We recognize that these moralities were an integral part of the way humanity structured power, enabling expansion in what was then a world of unlimited resources. We maintain that these moralities are not viable in a world of limit where an expanding humanity has become a core problem. Some solace and a guarded optimism may be found in realizing that deep structural change cannot come without the breakdown of old ways. It is only from this place of tension, backlash, and crisis that viable values that meet the movement of history can emerge. Thus these times, with their true dangers and real uncertainties, are a poignant, living example of the pressures of social evolution in action.

When people believed in the afterlife retributions of the old moral order, this did temper, or at least channel, expressions of violence. It did not, however, eliminate the injustices and ensuing hatreds produced by the social order of which it was an integral and justificatory part. Violence was sanctioned in war and in the ways hierarchies of power could protect designated rights. Throughout much of human history, killing, or the threat of it, has been the bottom line of power. This is still operative.

Fear is structured into all renunciate religions through proclaiming that some higher power is watching all actions (sometimes even thoughts) and will reward or punish them as deserved. This higher power is usually portrayed as a God that saves or damns, or an impersonal force such as karma giving better or worse next lifetimes. Here fear is woven throughout the web of morality in the form of "Do good and it will ultimately pay off; do bad and you'll be sorry." Such religions sometimes subtly let it be known that this relentlessly judgmental force must be feared, whether it be a stern father figure, a personification of destruction such as Shiva and Kali, or an abstract concept like the theory of karma.[4]

None of this works well anymore. As the old beliefs that maintained order disintegrate, another kind of fear arises—of purposelessness, chaos, and violence. Basically, what this boils down to is fear of each other. Given the hatreds and inequities produced by the old order, such fears are not unrealistic. Try telling a ghetto gang member that unless he stops being violent he will go to hell. His response could easily be, "I don't have far to go— I'm there already."

Every taboo is now being challenged and broken. We are living out the Freudian "return of the repressed"—Hitler, Vietnam, Hiroshima, purges in Russia and China, brutality, pain, and bloodshed on such a vast scale the mind cannot handle it. And on the more personal level, there is not a formally taboo behavior the mind can conceive of that isn't somewhere being acted out, and even publicly justified. In *Penthouse* magazine, a spokesman for a group of acknowledged child molesters came out with a declaration stating that initiating young children into sex is good for them as it frees them sexually. Satanism, rape, incest, and the glorification of pain in sadism are now being openly acknowledged, even romanticized. Some new value systems support a brittle hedonism and even extol an unabashed "me first" self-centeredness. This is exemplified by phrases in the popular culture such as: "The one who dies with the most toys wins," or "All I care about is what empowers me."

Who Defines Reality in Religions and Cults?

It is not surprising when old ways are breaking down that people seek other avenues for certainty, comfort, and protection. Charismatic leaders inevitably spring up in times of crisis and turmoil.

---

[4]"Do You Create Your Own Reality?" and "Oneness" in "The Power of Abstraction" contain succinct descriptions of how karma works.

In recent years, many people submitted themselves to a spectrum of spiritual teachers promising some form of salvation. Are gurus, as they claim to be, a necessary doorway to religious experiences that make life more profound? Or rather, are they filling deep needs and thus inadvertently pointing to trouble spots and lacks in the fabric of our culture, as well as revealing the depth of our conditioning to want authorities and mistrust ourselves?

Looking for saviors or holders of special wisdom as the way to lead humanity (or oneself) to salvation or survival has been ingrained in the old order. It is a core part of the unconscious authoritarianism deeply interwoven in the history, traditions, and myths of all complex cultures. Behind much of the appeal of such authorities lies the primitive and essentially childish hope of an external and magical answer to the existential problems and fears around living and dying. The guru/disciple relationship is a formal structure of extreme authoritarianism. It thus offers a quintessential exemplar of control and surrender, displaying mechanical processes that reinforce predilections toward submission. It also elucidates in *bas-relief* the workings of what may be called the cult mentality.

Here and throughout this book, the word "cult" is used in a specific way to refer to groups with an authoritarian structure where the leader's power is not constrained by scripture, tradition, or any other "higher" authority. This is a major difference between a cult and a traditional religion or sect that has become an accepted part of the culture. Probably all religions with an individual founder started as cults, becoming organized religions when, through widespread social acceptance, the structure itself and its symbols became more important than the individual leaders who succeeded the founder. Cults become religions whenever they build up traditions, a body of myths, parables, scriptures, and dogmas that are interpreted and protected by specialists (priests, etc.) who see themselves as the guardians of the truth, not the bringers of it.

Religious structures have as their ultimate authority either sacred writings or truths that are passed on orally, from generation to generation. The basic authority of religion is therefore tradition (statements, beliefs, and holy books from and about the past). This makes religious leaders the interpreters and perpetrators of tradition, much of which has been sacralized; thus they are only able to change things up to a point. Even the pope is constrained by the office he holds. As a one-time cardinal elected by peers, he is first among equals and not necessarily considered either morally or spiritually superior. He, too, must confess. Although the pope is theoretically the last word on spiritual matters in Catholicism, he is so only as an interpreter; the amount of reform or change he can actually bring forth is limited.

In a cult, absolute authority lies in a leader who has few if any external constraints. This means the leader (who is usually the founder) is not merely the interpreter but is also the creator of truth, and thus has free rein in what he proposes. Whether or not his authority rests upon a tradition or religion, he is revered as either God's unique vessel or as an actual manifestation of the living God or the god-force.

Like religions, cults offer meaning, purpose, identity, and community. But the feeling of unity is more intense in cults as their internal cohesiveness depends on protecting the purity of the group from outsiders. Thus there is relentless group pressure for loyalty and conformity. As social animals, many of our strongest feelings come from group alignment. Cults offer a powerful matrix that breaks through individual boundaries and amplifies energy. Often what grabs the person is not a specific leader or ideology, but rather the configuration of emotions that is part of the state of surrender itself. Gurus can arouse intense emotions as there is extraordinary passion in surrendering to what one perceives as a living God. The inbuilt potential for violence is likewise great. Should the guru become paranoid, greedy, or merely bored, as many do, they can get their disciples to do most anything.[5]

Eastern religions have a greater tendency to create leaders who do not have constraints, since the spiritually realized (the

---

[5]See "The Seductions of Surrender" and "Stages of Cults."

"enlightened ones") are held to be of a truly different order than ordinary people. Most gurus present themselves as being beyond the foibles resulting from ego.[6] Theoretically, Eastern religions offer the possibility of anyone achieving godhood and the infallibility this implies. In contrast, Christianity, Judaism, and Islam are transcendent dualisms where God is the creator of it all, and is a fundamentally different order of being. In Christ, God was uniquely portrayed as becoming partially human, but humans can never become God. Those mystics who felt otherwise were charged with heresy.

For many, Western religions have failed in offering a viable worldview. To understand the appeal of gurus for Westerners, one must understand the appeal of Eastern thought itself. In addition to promises of experiencing cosmic consciousness, Eastern religions offer three elements that are particularly appealing: 1) a perspective detached from the involvements of individuated life that ultimately sees everything as perfect; 2) practices that bring detachment from emotions and worldly desires; and 3) in karma/rebirth, a system that guarantees moral justice, the potential of continual improvement, and an open-ended existence. The idea of a detached cosmic perspective is new to most Westerners even though it appears in Western thought, Spinoza's "view from eternity" being an example. At first blush, it seems very unlike the emotional involvement with the personal God of Christianity. Actually, the guru becomes the disciple's personal living god, who can ignite even greater emotions than a god whose presence is not physically tangible.

We consider any worldview renunciate whose solutions to life's problems involve making what goes on in this world and this life secondary to some projected other kind of existence deemed more important and sacralized. This can at times alleviate personal despair, but historically has not—and from our perspective cannot—solve the problems that make renunciation appeal-

---

[6]"The Function of Enlightenment" in "Oneness, Enlightenment, and the Mystical Experience" covers this in greater depth.

ing.[7] Withdrawing from the world is much more appealing when there is somewhere to withdraw to. Increasingly, there is nowhere to go to escape external or internal disorder. Escaping through comforting beliefs is not a good model for survival.

A task of this book is to show that renunciate worldviews and their moralities are necessarily authoritarian, and why the solutions they generate have become a key part of the problem. This is so because the very construction of a category considered sacred automatically creates the non-sacred. Once this occurs, valuing sacrifice of the non-sacred to the sacred is inevitable, as are unchallengeable authorities that define how this is to be done. This paradigm has been a key controller on the planet for thousands of years, the results of which are for us the best testament that something else is needed. A blatant example is the Catholic Church making it difficult for a woman not to have children, because sacrificing her life and her body is part of God's will.[8]

The Guru Papers critiques the guru/disciple liaison because it is a clear-cut example of the old, no longer appropriate paradigm of spiritual authority. It is not that we doubt that some who are considered gurus have deeper insights than their followers. Yet even with the best intentions, assuming the role of spiritual authority for others sets in motion a system of interaction that is mechanical, predictable, and contains the essence of corruption. Another purpose of this book is to show that corruption is not simply the failure or weakness of a specific individual, but is structurally built into any authoritarian relationship, and less obviously, any renunciate morality.

---

[7]"Buddhism and the Abuse of Detachment" in *Control* discusses in depth the implications of renunciation.

[8]For more on the nature and limitations of renunciate religion, see "Dualism and Renunciation" in "Oneness" and "Symbol Systems and Power" in "The Power of Abstraction." "On Channeling Disembodied Authorities" gives a detailed exposition on how both authoritarianism and renunciation are disguised in certain current beliefs.

Surrender to a guru, though a way of filling a spiritual vacuum, is also one of the most powerful forms of mental and emotional control on the planet today. Especially insidious are the images of superiority tied to the presumption of greater wisdom, moral purity, or an enlightened state. Whether or not there is any reality behind these projections can be endlessly debated. The issue for us is not who has more wisdom or insight, but rather how this presumed wisdom is used. Asserting that one human being fundamentally knows what's best for another is authoritarian. If this is accepted, it sets up a chain of inevitable relational patterns that are detrimental to all players of the game.

Reexamining the Sacred

The yearnings to connect with something more profound than our individual lives may be called a religious or spiritual impulse. Religions have long been the way societies have structured this impulse. We do not question the need for people to connect with something more profound than their own personal dramas. We do question the viability of religions that present this world as a stepping stone to some other more important realm. Once this occurs, it is inevitable that religious experts delineate how to reach this other realm, and what must be sacrificed in this world to do so. This always includes renouncing self-centeredness—an endless task.

Once the spiritual impulse is channeled into any renunciate worldview, it makes those who share a belief in that structure feel connected. But this involves creating walls between "us" and "them," which historically has been the easy way to become mechanically bonded and fill the vacuum of meaning. This is especially tempting now that feelings of disconnection are rife. Uniting with each other and bringing meaning to existence in a way not based on a narrow group identity is one of the vital challenges of these times.

Because the power of traditional religions comes from furnishing unchallengeable answers about the unknown, they are inherently authoritarian. Religions deflect examination by ordaining faith and belief to be sacred, while maintaining that no ordinary person can know enough to take issue with the beliefs they put forth. A further hindrance to the intelligent examination of religious tradition is the social taboo against doing so. We do not question people's right to believe what they will. But the concept of religious tolerance is commonly extended to include not criticizing others' beliefs. This is partially because beliefs that are non-rational are considered not subject to rational examination. This may be true about the contents of a belief, but is not true about what effects operating out of a given belief have on the world. If a belief that sends children to war with the promise of a special paradise cannot be challenged as harmful, that concept of tolerance is for us intolerable.

We define tolerance simply as not trying to impose one's views on others through coercion. We also consider any view of tolerance that cuts off examination of anything the human mind can inquire into basically authoritarian. Why should religion, whose power is monumental, be exempt? We view ecological uncaringness, overpopulation, and uncared-for children as major threats to survival. In our conception of morality, structures that promote these are immoral. This, of course, is debatable, as it should be. Should a religion that makes birth control a sin not also be subject to examination and debate?

Indeed, the very act of making sacred certain actions, institutions, or ways of being is authoritarian, as it ensures that there can be no questioning. The potential for great abuse is inherent in any ideology closed to reason, feedback, or change based on changing circumstances. Officially placing something in the category of the sacred indicates that it needs protection and shoring up because of the fear it cannot stand on its own. Traditional concepts of the sacred set up an inherent dualism between what is sacred and what isn't. The hidden function of the sacred has been to get people to sacrifice to it. This has been a part of the same polarity that separated the spiritual from the worldly, which is the basis of all renunciate moralities. What most urgently needs to be reexamined in these fateful and dangerous times is, above all, that which has been held sacred.[9]

It is fashionable among some to say that truth, if it exists, cannot be known because all statements about it, and views of it, are couched in a language and cultural context which are essentially subjective. This is an understandable reaction against authoritarian absolutes and universals that masquerade as objective, while hiding self-interest. The downside of relativism is that it itself is a disguised absolute that inhibits even exploring whether there are or can be perspectives that go beyond the subjectivity of culture.

We hold that there are historically embedded pan-cultural truths that can reflect, however dimly, more than just the fabrications of vested interest, personal preference, or even cultural constructions. For us, one such truth is that the human species is now at risk because its new technological capacities for leveraging power have gone far beyond the constraints of the old moral systems. The truth of this can, of course, be challenged. But, nevertheless, the perception that the path humanity is on now risks extinction is either true or not. We cannot envision a more important topic for inquiry. People can only answer for themselves whether truth can be found and what it is. For us, humanity's hopes lie in the possibility that truth, whatever it may be in this time of crisis, will shine through.

---

[9]"The Power of Abstraction" examines the origin and development of the dualistic split between the spiritual and the mundane.

Gurus and Times of Upheaval

In times of upheaval or impending disaster, when people feel impotent to deal with the vast problems and uncertainties they face, the tendency to look for a leader who takes the responsibility out of their hands greatly increases. These saviors tend to be either political or spiritual, sometimes both.

Such is the case today. What is at risk is not only the security of individuals and cultures, but for the first time since the dawn of human history, our species itself is facing the possibility of extinction. The old morality and its institutions are breaking down, producing a spiritual vacuum, and with it alienation, meaninglessness, and moral confusion. Though such breakdown is necessary during periods of transition and is part of the impetus leading ideally to the creation of the new values, forms, and consciousness that will enable us to survive—still, while the breakdown is occurring, there is increasing fear, conflict, misery, violence, and chaos. Often when people are afraid, they regress to old values, behaviors, and emotional stances. Hence the political conservatism, religious fundamentalism, self-protectiveness, addictions, racism, hatred, cults, and "magical thinking" that can be observed all around us.

It is no wonder then that many people are looking to spiritual leaders to attempt to solve their problems. When one feels impotent the desire to surrender oneself to some higher power or authority is very great indeed. And yet in the very process of doing so, one often acts out patterns of dependency that are not at all conducive to meeting the challenges of these times. In fact, for this particular historical moment, the blind acceptance of authority—even if that authority has deeper wisdom—is not what is needed. Surrendering to authority sets up dangerous and powerfully ingrained patterns that become part of the psychic structures of both those who accept and those who become the authority.

Most people are uncomfortable with uncertainty; so when a previously held worldview loses credibility it is natural to seek another structured viewpoint to view the world from. For those who feel the answers provided by Western religions are bankrupt, Eastern religions are seductive for several reasons, among them: Eastern worldviews are more abstract and philosophically sophisticated, and thus also more congruent with modern science; they offer living human beings (albeit only a few special ones) as the vehicles for truth and wisdom; they offer techniques that can both alter consciousness and detach one from unwanted feelings, giving more emotional control; they promise direct access to religious or mystical experiences. Practices such as yoga and meditation have been refined over millennia to bring insights into such inner psychological states as fear, sorrow, and the nature of personal identity.[1]

A guru is a spiritual guide or teacher who through obedience to his guru is presumed to have attained spiritual realization, after which it is further presumed he can do the same for others if they likewise obey him. The tutorial method of religious instruction—the transmission of information from guru (Hinduism) or spiritual master (Buddhism) to disciple—was an integral part of maintaining Eastern traditions. Religious self-instruction was considered dubious at best because part of Eastern tradition asserts the need for a realized master to cut

---

[1] "East and West: Looking Within and Looking Without" in *Control* discusses what Eastern perspectives offer the West.

through self-delusion.[2]

In the East gurus have institutional status and are considered by believers to be a direct and unblemished expression of the divine. Gurus are the only living individuals to whom complete obedience on all matters is prescribed by the roles. As disciples are expected to surrender, gurus must also know how to keep and exercise control. Part One illustrates that though mystified, the methods gurus use to keep control are no different than in any other arena—the manipulation of fear and desire. In "spiritual" realms fear and desire can become as extreme as they get. When a living person becomes the focus of such emotions, the possibility of manipulation is correspondingly extreme. "Personal Masks" also shows the techniques the ancient guru tradition has refined over millennia for getting people to surrender control. The guru/disciple relationship provides the most extreme, clearcut and sophisticated example of a bond of dominance and submission not based on physical coercion. This still flourishing ancient tradition is a microcosm encapsulating the most extreme exercise of mental authoritarianism. Its appeal for some Westerners is a testament to the depths and tenacity of authoritarian conditioning. It displays in *bas-relief* the predilections toward authoritarianism that permeate the world at large.

In the rigid cultures of the East most people have little chance of moving out of the prescribed familial and social roles they were born to, except through the spiritual path which was the sanctioned (and only) way to "drop out." In order to explore the inner life at all it was necessary to remove oneself from the ordinary ties, binds, and activities that consumed life. The concept and role of spiritual master became the exemplar of renouncing the importance of worldly life. The idea is that one becomes a master of life (and death) by removing any hold that the vicissitudes of life had over one's internal states. Religious teachers who orally passed on the knowledge they acquired from

---

[2]See "The Function of Enlightenment" in "Oneness, Enlightenment, and the Mystical Experience."

either other teachers, inner practices, or both offered an alternative way of life that had at least the potential for greater depth of understanding; for only they had the time or inclination to delve into psychological and philosophical realms. The appeal of renunciation is that to the extent one can do it, it does bring control over emotional states. This "dropping out" really amounted to "dropping into" other socially sanctioned roles that were all encased in the category of spiritual—devotee, monk, wandering *saddhu,* or wilderness hermit.

Of course, the master/devotee tradition has not only produced advances in understanding but has also moved the hearts of many people through devotion, art, and literature. It offered an oasis from the grind of life and an opportunity to explore one's relation to the cosmos. In examining and critiquing it, we are not concerned with its historical appropriateness or past value. Rather, we wish to show why this or any authoritarian form is now not only counter-productive, but destructive. Understanding the appeal of gurus and the basic worldview they come from can help show why authoritarian means of disseminating information are no longer viable. Authoritarian mechanisms for information transmission have been a large part of what brought the world to where it is today. This book aims at describing why this mode can no longer answer the needs of a humanity that must mature to survive.

The guru/disciple relationship contains an essential assumption that makes it particularly susceptible to abuse: namely, that it is possible for a person to be totally immune from the corruptions of power. What this must also mean is that such a person is totally free of all self-interest, for self-interest necessarily entails the possibility of corruption. Our perspective is that no one, no matter how exalted in awareness and understanding, can totally escape the psychological fact that self-interest is an element in being human, and is also a necessary element in staying alive.

Regardless of whether or not it is possible for anyone to transcend self-interest and the capacity to be corrupted by power,

42

how could anyone (even—or especially—that person) be sure this is so? In political realms, the corruptions inherent in power are taken for granted. The power one person can have over another in so-called spiritual realms is far greater than any other, if one believes that person is the doorway to salvation. This power is so absolute that it can lead to excesses that are correspondingly extreme.

Many recent scandals have shown that those who have wielded such power routinely abuse it. It is often assumed that this is because somehow the wrong person was given more credibility than deserved. We wish to demonstrate that the corruption of so-called spiritual power does not simply occur because the wrong person is in power. Rather, this occurs whenever a role or structure bestows power through images of infallibility or moral superiority. The fault then does not lie in a given leader's shortcomings, but rather in the structure itself, through defining one person as more pure and spiritual, and thus superior to others.

If people believe a leader can save them, they are capable of any action ordered, including killing others and even themselves. Technology has expanded the potential abuse of power manyfold. Now through media images, leaders of all sorts can charismatically control far more people than ever before, without having any personal connection with them. A fundamentalist religious authority (now deceased) who took over an Islamic society exemplifies the very real danger of combining the extraordinary power of religion with political power. By literally giving them plastic keys to the gates of heaven, this leader was able to get young boys to die gladly as warriors for their salvation.

If humanity is to meet the extraordinary challenges it now faces, a context is needed that allows people to become self-corrective, responsible adults. Particularly in these times of upheaval, our deeply conditioned predilection to look to authorities to solve our problems must be seen for what it is—a part of human history that is no longer viable. Throughout the ages, this need for authorities has created hierarchies that have allowed power and privilege to justify and maintain themselves, without needing recourse to anything other than the masked vested interests of tradition itself. Tradition has always been used to reassure people's fear of chaos and of each other; it is also the cohesive force behind power and privilege. But now these traditions and institutions that once kept chaos at bay are at the root of disorder, since they are no longer able to meet the needs of a radically changing world. In times of upheaval the appeal of gurus[3] and authorities, whether "spiritual" or secular, is really reaching for an anchor of stability. The following chapters aim to show how and why any person, ideology, or structure that in the short or long run undermines a person's self-trust is part of the problem, not the solution.

---

[3]Although the concept of guru comes from a traditional Eastern framework, the dynamics of power in that position are largely applicable to any group with an unchallengeable leader. So throughout this book, the word "guru" is also used to refer to leaders (no matter what they are called) whose unchallengeability is not primarily based on physical coercion.

The Seductions
of Surrender

When a child is born, a very powerful constellation of factors occurs. Boundaries between self and others are as yet relatively indistinct and unformed; consequently there is a great deal of uncontrollable emotion. This includes a sense of being at the center of the universe, which can feel very powerful. The baby cries and the universe around it moves; it is the center of focus and attention. Being totally cared for, with no expectations from others, with no future to worry about or past to regret, is part of a unique moment that cannot last. Most people have had some time in this place—a day, a week, a month, or even longer. It is a place of innocence that contains a sense of basic well-being, of fundamental security, and also of power. That one has yet to face the specter of mortality is a significant factor in such innocence.

This experience—which lives deep in memory, not in an intellectual or symbolic way, but rather viscerally—can give rise to a nebulous sense of longing for its return. This is especially so if one's later life is unfulfilling. Often a large component of spiritual seeking is the desire for a place of no conflict, where a benign, all-powerful intelligence is taking care of things, and not incidentally, where one feels immortal again. Such yearnings are actually the deep want to return to that early place. This means that what many people are seeking in the name of spirituality is not really to grow and to further develop a sense of their relationship with the scheme of things—a journey into the unknown. What is actually being sought is a return to the known.[1]

Surrendering to an authority whose image of spirituality caters to such yearnings is perhaps the easiest way to simulate that bygone state of innocence. Since surrender is built into the structure of the guru/disciple relationship, it represents the epitome of submission to a living person. Surrender is not only the key to understanding this and other authoritarian modes, but the very act of surrendering has predictable psychological consequences that can explain why gurus have attracted people from many backgrounds. The guru/disciple framework offers a uniquely transparent window into the nature and appeal of authoritarian structures in general.

Unlike the West where only a transcendent God is considered infallible, much of Eastern religion postulates that people, perhaps anyone, can attain godhood through lifetimes of proper action (good karma). Thus the East links spirituality with either seeking or attaining such a state, which is often called enlightenment, i.e., being a cosmic or spiritual "knower." This creates two basic stances—seeker and knower. Should one delve into the mysteries of life and glean insights, it is natural to wish to share them. But taking on the role of knower fits into the predilection of seekers to want an authority they can trust. Being treated as a knower is one of the most seductive and difficult places to be. One is treated very specially—for what is more special than being considered a vessel of the truth? This special treatment hinges on fitting people's preconceptions of a spiritual knower, which means it is not propitious to acknowledge, even to oneself, that one may at times be uncertain or wrong.

In the spiritual world, those who rise to the top and are thought of as knowers tend to be exceptional people, as is the

---

[1]"Love Addiction" in "Love and Control: The Conditions Underlying Unconditional Love" shows how emotional surrender, whether in love or religion, can become a psychological addiction.

case in any area with much potential power, wealth, and influence. The need to appear right when presenting oneself as a spiritual knower is greater than in any other arena because knowing is what makes one essentially different from seekers. Admitting any fallibility not only removes one from that exalted place, but makes it difficult to compete with other presumed knowers who do claim infallibility. Part of being a knower is knowing that seekers are searching for certainty, and that if you don't offer it someone else will. The stance "I know a lot, but I can make mistakes" cannot compete with "I know everything that counts and never err about what's important." So those who play the knower role are under great pressure to put forth an image of certainty.

The concept of enlightenment contributes to gurus' need to be infallible. Enlightenment is conceived of as a static and absolute state which when reached is all-encompassing, leaving nowhere to go. Tied to this odd image of finality within an evolving cosmos is the presumption that a modern manifestation of an enlightened being would be saying pretty much the same things as were said thousands of years ago. If enlightenment could be influenced by the historical context, or could itself evolve, then one could never be sure that anyone had the last word. The view that puts enlightenment beyond history, change, and fallibility also reinforces the belief that neither the psychological facts of human existence (self-interest, fear, and desire, for example) nor the normal rules of behavior apply to enlightened knowers.[2]

In the traditional guru/disciple structure, disciples are expected to surrender their will to the guru. This is presented as necessary for the guru to lead the disciple to realizations that can only be achieved by giving up the mundane attachments previously accumulated. This, of course, includes material attachments; but more importantly, surrender is presented as the means of letting go of the more deep-seated psychological attachments,

---

[2]See "The Function of Enlightenment" in "Oneness, Enlightenment, and the Mystical Experience."

which include the very structure of personality and identity (what is called ego).

As surrender to a guru is an integral part of being a disciple, this offers a paradigm for examining the needs surrender fills, the emotions it generates, and why it appears to offer quick access to change. In our view, deciphering the mechanisms of surrender can only be done by viewing it in tandem with control.

Control and Surrender

Control, taking charge (or attempting to), and surrender, letting go, are two basic relational stances. Surrender is often presented as the antithesis of control, as giving it up. Surrender does not do away with control; rather, it shifts control somewhere else. This is because control and surrender are embedded in each other and always have some kind of relation. Like dominance and submission, control and surrender cannot exist in isolation without the other. Surrendering control usually means shifting from internal control to being controlled externally, whether by a person or ideology. But this shift is not clear-cut, for one must internalize the ideology to follow it, and the willingness to obey another is also internal. What one lets go of is only a level of self-control. There is still an aspect, often hidden, of being in control of surrendering.

As socialized animals, even internal controls, like values and conscience, have been at least partially implanted by an external social context. So, from our perspective, something is always in control, or at least more in control than something else. This is why we think it a mistake to consider control and surrender autonomous categories. Surrendering feels different than control because it involves opening one's boundaries. An irony is that the more total surrender appears, the more absolute the context of external control it occurs in.[3]

---

[3]See "Inducing Surrender" in "Guru Ploys." For more on control, see "Who Is in Control? The Authoritarian Roots of Addiction."

Hindu lore contains this adage, "No *shakti* without *bhakti*."
Shakti refers to a transcendent energy, while *bhakti* means devotion or surrender. What may be called transcendent experiences
do occur in love, art, religion, and even in something as seemingly mundane as sports—whenever one lets go of control, that
is, surrenders to something outside oneself. In team sports one
relinquishes individual control to be controlled by the group.
Anyone who has been involved in team sports may have experienced moments of feeling like part of a well-oiled machine, with
all the players magically acting as one. It's as if the totality were
directing all its parts—there are no mistakes. These high
moments in sports have a different quality of energy.

Surrender is one of the most powerful forces and emotional
states that a human being can touch into. Passion literally means
abandonment, letting go; thus surrender is a way to passion. It is
possible to surrender to many aspects of life: a person, an ideal,
one's art, a religion, a political system, the revolution, and even
the living moment. Surrender is so potent precisely because it
shifts control to an arena that is free, or more free, from one's
inner dramas and the conflicts involved in personal decisions.
If I surrender my heart to you, then being with you becomes
central in my life. If I give my life to music, spiritual realization,
whatever, then that dictates my movement. It becomes the focus
of my life, which eliminates many choices by making all else secondary. Surrender is a basic part of life, as is control. What is
being examined and taken issue with is surrender as a part of
authoritarian control.

In the East a guru is more than a teacher. He is a doorway
that supposedly allows one to enter into a more profound relationship with the spiritual. A necessary step becomes acknowledging the guru's specialness and mastery over that which one
wishes to attain. The message is that to be a really serious student, spiritual realization must be the primary concern. Therefore one's relationship with the guru must, in time, become
one's prime emotional bond, with all others viewed as secondary. In fact, typically other relationships are pejoratively

referred to as "attachments." Once the primary bond with the guru is established, a powerful configuration of factors comes into play.

The ostensible reason for fostering surrender is it detaches followers from certain deep conditionings presumed to be obstacles on the spiritual path. But it does not detach them from one of the most insidious and powerful conditionings of all—the predilection to look for an authority that one can trust more than oneself. On the contrary, gurus happily leave intact that basic conditioning. To be someone's authority is to be firmly implanted at the very center of their being. So although most gurus preach detachment, disciples become attached to having the guru as their center, whereas the guru becomes attached to the power of being others' center. These reciprocal attachments are ignored because attachment to the guru is considered spiritual; and the guru, who is presumed enlightened, is by definition supposed to be beyond attachments.

Scandals, Saints, and Self-Centeredness

In recent years, myriad scandals within different spiritual communities have come to light. The scandals expose that the leader, or the group with the leader's knowledge, was involved in behaviors contrary to the espoused message and values. In short, each instance involved an abuse of power. We will show why from our perspective these abuses were not merely isolated aberrations; rather the structure of surrendering to an authority not only increases the likelihood of corruption, but makes corruption nigh inevitable. Not surprisingly, the abuses were variations of the four routine corruptions of power:

1. Sexual abuse. Some of the more extreme abuses include child molestation, rape, and promulgating prostitution to support the leader and group. Then there is the deceit that is seemingly innocuous to some people, involving a pre-

tense of celibacy or monogamy while having clandestine sexual activity.[4]

2. Material abuse. This involves the different ways the concerns for wealth and luxurious living contradict the stated values of austerity or detachment—secret bank accounts, cultivating the wealthy, flamboyant lifestyles, expensive cars and planes, etc. Commonly the leader and the inner circle lead extravagant lives of opulence, while the outer circle labors hard for meager material reward.

3. The abuse of power. This includes using and abusing others for one's own enhancement and to preserve power. Behind images of peace, altruism, love, non-violence, and saving the world, many groups used threats and violence to maintain obedience and protect themselves against what they perceived as danger to the group. One leader even sent "hit" men to physically punish errant disciples. There have been incidences of death threats and attacks aimed at anyone who was thought to undermine the group; this included former followers, those considering leaving, and those who directly challenge the beliefs. Abuses of power are just another indication of the lie within the guru's identity, which is supposedly beyond self-interest.

4. Self-abuse. The conscious messages are clear: the body is the temple of spirit and must be so treated; a healthy body is the result of a healthy mind and spirit; tranquillity, compassion, and emotional control are signs of arrival. Yet many leaders display the opposite: drunkenness, obesity, vindictiveness, rages, and physical ailments that in others would be called psychosomatic, such as allergies, ulcers, or high blood pressure. In fact, a close examination of the history, past and present, of many religious leaders shows a high incidence of what might be termed self-destructive indicators.

---

[4]See "Gurus and Sexual Manipulation" on why sexual misconduct is not only a deep betrayal of trust, but also a core lie about the guru's very identity and teachings.

When abuses are publicly exposed the leader either denies or justifies the behaviors by saying that "enemies of the truth" or "the forces of evil" are trying to subvert his true message. Core members of the group have a huge vested interest in believing him, as their identity is wrapped up in believing in his righteousness. Those who begin to doubt him at first become confused and depressed, and later feel betrayed and angry. The ways people deny and justify are similar: Since supposedly no one who is not enlightened can truly understand the motives of one who is, any criticism can be discounted as a limited perspective. Also any behavior on the part of the guru, no matter how base, can be imputed to be some secret teaching or message that needs deciphering.

By holding gurus as perfect and thus beyond ordinary explanations, their presumed specialness can be used to justify anything. Some deeper, occult reason can always be ascribed to anything a guru does: The guru is said to take on the karma of others, and that is why his body has whatever problems it has. The guru is obese or unhealthy because he is too kind to turn down offerings; besides, he gives so much that a little excess is understandable. He punishes those who disobey him not out of anger but out of necessity, as a good father would. He uses sex to teach about energy and detachment. He lives an opulent life to break people's simplistic preconceptions of what ego-loss should look like; it also shows how detached and unconcerned he is about what others think. For after all, "Once enlightened, one can do anything." Believing this dictum makes any action justifiable.

People justify and rationalize in gurus what in others would be considered unacceptable because they have a huge emotional investment in believing their guru is both pure and right. Why? Why do people need images of perfection and omniscience? This goes back to the whole guru/disciple relationship being predicated on surrender. Surrender of great magnitude requires correspondingly great images of perfection. It would be difficult to surrender to one whose motives were not thought to be pure, which has come to mean untainted by self-centeredness. How can one surrender to a person who might put his self-interest first? Also it is difficult to surrender to someone who can make mistakes, especially mistakes that could have significant impact on one's life. Consequently, the guru can never be wrong, make mistakes, be self-centered, or lose emotional control. He doesn't get angry, he "uses" anger to teach.

There is another equally important, crucial to understand reason why people want so much to believe that someone, somewhere, does not have the common foibles of humanity—that it is possible for a few special people to be above it all. Instead of enumerating the many ways human beings heap uncaringness on each other, let's categorize them as all containing aspects of self-centeredness. Most moral judgments pertain to the wrongness of particular expressions of self-centeredness. Furthermore, since unmitigated self-centeredness lies underneath acts of callous violence, it itself is often simplistically made the culprit. In this line of thinking, to be a better human being is to be less self-centered; and to be the best possible person is not to be self-centered at all.

The way spiritual growth is traditionally presented involves getting rid of the aspects of oneself that are disliked or disapproved of. Here becoming a better person means tempering such self-centered expressions as jealousy, competitiveness, pettiness, etc. So for there to be someone who is free of such things acts as a motivator for bettering and controlling oneself. That's why many people need to believe in saints. (The traditional meaning of saint is someone who has transcended the ordinary manifestations of self-centeredness.) Saints serve as ideal examples, giving hope that others, too, can at least become better, if not perfect.[5]

It is difficult for an intelligent, caring person to look clearly at self-centeredness without experiencing some discomfort. Obvi-

---

[5]"Who Is in Control?" describes the consequences of internalizing an unlivable morality. "What is Selfless Service Serving?" (in *Control*) gives an in-depth explanation of why making selflessness the all-important virtue not only does not work, but contains the seeds of corruption.

ously all the judged inequities in the world are a product of it, and the ways we hurt each other contain it. All the major problems on the planet (ecology, politics, starvation, violence, racism, chauvinism, and crime) likewise display it. Renunciate religions control people through the guilt they instill around self-centeredness; and communist regimes, at least theoretically, tried to legislate and coerce it away, believing it to be a product of wrong social conditioning. No wonder then that many on spiritual paths are searching for a way out of the problems and discomfort that self-centeredness brings. In the East, ego-loss is looked upon as the necessary doorway to a different and sublime relationship with the spiritual. This involves the goal of eliminating self-centeredness through eliminating the self. Detaching from the cravings of ego is the origin of the spiritual ideal of detachment.

Christianity demands the acknowledgment that humans are sinners (read self-centered), and that salvation comes through accepting Christ and the morality he is purported to have put forth. Christ is viewed as the ultimate in selflessness, for he sacrificed himself to save humanity and pay for its sins. A core message of the New Testament is that by surrendering to Christ and his dictates, one can curb self-centeredness enough to save one's soul. That interest in one's own salvation is totally self-centered is a conundrum rarely explored. Surrender to Christ and to a guru have similar dynamics, as they both bring about feelings of passion, a sense of purpose, and the immediate reduction of conflict and tension. It is difficult for disciples to avoid the trap of using their new-found good feelings and relatively peaceful emotional state as verification that the guru and his worldview are essentially correct. As many do, they use "feeling better" as their litmus test for truth.

The power of Eastern religions and the gurus that represent them is that they offer a living Christ-like figure to worship, and also hold out the promise that anyone who does the proper practices could conceivably reach that high state, too. The path most often recommended and presented as the easiest, most direct route is called *bhakti* or devotion, which involves worshipping and surrendering to the guru as a manifestation of God. Interestingly, the more one surrenders to another, the less self-centered one actually feels, because one appears to be making that someone or something more important than oneself. This is why surrendering to a guru is often presented as the easiest way of becoming more selfless. Along with devotion, working hard for the guru and his cause (sometimes referred to as "karma yoga") also makes one feel less self-centered.

Recognizing Authoritarian Control

Surrendering to a guru brings instant intimacy with all who share the same values. In a world where traditional values are crumbling, bringing brittle, hedonistic ways of relating, many feel alone and disconnected. Acceptance by and identification with the group induce a loosening of personal boundaries. This opening consequently increases the emotional content of one's life, bringing purpose, meaning, and hope. It is no wonder that those who join such groups rave about how much better they feel than previously. But this quick, one-dimensional bonding is based solely upon a shared ideology. No matter how intense and secure it feels, should one leave the fold, it evaporates as quickly as it formed.

Surrender is the glue that binds guru and disciple. Being a disciple offers the closest approximation (outside of mental institutions) to the special configuration of infancy. Surrender is a route that enables disciples to experience again, at least partially, the conflict-free innocence that is the source of their atavistic longings. Among these, perhaps most important is the feeling of once again being totally cared for. Surrendering to any authority brings this about to some extent, but with a guru it reaches vast dimensions. The guru reinforces this by letting it be known that all who follow him are and will be especially protected. For the follower, this feels like being protected by God.

This dependent state satisfies other longings that stem from infancy. Once again, one experiences being at the center of the universe—if not directly (the guru occupies that space), at least closer to the center than one could have thought possible. The guru also puts out the image of the totally accepting parent—the parent one never had but always wanted. So disciples believe they are loved unconditionally, even though this love is conditional on continued surrender. Disciples in the throes of surrender feel they have given up their past, and do not, consciously at least, fear the future. In addition, they feel more powerful through believing that the guru and the group are destined to greatly influence the world. Feeling totally cared for and accepted, at the universe's center, powerful, and seemingly unafraid of the future are all achieved at the price of giving one's power to another, thus remaining essentially a child.

Surrendering to an authority who dictates what's right is a quick, mechanical route to feeling more virtuous. It is a fast track for taking on a moral system and to some extent following it. But more, that act of surrender itself can feel like giving up or at least diminishing one's ego, which is presented as a sign of spiritual progress. All renunciate moral systems have as prime virtues selflessness and obedience to some higher authority. If confused or in conflict, conforming to programming can make one feel immediately better. Obedience itself can feel selfless. The conditioning here runs deep. Children are praised for obedience, which fundamentally means doing what the parent wants instead of what they want. When disobedient, a child is often called selfish, which is never a compliment. Surrendering to an authority and then being rewarded for it is part of being a child. It may be true that there is no way out of this. Yet there is a world of difference between parenting aimed at holding on to authority, and parenting that leads children to self-trust. We are certain that children raised to trust themselves would be far less susceptible to authoritarian control. No matter how much better one initially feels, anything that undermines self-trust in the long run is detrimental to becoming an adult.[6]

---

[6]"The Ambiguity of Parental Authority" in *Control* goes into this in depth.

Disciples usually become more attached to the psychological state that surrender brings than to the guru, whom they never really get to know as a person. Repudiation of the guru (or even doubt and questioning) means a return to earlier conflict, confusion, and meaninglessness. The deeper the surrender, and the more energy and commitment they put into the guru, the greater their emotional investment is. Disciples will thus put up with a great deal of contradictory and aberrant behavior on the guru's part, for doubting him literally means having their world fall apart.

This is why many who are involved in authoritarian surrender adamantly deny they are. Those who see the dissembling in other gurus or leaders can find countless ways to believe that their guru is different. It is not at all unusual to be in an authoritarian relationship and not know it. In fact, knowing it can interfere with surrender. Any of the following are strong indications of belonging to an authoritarian group:

1. No deviation from the party line is allowed. Anyone who has thoughts or feelings contrary to the accepted perspective is made to feel wrong or bad for having them.

2. Whatever the authority does is regarded as perfect or right. Thus behaviors that would be questioned in others are made to seem different and proper.

3. One trusts that the leader or others in the group know what's best.

4. It is difficult to communicate with anyone not in the group.

5. One finds oneself defending actions of the leader (or other members) without having firsthand knowledge of what occurred.

6. At times one is confused and fearful without knowing why. This is a sign that doubts are being repressed.

The age-old inquiry that asks "Who am I?" looks inside for self-discovery. The process of digging deeper into oneself reveals there are self-images constructed out of the past that are part of one's identity. The true meaning of spiritual surrender involves letting go of self-defining images that limit who one is and can be. Within this inner inquiry one also comes to realize that one is part of a larger context. Surrendering to those who present themselves as a better or more real representative of that larger context perverts the true beauty and meaning of surrender. On the contrary, surrendering to another as the gateway to salvation keeps people dependent, childish, and living second-handedly. Surrender as an adult encompasses realizing that all of us are an interwoven part of a larger process that both creates and is created by its components. This involves being able both to control life and to surrender to what life offers. It does not involve giving up one's power or identity.

The only way any living system works well is to have information flowing freely between its parts and its environment. This is particularly essential with human beings, in order to counteract the inbuilt nature of subjectivity and the biasing filters of self-interest. The guru/disciple relationship, which is inherently authoritarian, cuts off the necessary flow of information for both, creating a feedback-proof system. If any degree of objectivity can ever be obtained, it is only through open minds that change with changing information.

The thoughts in this book could always be written off as unspiritual, egotistical, and coming from a lower plane of understanding. Ultimately there is no way to prove whose perspective is more accurate. What can be shown, however, is whether the process involved in establishing a given worldview is authoritarian, and what the implications of this process are. The tragedy that all authoritarian structures breed, particularly so-called spiritual ones, comes from giving absolute priority to another's viewpoint. This involves mistakenly identifying as spiritual the (usually temporary) conflict-free emotions and passions that come from surrendering to an authority. The tragedy is compounded in our times because our survival as a species depends upon adults coming to the fore who can break the shackles of old authority and tradition, creating new forms of relating to each other and to the planet we live on. In order to do this, we must use all we have: our bodies, our emotions, our minds, and all types of information from the world around us. Blind surrender to authority is an emotional indulgence and illusory security the species can no longer afford.

Guru Ploys

Surrender lies at the core of the traditional guru/disciple relationship and is in varying degrees a part of any authoritarian structure. Ideally disciples surrender totally to the will of the guru, as Christians are supposed to surrender to the will of God. Gurus are thus able to wield extreme authoritarian power over their disciples. A guru, to be a guru, must know how to move people into a psychological state of surrender and keep them there. Gurus know that those who show any interest in them rarely do so out of mere curiosity, but want something they are lacking. What many people crave these days is a sense of connection or union with something they consider sufficiently profound to give their lives meaning. The very act of surrender initially brings this about.

Inducing Surrender

Psychological authoritarianism is based on manipulating desire and fear. Hence the motivational techniques utilized to induce and perpetuate surrender are the usual promises of rewards (worldly or otherworldly) and threats of punishments. Getting people to surrender leans more heavily on the reward side, while keeping them there depends more on emphasizing the dire results of leaving the guru. The focus of this chapter is to reveal the ways surrender can be mechanically induced. We are not intimating that all gurus are consciously aware of their manipulations. Some, especially those immersed in tradition, could be merely repeating what they were taught and what was done with them by their own guru. Those who at one time had a guru are particularly inclined to believe surrender is an essential component in transmitting their esoteric knowledge.

Traditional gurus teach what they were taught. Most gurus' training in dealing with disciples is through example—watching their own guru. They learn to recognize, reinforce, and reward surrender, and to negate non-surrender. Aside from the more tangible rewards, they reinforce devotion with attention and approval, and punish its lack by withdrawing them. Though some gurus say that doubts are healthy, they subtly punish them. Doubt is not the way to get into the inner circle. Believing surrender is essential for transmitting their teachings, some gurus could be aware they are manipulating people to surrender, but think they are doing so "for their own good." (If this were in fact true, it would mean that deep truths are only accessible via an authoritarian mode.) This can not only justify manipulation, but also justify dissembling in order to help eliminate people's doubts—all this being done in the name of fostering spiritual growth.

In the initial seduction phase, the potential disciple becomes the focus of the guru's or group's attention and is made to feel very important. Then enticements are dangled in the form of testimonials, promises of extraordinary experiences, and offers of unqualified friendship and care—heady stuff. A convincing persuasion is that devotees not only claim to feel so much better now than before, but to those who have known them previously, they do in fact appear happier. Once an initial commitment has been made, techniques geared at disorientation come into play. This is done through undermining both self-trust and one's previous attachments and support systems. Critical thought and relying upon previous experience are made to appear the source of one's past or current problems.[1] One spiritual leader claims to be the real parent, while labeling the biological parents the "devil parents."

---

[1] "The Assault on Reason" describes some key functions of critical thought and the effects of undermining it.

The most enticing message to induce surrender is that only in this way can one achieve true spiritual advancement. Two common arguments used to deal with resistance contain promises of "knowing God" or "fulfilling karmic destiny." The first makes one feel inadequate because of the inability to commit; the second emphasizes the guru's superior position and disarms fears of making a mistake:

1. "What is important is not the guru or whether you become my disciple. What most limits you is your great difficulty with commitment to anything. Someday you must face whether you will ever move beyond your endless indecision and have the courage to give yourself totally to something. Do you think that knowing God can come from half-measures?"

2. "How can anyone who is half-asleep know who is awake and who is not? How can a disciple know what is in the heart of the guru? If your heart is open to the guru, you fulfill your karmic destiny. If the guru betrays his disciples' trust, that is his bad karma, not theirs. But what man of wisdom would sow the seeds of his own demise?"

At some point disciplines or techniques are given that have a specified goal and predicted end result. For example, people are told that through meditating in a specified way they will eventually experience blue lights or see the guru's face, or some other internal occurrence. What the promise is matters little because the mind can eventually construct any image it focuses upon. One is also told that regular practice will eventually bring higher states of consciousness and possibly even enlightenment, though this can take years or lifetimes.[2]

---

[2]Meditation techniques are often presented as devoid of any ideology or programming. The section on Buddhism in *Control* shows the ways even the most seemingly simple and "pure" techniques can contain hidden authoritarian prescriptions and be used surreptitiously to program a given worldview.

Once a disciple has had the predicted experience, the guru and group reinforce belief in its importance. The first mini-experience (say of blue lights) is presented as a significant step on the spiritual path. Having a mini-experience gives hope that grander ones will eventually occur. The experiences derived from the practices are then used as verification of both the guru's power and the truth of his worldview. But all this actually proves is that these experiences can be mechanically induced through mental techniques, and thus are predictable. People are often further conditioned to look at the guru as the fount or source of their newfound positive feelings. They are taught to use the guru's picture before meditation to trigger memories of emotional states that occurred in the presence of the guru.

The process of surrendering to a guru can be gradual, like peeling an onion, as people surrender more and more deeply over time. Often, however, a powerful and relatively quick conversion experience occurs wherein people drop all resistance, totally accepting the guru's teachings. Quick, sometimes unexpected conversions can happen within any belief system, although they generally occur in religious frameworks. This "seeing the light" can make one feel free of old baggage, thus new and even reborn. A conversion experience often brings tremendous release and intense emotion, as it involves letting go of one's old identity and taking on a new one. The past is automatically reinterpreted in the light of whatever value system and worldview one has converted to. People use these powerful feelings to validate their new beliefs. These beliefs are the source of the euphoria, but not necessarily because they are true. Any new worldview will do, as it is the conversion experience itself, not the validity of specific beliefs, that is the real source of the emotions. The guru promises, either directly or indirectly, that surrendering to him will bring something wonderful, and he is found to be right. People then conclude the guru must indeed be an enlightened master.

Many cults and evangelical fundamentalist religions not only promote conversion experiences but rely on them for much of their credibility. Some New Age groups promote conversions in their "trainings," claiming to be non-authoritarian because people supposedly personally experience the truth of their belief systems. However, something else is going on here. The very fact that so many different types of groups, with such radically different belief systems, can do this shows that surrendering to any leader or ideology can bring powerful feelings and an instant new identity. The feeling of renewal often includes believing that one has wiped one's moral slate clean. The power of conversion experiences lies in the psychological shift from confusion to certainty. The new beliefs become essential to hold and defend lest all the good feelings that come from certainty vanish.

The price paid for these good feelings is succumbing to one of the oldest forms of authoritarian mind control. Its power is such that it is not unusual for people to defend the sanctity of the authority with their lives if necessary. Being reborn in this way eventually closes people to everything that does not conform to their new, rigidly held worldview. Although one's individual boundaries are open to the group, the group's boundaries are closed to outsiders. Ultimately one only accepts and feels comfortable with those either within the system or open to proselytization.

Maintaining Dominance

Surrender to authority is an integral part of the psychology of authoritarian hierarchy. Hierarchies of power, especially those that purport to be spiritual, are based on a hierarchy of value where the leader is considered better, purer, or essentially different. Next comes the heir-apparent or inner circle. This creates separation between those at different levels, and also between the group as a whole and those outside the hierarchy. Surrendering to a guru thus involves surrendering to a hierarchical mode of relating that has within it dominance and submission.[3]

---

[3]See "The Attractions of Cult Hierarchy."

After the newness of conversion wears off, some doubt may return. To maintain allegiance, a support system that reinforces people's new identity is crucial. Power within the group is gained by deepening surrender to the guru, and members reward each other for making the group the priority. Deepening surrender does feel like letting go of ego and is defined by the guru as spiritual progress. Secrecy and arousing desire are important parts of the seduction. The guru dangles carrots of esoteric knowledge that he will transmit when he deems the disciple "ready." Waiting for each new piece of hidden knowledge not only keeps devotees around, but receiving pieces of it (one never gets it all) confirms their worthiness and specialness. Now they, too, have knowledge that others do not.

Any conflict disciples have about submitting to the guru's authority is defined pejoratively as resistance to a higher truth, the intrusion of ego, or a sign of unwillingness to give up attachments. Since surrender initially alleviates conflict and brings extremely good feelings, it is a powerful form of conditioning. If people end up feeling good and more open, they mistakenly conclude that whatever promoted it must also be true and good. Thus "feeling good" and opening boundaries are erroneously equated with truth. Conversely, anything that contradicts the guru's point of view is labeled "negativity"; so information that runs counter to accepted beliefs is repressed and punished. This ploy conveniently prevents negative feelings from being used as feedback that something might be amiss.

People whose power is based on the surrender of others develop a repertoire of techniques for deflecting and undermining anything that questions or challenges their status, behavior, or beliefs. They ridicule or try to confuse people who ask challenging questions. Throwing the question back at the questioner is a common, easy-to-use ploy. This is done by attempting to show how the question displays some lack in the questioner. For example, should someone ask how it is that one whose message promotes austerity lives so lavishly, this type of reply is usual: "You do not understand the true nature of austerity, which has nothing to do with external circumstances. True austerity is a state totally free from attachments and comparison. Do you think any of this matters to me? Because this matters to you and you compare yourself with others, you are not free. The universe supports the truly liberated as a matter of course." The message here not only faults the questioner, but intimates that through the guru's teachings, one can eventually have it all, too.

Another ploy is calling whatever seems to be problematic a "test of faith." As these tests become more extreme, the release that passing the test brings is also more intense. This is why it is possible for the leader to get his increasingly bizarre behaviors accepted. Anything can be looked upon as a test of faith. Once reason has been undermined, there's no way logically to refute this system—that's why people who are ordinarily considered highly intelligent can become involved in believing, doing, and justifying just about anything.

A number of gurus have made statements to the effect that disobedience or disrespect of the guru has more severe negative spiritual consequences than other forms of morally unacceptable behaviors. One even said that such disrespect can bring thousands of lifetimes of pain and suffering. Whatever else is involved, it should be obvious that fear and threats are being used here for control. As the guru's power is dependent on the disciples' surrender, he does what is necessary to maintain that state. Still another ploy is parceling out, or taking away, power over others in the group.

Mysterious or supernatural powers have always been used to validate religious authorities. Even today many people operate under a basic assumption that the ability to perform some act that defies ordinary explanation means the person who does this has an inside track to truth, or "higher" truth. Should anyone be seen floating (or believed to have been floating) over the ground, many people would take this person's words and opinions on other things very seriously.

Special powers people are reputed to have include healing, transmitting energy that gives others special experiences, and feats of magic such as materializing objects. One guru promised people levitation and invisibility through his practices. With such phenomena, the usual concerns involve what's really going on. Are these powers magical, or some kind of ESP, or chicanery that depends on people's gullibility and readiness to believe? Is the source of energy transmissions in the guru, or within a relational matrix where the receivers have a particular openness to receive? Is experiencing intense energy a sign of spirituality, or is the experience in the same vein as young ladies who swoon in the presence of rock stars? And then there is the question of whether special traits are necessarily an indication of special wisdom.

Our interest is not so much in explanations of the nature of these phenomena, but in how they are used by those who claim to do them. The reality and source of magical events can be endlessly debated. What can be easily seen, however, is whether they are being used to gain dominance, bolster credibility in other areas, make people worshipful, and create a context where the "miracle worker" becomes an unchallengeable authority. When magic lies at the base of authority, no matter how elevated the people appear, they are engaged in perhaps the oldest ploy of authoritarian mind control.

Whenever powers are utilized as credentials to disarm reason and make people blind followers, there is little wisdom there. The idea that wisdom is justified by magical ability is even questioned within traditional Eastern thought. Trying to cultivate or being enthralled with special powers is considered one of the great dangers of the spiritual path. The major use of the miraculous has been to impress. For us the real mystery is why people display their purported powers in so many irrelevant or even trivial ways. Although healing individuals, however it's done, is a fine thing, it does not have the great planetary impact one might expect from one claiming to be God's most special representative. A world on the brink of self-destruction can use all the help it can get. Bottom line, those who use anything seemingly out of the ordinary to get others to bow down to them should be held suspect.[4]

The guru's specialness is presented as the result of many lifetimes of purification. So it is tacitly implied that one's advancement can never approach the guru's exalted state—at least not in this lifetime. It is far easier to surrender to a projection of perfection than to someone who is essentially like you. Thus gurus routinely take on images that people have been conditioned to associate with divinity: all-wise, all-good, all-powerful, or some approximation thereof. They all claim to be able to lead people to salvation, enlightenment, bliss, self-knowledge, immortality, peace, an end to sorrow, and ultimately being one with God. These states are conveniently as difficult to reach as they are compelling. Gurus also claim to bestow unconditional love on those who surrender to them, while actually whatever emotional connection exists is conditional on surrender and obedience. They cultivate images that cater to the disciples' preconceived ideas of spirituality as selfless purity. In short, gurus basically tell disciples what they want to hear, including how special and wise they are for surrendering to them.

The deceit underlying most ploys is that the guru has no self-interest at all. The traditional ideal of enlightenment allows this deceit free reign because the guru is placed in a category beyond the knowledge and judgment of others. From here gurus can rationalize any contradictory behavior. The traditional idea that once enlightened, one can do anything is also attractive to disciples who secretly hope this is where their sacrifices will eventually lead them. Tied into this is the Oneness worldview that sees the unity of all existence as the ultimate reality. Within this framework, separation or individuation is considered either an out-and-out illusion or at best less real than unity. The guru presents himself, and is viewed by his followers, as an ego-less manifestation of this unity. Thus the concepts of Oneness and enlightenment work in tandem to

---

[4]See "On Channeling Disembodied Authorities." The chapter on magic in *Control* elaborates on these ideas.

create a closed system where each validates the other: the One-ness ideology postulates that a few special people are enlight-ened, who in turn verify the ideology of Oneness.

To be thought enlightened, one must appear not only cer-tain that one is, but certain about most everything else, too. Cer-tainty in areas where others are uncertain and have strong desires automatically sets up the guru's dominance. Since those with-out self-trust look for certainty in others, power is just there for the taking by anyone who puts out a message that tells people, with certitude, what they want to hear. In addition, to get fol-lowers what is needed is a message promising desires will be realized, and facility in handling people's challenges and confu-sions. Certainty combined with the traditional Oneness frame-work gives the guru a relatively easy-to-maintain position of unassailability. Mouthing words of Oneness such as "We are all one" or "Everything is perfect" is easy to do and can deflect any challenge or doubt. Problems arising from individuated life can be made to appear trivial, and a sign that the questioner has serious "ego problems." Deflecting everything back to others' lacks is a simple, age-old ploy of anyone in a position of unchal-lengeability.[5]

Another related ploy is placing high value on detachment, which also derives from the Oneness worldview. If unity is the basic reality, then being attached to any individual expression of it is said to obstruct achieving enlightenment. Not coinci-dentally, this serves as a convenient concept to get people to give everything to the guru, including themselves. And indeed, gurus urge people to detach from everything but them. The message is "You can't become enlightened if you're stuck on the material plane with attachments." To be attached is presented as being ego-bound. Preaching renunciation and self-sacrifice is by def-

---

[5]"Oneness, Enlightenment, and the Mystical Experience" discusses the function of enlightenment, and why it is a mistake to try to solve the problems of individuated life with a paradigm of unity that does not give equal weight to diversity.

inition authoritarian—it means an authority telling you what you're supposed to renounce. If a person buys this ideology, then detaching from possessions, relationships, and even one's identity can at first make one feel better because they are the usual sources of psychological pain.[6]

Taking on beliefs because they alleviate conflict is part of the unconscious code underlying authoritarian control.[7] In our view, any immediate solutions or solace that come from authoritarian control become tomorrow's problems.

---

[6]"Buddhism and the Abuse of Detachment" in *Control* contains a detailed analysis of the problems with cultivating detachment.

[7]"Who Is in Control? The Authoritarian Roots of Addiction" describes aspects of this code in detail, much of which is unconscious.

The Assault on Reason

To maintain mental control it is necessary to undermine self-trust. This is insidiously done by removing the ways people can build trust in themselves. Self-trust is built by utilizing one's own personal, firsthand experience as feedback. It is also built by sharpening mental and perceptual tools and frameworks in order to process, integrate, and evaluate one's relation to the external world, as well as to inner dramas.

It is commonly assumed that the nature of spirituality is not only fundamentally different from ordinary experience, but that this difference is vastly superior. From this it is concluded that the tests of truth or meaning used for ordinary experience are not relevant for the so-called higher truths that gurus and religion offer. This age-old separation of the spiritual from the worldly is deeply embedded in all of civilization. We view this split as tragic, and at the core of the fragmentation prevalent in the contemporary human psyche. The inner battle between the presumed higher and lower (or good and bad) parts of oneself often binds people with conflict by making them unable to accept themselves as whole human beings.[1]

We are in no way negating the occurrence and importance of transcendent experiences that cannot be encapsulated by thought. Actually any experience, by its nature, is different from the words that try to describe it. This includes the meaning of the

---

[1]See "Who Is in Control? The Authoritarian Roots of Addiction" on the inner battle.

color red, as well as the essence of what love is. That reason has limits is also true. But to conclude that reason is therefore useless or even harmful in integrating all these experiences is not true. Reason is not only a useful and necessary tool to sort things out, but it is insidiously dangerous to reject it.

The Eastern view of enlightenment as beyond reason allows gurus to undermine reason.[2] This precept alone makes the guru dangerously feedback-proof, for he automatically escapes accountability for any behavior. If pressed, the guru can easily reply, "You can't possibly understand what I'm really doing because you're not enlightened." This stance, if believed, makes acceptable any incongruity between ideals and action. The guru can reverse any challenge or criticism by saying, "It's your problem; your ego is getting in the way." He, of course, has no ego. Common phrases used as barriers against anything that questions spiritual authority are: "That's merely mental" (or analytical, rational, psychological). "Your ego is experiencing resistance." "You're coming from the head instead of the heart." "That's a low-level consideration of the material world."[3]

Once critical faculties are disarmed, followers can accept the most bizarre and inconsistent behaviors: Gurus preach the unity of all being, while isolating themselves from all who do not agree with them. They preach austerity and live lavishly. They preach equality and demand deference from their followers, who, following the lead of their idol, manage to feel superior to those deemed less spiritual. Anything the guru does can be viewed as a test of faith and commitment.

Gurus undercut reason as a path to understanding. When they do allow discursive inquiry, they often place the highest value on paradox. Paradox easily lends itself to mental manipulation. No matter what position you take, you are always shown to be missing the point; the point being that the guru knows something you do not. Paradox is usually accomplished by shift-

---

[2]See "Oneness, Enlightenment, and the Mystical Experience."
[3]"Guru Ploys" gives other examples of disarming reason.

ing levels of abstraction. In esoteric "spirituality," this shift is from the realm of individuated existence to the abstract level of an overall unity. For example, when viewing existence as comprised of separate entities, individual people are the locus of suffering. The concept of unity does away with individuals. By combining the different levels and ignoring that they are different, paradoxical statements can be made, such as "There is suffering, yet no one suffers" and "All imperfection is perfect." By changing the context in this way, almost anything can be made into a paradox, thereby intimating special wisdom. Paradox can also be used to justify any behavior by saying there is a hidden meaning that is part of the paradoxical nature of things, which of course, only the guru adequately understands.[4]

With some, it is fashionable to denigrate reason and elevate emotion or intuition in an attempt to transcend the dryness of mechanistic science and linear thought. But using emotion or intuition without reason is as one-sided and limited as using reason alone. For just as the head without the heart is barren, the heart without the head is rigid or chaotic. Living creatively is the art of combining passion with understanding. Without reason, one easily becomes a "true believer" who takes on beliefs that generate wanted emotions. Here, when thought is used, it functions to protect these beliefs by building an impregnable, closed system that is impenetrable to logic, experiences that do not fit, and inconsistencies (whether behavioral or mental).

Sanity involves the capacity to respond to information, internal and external, in a way that contains the possibility of change. Interfering with this process is one of the most subtle and basic abuses of authority—that is, the denial of, or even assault on, the followers' basic experiences and discriminatory capacities. This allows a leader to manipulate even highly educated people, espe-

---

[4]For more on paradox, see "The One-Sidedness of Oneness" in "Oneness." The final section of "The Power of Abstraction" discusses the nature of "the spiritual paradox." The section on Buddhism in *Control* goes into the authoritarian uses of paradox (particularly in Zen) in more detail.

cially if their intelligence did not bring them fulfillment.

Reason does not guarantee wisdom. It is, however, a tool for integrating experience, which is necessary for self-trust, without which there can be little wisdom. When critical intelligence is labeled unspiritual, or a hindrance to higher truths, what is left? There is little option but to take the word or worldview of some higher authority.

Stages of Cults
Proselytizing to Paranoia

Most cults follow a predictable progression of two distinct stages, which indicates that what is involved is more a function of how authoritarian structures work than of the particular teachings of a given guru. The similarity of these stages among diverse groups also demonstrates how being a cult leader creates a track that is difficult, if not impossible, to escape.

Messianic Proselytizing

Cults generally put out a similar message, each proclaiming their specialness. The leader and the group are touted to be at the cutting edge of awareness, spirituality, evolution (whatever). They are the heralds of a new age which will bring a transformative quality to living and solve the world's problems. As long as the movement is gaining in strength and membership, this attitude is reinforced. Believing they are on the crest of planetary change, the feeling and overall mien within the group and leader is one of optimism and satisfaction. Their stance toward outsiders is of benign superiority. Others will catch up or see the light in due time.

This first stage is messianic with the message being that all labors of the organization, including the guru's, are aimed at a higher purpose beyond the group, such as saving mankind. During this phase the guru is confident that he will eventually be acknowledged as the one who will lead the world out of darkness. The major emphasis is on proselytizing to bring in new converts. The continual increase in numbers satisfies the guru's need for power and adulation. While there is still hope of becoming the acknowledged herald of a new order, he remains happy and relatively benign in his treatment of those who have surrendered to him.

As long as the guru still sees the possibility of realizing his ambitions, the way he exercises power is through rewarding the enthusiasms of his followers with praise and positions in his hierarchy. He also whets and manipulates desire by offering "carrots," and promising that through him the disciples' desires will be realized, possibly even in this lifetime. The group itself becomes an echo of the guru, with the members filling each other's needs. Within the community there is a sense of both intimacy and potency, and a celebratory, party-like atmosphere often reigns. Everything seems perfect: everyone is moving along the appropriate spiritual path. The guru is relatively accessible, charming, even fun. All dreams are realizable—even wonderful possibilities beyond one's ken.

The energy and excitement of proselytizing, conquest, gaining public attention, and of newcomers flocking to the group are what makes a cult feel vital and prosperous. Cults need a continuous stream of recruits and potential converts to reinforce the belief that they're "where it's at"—the vanguard of spirituality on the planet. Proselytizing is an engaging form of seduction that brings both reaffirmation and credit for "doing good." Feeling in the vanguard fuels moral superiority and cuts insiders off emotionally from outsiders, which binds them more deeply to each other. Because cults are relatively closed systems, proselytizing is their main form of communication with the outside world. New members are also a needed source of revenue.

All the major cult-like organizations that have captured people's minds have used similar approaches for marketing themselves. What most proselytizing groups face is how to sell their beliefs without appearing to do so. Recruiting is therefore always done in the name of helping or doing some kind of good. The underlying message these groups give to their members is that since they are on the cutting edge of evolution, to care about others is to get them to join. New recruits attend testimonial sessions with older members as part of the indoctrination. They are treated very specially and made to feel important, and then are typically pressured to "share their experiences" with others.

What such sharing really amounts to is a more oblique form of proselytizing that cleverly accomplishes several things: It obviously can bring in more new people, but less obviously, the more new or potential members share their experiences with outsiders, trying to explain and defend why the group attracts them, the more they themselves identify with the group. New members have great enthusiasm, but are often not yet emotionally tied to the group. In this context, proselytizing itself is a subtle kind of indoctrination, as the very act of "sharing" moves one to identify more with the group.

A particular form of seduction that the group participates in with those flirting with joining is similar to sexual conquest. The group pours an enormous amount of focused energy and attention into potential recruits until they surrender to the group's authority, which of course has the guru and his belief system at its center. When someone does surrender, everyone celebrates the new bonding. This is a bit like a new marriage, and for the recruit, it is the honeymoon phase. This lasts as long as it does, and then the focus of the group shifts elsewhere. (This also happens in romantic love, for after the conquest the wooer's interest and focus often move somewhere else.) When the honeymoon is over, the new converts must shift roles—from being the wooed to being the wooer.

Through proselytizing, the insidious pleasures of seduction, conquest, and dominance also ensnare the recruiters into the group more deeply. The more power proselytizers gain in interaction with outsiders, through being the focus of attention and the holders of mysterious knowledge, the more this makes them—the wooers—feel special. The better they are at evoking the listener's curiosity and desire, the better it makes them feel about themselves. These good feelings further reinforce their conviction of being on the right path. People typically use this new source of power, with its inbuilt pleasures, as verification that they have indeed found truth, thus becoming more confident they are right.

Power and certainty do feel better than weakness and confusion. Unfortunately, such feelings make self-delusion more rather than less likely. When dealing with others who are less certain, simply having certainty gives dominance. The more certain one is, the stronger one feels, which does attract others. This in turn reinforces one's certainty, creating a self-propelling loop that can feel great. It is extraordinarily difficult not to become attached to the beliefs that promote one's power. In order to sell well, it is most helpful to believe in the product. Conveniently, the more vested interest one has in a product, the easier it is to believe in it.

Apocalyptic Paranoia

A time inevitably comes when the popularity and power of the group plateaus and then begins to wane. Eventually it becomes obvious that the guru is not going to take over the world, at least not in the immediate future. When the realization comes that humanity is too stupid or blind to acknowledge the higher authority and wisdom of the guru, the apocalyptic phase enters and the party is over. Then one of two things generally happens: The first is that the guru's message turns pessimistic or doomsday, voicing something like this: "Soon civilization is going to break down and face amazing disasters—except for us, who are wisely withdrawing to protect ourselves and retain our purity. This group will survive as a pocket of light amidst the darkness; then afterwards we will lead forth a new age."

The other possibility is that in order to attract more people, the guru makes increasingly extreme promises and bizarre claims that offer occult powers, quick enlightenment, or even wish-fulfillment in the mundane sphere around wealth, love, and power. One guru went so far as to promise levitation and invisibility; another group claims that through proper daily chanting, people can achieve their every desire, getting anything they want—anything. They justify such pandering to greed by saying that realizing all desires is the fastest path to detachment from desire. Either of these tacks—predicting disaster or making grand promises—is counter-productive in the long run, since most people would prefer to align with an optimistic viewpoint and are taken aback by outrageous claims.

The attitude of benign superiority toward outsiders characteristic of the expansionistic phase dramatically shifts when the group turns apocalyptic. It is the outsiders who will receive the brunt of whatever cataclysm the guru claims will come. Now there are dire warnings about "the dangers of associating with anyone not on this path." The fervor shifts from world-saving to a holocaust mentality focused on the survival and protection of the group. Any member who leaves threatens the cohesiveness of the whole group. This mounting mistrust is not totally paranoid (there is some reason for it) because as the group becomes more closed and bizarre, outsiders react more negatively. Disciples are often asked to put aside temporarily their concerns for their own spiritual advancement, and to work hard to become a pocket of light that will survive the holocaust. Proselytizing turns to entrenchment. One guru had everyone busy building bomb shelters. At this point, cults often have members learn martial arts or begin stockpiling weapons. Fear now becomes the primary mechanism of the leader and group to maintain power and cohesion.

The transition from optimistic expansionism to the paranoid doomsday mode involves a heavy turnover of people. Those not really "serious" leave, and others begin surreptitiously to question the leader's omniscience. In an attempt to counteract this, the group becomes more militaristic, demanding even greater obedience. Even when a cult is no longer expanding, some recruiting of new members still occurs to balance off the losses of old ones during the turnover of this phase. But a cult in decline has more trouble selling itself. It no longer looks that enticing or special. Nevertheless, members still manage to feel special since they are convinced they have been singled out to survive.

Members and the guru become withdrawn and the focus gets more internal, insular, and isolating. Internecine squabbling and power struggles replace external conquest. When the guru realizes that most people are not going to acknowledge him, he often compensates (if he can afford it) by building monumental edifices that proclaim his greatness. This includes monuments or temples, buildings, model communities, and "learning centers." The fun is over. The rewards are now put into the distant future (including future lives) and are achievable only through hard work. This not only keeps disciples busy and distracted, but it is necessary because the flow of resources that came with expansion has greatly diminished. This glorification of work always involves improving the leader's property (the commune or ashram), increasing his wealth, or some grandiose project.

Whenever a guru's power needs are not being satisfied by expansion, he generally seeks more adulation from and control over those who have surrendered to him. He does so by dictating more directly how they spend their daily lives. Needing now more than ever to be his disciples' prime emotional bond, the guru undermines anything that interferes with this.[1] Though the guru needs his disciples even more attached to him, he becomes more remote, sending his dictates down the line. Subtle or not so subtle warnings proliferate about the disastrous consequences of disobedience and of trusting outsiders. Statements like this become prevalent: "Disobedience to the guru brings countless lifetimes of suffering." "How can you expect enlightenment or salvation if you are not obedient and do not work hard for it?" "You must not pollute yourself by associating with those who are not spiritually developed."

---

[1]"Gurus and Sexual Manipulation" describes a variety of ways this is done.

Although the guru usually preaches the unity of all humanity, he becomes increasingly more separate. His message is of love, but he shows little concern for those under him, as they have become mere tools for his ambitions. Often he consciously or unconsciously blames those around him for the failure of his messianic aspirations. As the group's isolation increases, so does its paranoia toward outsiders, which can trigger violence. Those who drop out are often threatened, violently punished, or sometimes even murdered. This stage commonly results in scandal and tragedy.

Authoritarian groups with a leader who has few constraints (our definition of a cult) derive their intense feelings of loyalty and unity from erecting huge walls between insiders and outsiders.[2] This is an easy, mechanical route to intimacy that will be attractive as long as alienation is rife. Such rigid boundaries render cults both brittle and easily threatened, leaving only either proselytizing or paranoia as ways of relating to others. The potential for violence and abuse in an authoritarian cult is always there, not only because whatever the leader says goes, but also because outsiders are made into "the Other," which has always been used to justify violence.[3]

---

[2] We define "cult" as a group where the leader is unchallengeable and considered infallible. The term "guru" is used generically for any such leader. See "Religion, Cults, and the Spiritual Vacuum" for more on cults and gurus, and a comparison of cults and religion.

[3] See "Jim Jones and the Jonestown Mass Suicide."

The Attractions
of Cult Hierarchy

mages of omniscience and perfection automatically generate hierarchical relations. The structure of the organization that disciples must fit into is always pyramidal, with of course the leader on top. Next comes the very close inner circle of a few people who also become teachers and surrogate leaders in the guru's absence, then an administrative hierarchy, and so forth. Both gurus and disciples use hierarchical relationships for power. Everyone on the hierarchy gets their feelings of power and specialness from where they are positioned. Even those on the lowest rung can feel superior to those who have not had the intelligence to become members. A hierarchy is a way of organizing power; it also is a vehicle for filling needs as it creates goals and meaning.

It might appear that we are critical of hierarchy in general. This is not so. It is common in certain circles to blame hierarchy for many of the world's problems and injustices, particularly because hierarchy has been universally used to maintain power and privilege. Once it enters a culture, however, there is no going back. This is because it is a unique social tool for organizing and directing large numbers of people. Hierarchies enable a society to specialize and grow, and then are needed to organize the larger population.

Though humanity is stuck with hierarchy, it need not be intrinsically authoritarian nor unjust. Because authoritarianism is hierarchical by its nature, it is easy to assume the reverse, that hierarchy is necessarily authoritarian. This assumption is made because authoritarian hierarchy has been, and still is by far, the predominant planetary mode of social organization. It is the water we swim in. Authoritarian hierarchies are propped up with an authoritarian worldview and morality. No matter their stated rationale, their main purpose always becomes self-perpetuation, which inevitably corrupts them.[1]

Participation in an authoritarian hierarchy is an easy route to purpose and meaning that also offers security, if one follows the rules. Moving up the rungs brings power and respect. All this, however, is totally dependent upon accepting the ultimate power of the leader. This, of course, brings a deep attachment to and dependency on both the hierarchical structure and the leader on top. Religious hierarchies often put out a message (sometimes covert) that position on the hierarchy is related to spiritual advancement. With gurus, this is measured by the depth of the disciple's surrender, which translates to willing obedience and self-sacrifice. Deeper devotion to the guru is prescribed as the fast track not only to spiritual goals, but also to moving up the hierarchy.

The organization's hierarchical structure neatly fits the disciples' psychological needs to make progress, and to be able to evaluate themselves (measure their progress) with regard to others. Whatever one's position, one can feel better than those who have not progressed as far. Many people are conditioned to continually improve and move toward a higher goal as their deepest source of meaning. The need to prove one's worth continually is often an indication of an implanted authoritarian morality, with an inner authoritarian who judges oneself to be not good enough.[2] This leads people to seek an external authority for some kind of bene-

---

[1]See "Authority, Hierarchy, and Power" on how a hierarchy can be non-authoritarian.

[2]See "Who Is in Control? The Authoritarian Roots of Addiction" for an explanation of the source of inadequacy behind the continual striving to improve.

diction. Since spiritual hierarchies contain ready-made steps for advancement, they offer quick access to feeling better through improving. Gurus put out enticing hints about the next rung of the spiritual ladder. This reinforces one of the emotions people easily get attached to—yearning. Yearning, looking up to, and step-by-step goals toward attaining the ideal are interconnected parts of the psychology underlying spiritual hierarchy.

To those observing such authoritarian groups from the outside, it appears that members give up their power to the leader. But most disciples did not have very much personal power to begin with. What in fact has been given up is their power and self-determination. Since for many their previous choices did not bring them what they wanted, giving up self-determination does not at first seem like much of a loss.

People are especially vulnerable to charismatic leaders during times of crisis or major life change. Most often those who enter into this kind of authoritarian group are having problems bringing meaning, human connection, and good feelings into their lives, all of which become instantly available upon joining. What they also gain is a sense of power, usually greater than any they previously had. Although seemingly relinquishing their power, they actually trade what little personal power they had to piggyback on the guru's power. Occasionally people who did have power elsewhere forsake their old lives to become disciples, largely because their previous successes were unsatisfying. Interestingly, these people usually end up in the guru's inner circle. The higher up one is in the organization, the more one's power and even livelihood are hooked into it and the guru. This makes it very difficult not to accept, rationalize, or deny any incongruent, greedy, or corrupt behavior on the part of the guru or the organization as a whole.

Typically the guru lets it be known that he is on the crest of evolutionary awareness (or whatever is held important), and that anyone who joins him can participate in being on the wave of history. Competitiveness is built into the posture of being on the cutting edge. In order to get and keep members, each group must believe in and defend its superior position, and claim to be the best at doing whatever is valued.[3]

People don't want a second-rate guru; they want the one who seems the best. Since purity is the standard of measurement—the gold or Greenwich meridian time of the guru world—each guru has to claim the most superlative traits. This is naturally a breeding ground for hypocrisy, lies, and the cultivation of false images of purity. Gurus are thus forced to assume the role of the highest, the best, the most enlightened, the most loving, the most selfless, the purest representative of the most profound truths; for if they did not, people would go to one who does. Consequently, it is largely impossible for a guru to permit himself real intimacy, which in adults requires a context of equality. All his relationships must be hierarchical, since that is the foundation of his attraction and power.

It is ironic how deeply competition is built into this profession that characteristically so strongly condemns it. We are not taking gurus to task for being competitive in and of itself. Rather, we are critical of the claims gurus make of being beyond it. Insofar as gurus wish to remain on top of the hierarchy, they must compete and win against all challenges. By presenting themselves as beyond competition, gurus promote a system of values that denigrates competition. Any who compete with them are deemed wrong for doing so. This is one of the ways gurus use competition to remain on top without appearing to do so.[4]

As is the case in all highly competitive activities, those who rise to the top are extremely good at what they do. They are most usually charismatic people who are masters at manipulating image and emotion. The manipulation of images is the game played in most effective advertising; proselytizing and advertising are cut from the same cloth. The enormous attention given to appearance leads to a concern for packaging rather than what's

---

[3]See "Stages of Cults" for more on the messianic phase of such groups.
[4]See "Guru Ploys" for other ways gurus maintain dominance.

inside the package. Focusing on image is essentially shallow; the depth of a spiritual teaching is usually inversely proportional to the amount of its accouterments, costumes, pomp, titles, and sacred symbols.

The nature of such so-called spiritual hierarchies is that everyone at every level has a role to play and an image to keep up. This is especially true of the guru, who not only defines how those under him are to appear, but must himself present the image his disciples want and need. Since the roles are so highly defined, the people who fill them are somewhat interchangeable. Hierarchies in general foster modularity since what counts is fitting into their rungs and roles. The disciple role can be filled by anyone who properly surrenders to the guru. Since adulation from any one person eventually becomes boring, gurus do not need any specific disciple—they need lots of them. Gurus do give special attention to those with wealth or power; having celebrities in one's entourage increases coffers, influence, and membership. What appears to be a strong personal bond between guru and disciple is illusory, as it depends solely upon the disciple acknowledging the guru's authority. Should that break, little remains.

The role of guru is likewise fairly modular. What matters to disciples is having an idealized image of perfection to surrender to. Such images do come in different flavors that appeal to different kinds of people: the stern but caring parent; the cosmic jokester; the fount of love and acceptance; the knower; the (seemingly) liberating iconoclast who frees people from inhibitions; and the partying "you can have it all" type. (The last two often go together.) These different styles each attract a different clientele. For example, the stern parent tends to attract the alienated young; the knower could appeal to intellectuals whose intellect has not given them a great deal of comfort; the iconoclast naturally attracts rebels.

What the guru is really like is difficult to ascertain. Those at the top usually display contentment and equanimity, which are mistakenly taken as signs of spirituality. Successful gurus, like monarchs of old, have their every whim catered to and are total-ly taken care of. And although many say they do not need any special treatment and would be as happy in a cave, the power and adulation at their disposal are more seductive than any drug. It is not surprising they appear turned on, especially in public.

Looking carefully at a guru's inner circle is extremely reveal-ing. Those closest to him, his most dedicated students, display better than anything else where his teaching leads after years of exposure. What is also displayed is who he prefers to have around him: Are they strong and interesting in their own right, or are they boring sycophants who continually feed his ego? Do dis-ciples ever "graduate" and become self-defining adults, or do they remain obedient and tied to the guru? It is also very enlight-ening to observe how gurus treat and refer to those who leave their fold.

The person at the apex of a hierarchical pyramid, whose pow-er is a function of being in that position, cannot show weakness or real commonality with those below. Many gurus vociferous-ly claim that they discourage worshipful attitudes in their fol-lowers, "Alas to no avail." This is another manipulation of image, the reality being that gurus are powerful enough to construct whatever environment around them they want. Especially in sit-uations involving power, it is most important to pay more atten-tion to what people do than to what they say.

Gurus and Sexual Manipulation

Social orders always deemed it necessary to control people's sexuality when wealth and power were passed from one generation to the next through inheritance and structures of legitimacy. In modern societies technological breakthroughs in birth control have loosened, but not eliminated, sexual control. A primary social function of religion has been to serve as the moral underpinning that regulates sexual acceptability. To control a person sexually is to have control over a basic aspect of human life. Sexuality is a deep power in human beings that underlies attraction; attraction, the capacity to command attention, is one key to personal power. Thus to exercise sexual control is to have real power over individuals and society as a whole, through structuring the most basic connections of mating and reproduction.

Religions all want everyone's major emotional bond to be with whatever god figure the religion presents. If the most important thing is salvation—whether of one's soul as in the West, or progressing along the reincarnative chain as in the East—then anything that detracts from this is looked upon as detrimental. This is one reason why sexuality is often regarded as low, carnal, animal, even dirty; for sexuality, if left unfettered, risks putting people out of control—and more importantly, out of religion's control. Thus religions came to define which expressions of sexuality were (and for many still are) acceptable, and also to provide

91

sublimated outlets through ritual and worship. Yet sex is so basic that ideology alone is not strong enough to control it. Fear and guilt must also be used as control mechanisms of repression.

Gurus likewise do many things to ensure that their disciples' prime emotional allegiance is toward them. In the realm of sexuality, the two prevalent ways control is exerted are through promulgating either celibacy or promiscuity. Although seemingly opposite, both serve the same function: they minimize the possibilities of people bonding deeply with each other, thus reducing factors that compete with the guru for attention.

Celibacy, or at least the image of it, is the easiest route for a guru to obtain this power of being the central emotional focus for large numbers of people. The very nature of sexual connection has within it preference, at least in the moment. For a guru to become sexually involved with some and not others causes a hierarchy of preference. Since the guru's appeal is his ostensible offer of unconditional love to all, this causes an undercurrent of jealousy and resentment among the followers. Celibacy does allow one to maintain a certain kind of control of one's energy and emotions. It also conforms with images of purity. Therefore, it is far easier for a guru to gain and maintain power if he is celibate—or pretends to be.

Celibacy undermines coupling when presented as a higher state than sexual intimacy. This, in effect, gets people in couples to surrender to the guru rather than to each other. Gurus can exercise control over their followers in the most basic areas by decreeing whether coupling is allowed, who marries whom, how often and in what circumstances sex is permitted, whether couples can cohabit, and even whether they reproduce and how to raise the children. Some gurus actively discourage having children or separate parents from them, which is done to decrease distractions from devotion to the guru. One even let it be known that having more children was undesirable, and encouraged vasectomies and tube-tying. Similarly, to counteract family influence, gurus often try to undermine disciples' ties with their own parents.

The Betrayal of Trust

When a religion is transplanted from a conservative culture to a more experimental one, its leaders are no longer constrained by tradition. The West's looser mores make sexuality practically irresistible for foreign gurus from rigidly patriarchal cultures in which the sexes were separated and closely monitored. The availability of sexy, adoring female disciples is a temptation few (if any) can resist.[1] Without deep cultural constraints against it, sex scandals go with the occupation of guru because of its emotional isolation and eventual boredom. Disciples are just there to serve and amuse the guru who, after all, gives them so much. The guru's temptation is exacerbated by the deep conditioning in many women to be attracted to men in power.

Below are some of the more extreme examples of sexual abuse that have been exposed:

1. Religious leaders using their exalted position to seduce, pressure, or coerce disciples sexually, some even at puberty. This is compounded by the fact that they most usually preach either celibacy or marital fidelity.

2. Incidents of rape and creating "love slaves."

3. Using sex and romantic seduction by other members to entice people to join.

4. Separation of parents from their children, sometimes with accompanying child abuse and molestation.

5. Encouraging prostitution to support the group.

---

[1]This chapter focuses on male gurus, as all the sex scandals we are aware of involve male spiritual leaders. There are a number of reasons for this that are beyond the scope of this chapter to examine, among them: women being turned on to powerful men eroticizes the male teacher role; casual sex is less socially acceptable in women; and women in power in general have to be more impeccable.

Openly promiscuous gurus utilize their power to create what amounts to a harem for their pleasure. The real motives behind their sexual excursions are often masked by such words as "teaching" or "honoring" their disciples. One famous guru had a procurer. (This disciple, later sadly disillusioned, described herself as having been his pimp.) He would specify certain physical traits for a given evening (blond, large breasts, petite, etc.) and she would round someone up for his nightly pleasure. When asked how she justified this to herself, she said that at the time she thought of him as godlike and God can do anything. The view that once enlightened a person can do anything also justifies anything. (After all, what good is it to be God if you can't do what you want?) Also, he gave so much of himself he deserved whatever it took to make him happy. This ultimate male fantasy apparently did not suffice to make him happy. He was notoriously self-destructive and died young.

Having sex with one's disciples whether secretly or openly is a real betrayal of trust because:

1. The guru is putting his own needs and pleasures first, which is an exploitation. "Honoring" a disciple with sex is a form of unabashed dominance—how can a disciple refuse who is committed to serve and obey?

2. Rewarding women for their sexuality taps into and reinforces deep lines of conditioning. Traditionally women's power has been related to sex. So women, especially the good-looking ones gurus seem to choose, generally have deep patterns that link their power and self-worth into their sexuality. Gurus, like fathers, are in a context that gives them enormous power because of their disciples' needs, trust, and dependency. One reason incest is a betrayal of trust is what a daughter needs from her father is a sense of self-worth not specifically linked to her sexuality. Sex with a guru is similarly incestuous because a guru ostensibly functions as a spiritual father to whom one's growth is entrusted. Having sex with a parental figure rein-

forces using sex for power. This is not what young women (or men) need for their development. When the guru drops them, which eventually he does, feelings of shame and betrayal usually result that leave deep scars.

3. Sexuality with disciples (whether overt or covert) sets up hierarchies of preference where disciples compete for status through who is attracting the guru more. If covert, it also creates lies and secrecy among disciples.

Psychotherapists face a similar context of power, trust, and dependency, though not as absolute. They, too, operate as parental and authority figures, both of which are easy to use to stimulate erotic feelings in a vulnerable client. Professional ethics aside, although theoretically it may not be impossible for a therapist to develop a viable intimate sexual relationship with a client, the probability of betraying the same kind of trust is great. This is especially true if the therapist treats the liaison casually, or if the sex is presented as part of the therapy done for the client's good.

Gurus who preach celibacy while secretly engaging in sexuality present sex as an esoteric initiation ritual or advanced spiritual exercise that must be kept hidden. This makes the disciple feel special while colluding in an enormous lie and manipulation that has severe emotional repercussions.

The implications of a spiritual teacher lying about sex are often deflected by focusing on the sex instead of the lying. Here some people actually feel good about the guru's behavior in that it validates for them that there's nothing wrong with sex after all. We have also heard people say they were glad that he "got some."

Lying about sex is so rampant in every culture that structures what is sexually permitted it is commonplace to be inured to it and accept such lying as a given, or a peccadillo. But it is the lie, not the sex, that's the real issue. The lie indicates the guru's entire persona is a lie, that his image as selfless and being beyond ego is a core deception. Many think that though a guru lies about his personal behavior, his message is still essentially true.

Lying here as elsewhere is done to cover up self-interest. If the guru's message is that purity without self-interest is the ultimate achievement, not only did he not achieve it, but he does not even know if it is achievable. If being self-centered is an unavoidable aspect of being human, then any ideology that denies this will necessarily corrupt its promoters and believers. This why images of purity corrupt.

Spiritual Hedonism

Cross-fertilization between East and West has produced a strange hybrid—a new breed of guru who combines hedonism with detachment. The rationale takes this form: Detachment from desire is still presented as the key to spiritual progress, but the quickest path to this is said to be not through asceticism, but rather by experiencing all desires. These particular gurus depict what they are doing as modernizing ancient esoteric methodologies (sometimes referred to as "tantric") that attempted to bring self-realization through ritualistically breaking taboos. In the name of freeing people from their limitations and "hangups," this path is presented as the fastest track for contemporary Westerners to achieve spiritual goals, without undo austerity. The intoxicating message is that "You can have it all"—live out hidden desires and fantasies, experience any pleasure, break taboos around sex and even violence—and be spiritual besides. The assumption is that if one has or cultivates the right attitude (detachment), then "Anything goes." This seductive, seemingly liberating stance of the you-can-have-it-all gurus has attracted many highly intelligent, experimental people.

Most people's deepest inhibitions revolve around sexuality, aggression, and violence because it is here that the deepest taboos lie. One guru utilized "workshops" where various expressions of sex, rage, and intimidation were used to break through people's boundaries. Bones were broken and group, impersonal, and even forced sex occurred. This is indeed a fast track to breaking down personality. By telling people this was a path to liberation, deep taboos could be broken without initial guilt. This brings not only powerful feelings as energy is released, but also the experience of a particular kind of freedom—freedom from repression. Dramatic shifts of identity coupled with intense emotions are easy to interpret as profound breakthroughs. Although breaking down personality in this fashion can seem like a breakthrough, it contains an inherent hidden trap: It is the authority of the guru that gives permission to "act out." Thus only through accepting the guru's values and worldview can the hurtful aspects of such actions be ignored and condoned.

Having been stripped of their values, these newly "liberated" people are in a fragile state until new values and a new sense of identity can be integrated. Having "emptied" them, it's easy for the guru to step in at this crucial moment and put his persona, values, and ideology at their center. So the followers' new identity forms around surrender to him, a father figure, the one they now trust above all others—even themselves—because he supposedly liberated them in bestowing this great sense of freedom. This kind of freedom is the real illusion. Here direction and permission from an authority, combined with group pressure, moved many to act out in ways they were not capable of integrating without accepting the guru as the ultimate source of truth. What did not change is the underlying authoritarian personality structure, which was, if anything, reinforced.

Most often those who became involved in such groups could not conceive of themselves as subject to authoritarian manipulation. They saw themselves rather as true spiritual adventurers, unafraid to push against the boundaries of convention. For them, the very fact that they were capable of going beyond social constraints was a sign of liberation. (They were also told this by the guru.) That many discontented and innovative people were unwittingly seduced into submission and conformity (visible only to others) indicates the depth of people's susceptibility to authoritarian control.

To rebel against one authority (society) by accepting another (a leader who gives permission to rebel) merely shifts allegiance, while giving the illusion of liberation. There are different ways of unleashing the repressed in oneself. Surrendering to a guru who facilitates this is one of them. However, this is very risky. Here these repressed aspects are highly manipulable because their allowability is dependent upon permission from an authority. The authority then ultimately defines what is permissible. This is how people can come to lie, steal, and even kill for the glory of God, or the guru.

Bringing up repressed desires can be useful in a context that fosters integration. The guru/disciple relationship is not such a context because it does not allow people to integrate their own experiences. Rather a new identity, that of disciple, is given as the means for integration. An identity that is dependent on the authority of another is not only fragile, but it is not a truly deep inner restructuring. The content may look different, which includes taking on a different worldview and values (the guru's). However, the deepest structures of personality, especially how the person integrates experience and looks for validation, remain not only unchanged, but are often strengthened by this essentially authoritarian relationship.

The contents of a personality (beliefs, values, a worldview), though resistant, change far more easily than the underlying form or context, which in many is unconsciously authoritarian. This is not surprising given that so much of culture is transmitted as a given, not to be questioned, meaning that our heritage, too, is unconsciously authoritarian.[2] Seemingly dramatic shifts that involve switching quickly from one authoritarian system to another are not that difficult. (Many disillusioned Marxists shifted their utopian hopes to the spiritual world.) Utilizing sex (or violence) to push limits is indeed a quick way to undermine people's identity and move them, but to where? We consider this truly unethical, not only because it fails to take into account how it hurts others, but because the very quick-

---

[2]The section on "The Roots of Authoritarianism" in *Control* describes this in depth.

ness of it leaves people awash and subject to easy manipulation. This is but another example of the great myth that an external authority can be the source of inner freedom.[3]

Extremes in emotionally disconnected sex also disconnect the desire for closeness with another, especially when intimacy is pejoratively labeled "attachment." This makes it easy for the guru to be the central emotional bond. As a result, many disciples gradually give less importance to sex, some even drifting into celibacy. They take this as a sign of their spiritual progress. For after all, they had tried sex to their heart's content and seemed to have outgrown it, evolving into a supposedly more spiritual detachment—precisely as predicted and promised. Not coincidentally, this also increased their faith in the guru's wisdom and made them more available to work harder on whatever agenda the guru prescribed. This answers the riddle of how promoting detached promiscuity eventually turns dedicated hedonists into dedicated workers.

Fostering promiscuity, impersonal sex, and interchangeable sexual partners accomplishes the same agenda as celibacy. It trivializes sexual attraction and undermines coupling. Casual, disconnected, modular sex eventually leaves people satiated, jaded, and often hurt. They become fearful of forming deep relationships, which fits neatly into the guru's need to have disciples detached from everything but him.

Throughout all this sexual manipulation, the underlying authoritarian personality structure not only remains intact and unconscious, but is greatly buttressed. For now it's not just messages implanted in one's mind long ago that impose "shoulds" and internal control; it's a living authority figure who wields the absolute power of active mind control. This includes the power to make people who are being callously manipulated believe they are freer than everyone else.

---

[3]See "Who Is in Control? The Authoritarian Roots of Addiction" for an in-depth analysis of the dynamics of authoritarian psychology.

Gurus, Psychotherapy, and the Unconscious

Both the East and the West have long traditions valuing an internal journey to self-awareness. Eastern religion has developed different methodologies and meditations aimed at leading people to self-realization or selfless-realization. In the West, Socrates championed the idea that in order to know anything one must first "know thyself." The question is what is the nature of this self that one is to know, realize, or transcend?

The prevalent idea in the East is that the self is either a limited structure to be transcended (Hinduism) or a false construction to be transcended (Buddhism). Since for Hinduism and Buddhism it is the human mind that constructs notions of limited or false identity, their practices are largely aimed at reversing this. Both promote the idea that the ultimate achievement is an awareness that is totally selfless, with the corollary the more selfless the better. Consequently, the East's interest in the machinations of the self or ego is not an unbiased exploration, but has an agenda to reduce or eliminate the self's influence in order to achieve selflessness or ego-loss.

Sophisticated thinkers within Buddhism were (and are) aware that unconscious elements exist in the mind. But their interest in the unconscious is cloaked in an ideology that believes it is not only possible to become totally selfless, but once having done so, one is also totally conscious and no longer moved by unconscious factors. If there were even the possibility that a totally realized being had an unconscious, how could anyone (including the realized one) be certain that all motives and actions were pure and selfless?

Whether it is possible to become or be totally egoless or selfless can be debated. Buddhism states that it is possible; our position is that the selfless and self-centered, altruism and egoism, are embedded in each other and essentially inseparable. This does not mean that altruistic acts are all reducible to hidden egoism, but rather they are two poles of an interwoven process that can only be defined in relation to the other. We see self-centeredness as an inescapable element in existence. If giving gave nothing in return, there would even be far less of it than there is.

Those who insist absolute selflessness is obtainable can always say that anyone who has not obtained it cannot know for sure it isn't obtainable; and they can always deflect other points of view by saying they are limited by ego. Similarly, we can always say that those who think they have reached a permanent egoless state are deluding themselves, and point to what seems to us obvious manifestations of ego.

Though this debate is not resolvable, it does serve to illuminate why any who claim total selflessness must also claim being totally conscious. Many gurus and spiritual authorities negate, make light of, or even ridicule the use and value of Western psychotherapy because its concepts of the unconscious undermine their authority and power. To acknowledge that unconscious factors may be operative in oneself means that one cannot be totally sure one is selfless.

What we call the unconscious is not only the repository of early traumas, forgotten memories, genetic proclivities, and perhaps even primitive, archaic, and archetypal structures. It is also being continually created by selective processes that filter the way information is kept out, taken in, and also expressed to others. One may speak perfect English and know when mistakes are made without consciously knowing the rules of English grammar. Yet it is these unconscious rules that structure how one speaks and filter what one hears. All perception involves a selective process whereby in any given instant one is focusing on this rather than that. The selection of attention, that is, why one's attention is here rather than there, is usually not conscious.

In our view, one of the most powerful unconscious selective filters involves keeping out, denying, or repressing that which can cause discomfort; the more extreme the discomfort, the more likely filtering will occur. An area of very extreme discomfort for most people is anything that does not match their ideals of how to be and basic self-conceptions of who they are. It is difficult even to want to see things about oneself that one doesn't like. Self-identity—who and what one thinks one is—is a pillar of personality. The human mind is an image-builder that uses the present to attempt to create the future out of the past. The selective process that lets things in that verify self-images while keeping out what undermines them is itself unconscious. Actually, self-images themselves are filtering systems that only work well if one is not aware filtering is going on.

Usually what is repressed or filtered out are motives and behaviors that do not match one's ideals. If one has values against controlling others, then one will translate the ways one exercises control (or tries to) into rights, duties, or fostering virtue for the other's own good. These all involve moral justifications for control. This means control is often disguised, especially in personal relationships. In any relationship, it is dangerous to ignore power and control. This is especially so in the guru/disciple relationship where ideals of selflessness make authoritarian manipulation easy by masking them.[1]

Western psychology has various theories about the nature and workings of the unconscious, each emphasizing the importance of different elements: sex, power, archetypes, security, etc. They all agree in attributing significant unconscious motiva-

---

[1] "Love and Control: The Conditions Underlying Unconditional Love" discusses in depth the problematic ramifications of selfless ideals on relationships.

tions to why people do what they do. Leaving aside which theory is right or more right, the important question here is: Does using the concept of the unconscious better explain human behavior; and if it does, can anyone ever know with certainty that in any given moment there are no unconscious factors at play? We believe every self-examining person has, at one time or other, realized that they are more conscious than they were, which means they were less conscious previously. This is enough to validate some conception of unconsciousness. We also think that because the unconscious is unconscious, assuming that one is beyond its reach can only make one less alert to its power.

Spiritual authorities who present themselves as unchallengeable purveyors of the truth undermine Western frameworks of the unconscious because they cannot acknowledge that they, too, may be in its sway. Neither do they want their disciples to question too deeply their own motives. To attract followers, gurus must present themselves as enlightened (without ego), which includes not having an unconscious. There is good reason for this: To surrender totally to another it is essential to believe that the recipient of such trust is not motivated by self-interest. Being ego-less is the only way self-interest could not be a motivating factor. The possibility of unconscious elements in the guru would mean there could be unacknowledged or secret self-interest. It would be most difficult to have absolute faith in the pronouncements of a teacher one suspected of having unconscious motivations.

A largely unconscious process that can occur in any context where one person helps another is called transference. What this refers to is the transferring, projecting, or cathecting of an old and unresolved emotional configuration onto a person who, because of either personality or position, can easily ignite and take on these emotionally charged images. For example, longings for being taken care of, unconditional love, and approval are readily transferred to anyone people believe can help them become more fulfilled or realized. Counter-transference occurs when the teacher, therapist, or helper unconsciously buys into the transference of others. The helping stance "I know what's best for you" maximizes both transference and counter-transference. Good therapists know their clients transfer unresolved emotional issues, especially related to parents and authority, to them. Gurus as well as therapists naturally take on such parental projections because of the nature of their role as helpers. A primary goal in therapy is to free clients from their need to transfer unresolved issues onto others. This need makes people particularly susceptible to authoritarian control. Good therapists aim at being very conscious of how they deal with transference.

Because of the nature of the relationship which demands total surrender, gurus do exactly the opposite. They cultivate and reward transference, for a parental type of authority is at the very core of the guru's power over disciples. The power to name, arrange marriages, and dictate duties and behavior are ultimates in parental authority, especially in traditional societies like the East. To give someone the power to name or marry you is to profoundly accept their parental role in defining who you are. The ostensible motivation behind this has to do with an attempt to break the ties of the past so the person can become "new." A deeper reason is that this aids the guru in becoming the center of the person's emotional life, which facilitates surrender.

Turning one's back to all of the past is not so easily done. What remains are predilections and patterns around authority, which are transferred to the new authority. There is the hope that the guru will be the perfect or idealized parent one never had—a veritable fount of unconditional love. But this so-called unconditional love is conditional upon surrendering to the guru and accepting his authority. Transference that is reinforced such that it becomes a way of life ensures the client, student, or disciple will remain fundamentally childish.[2]

Renunciate ideals of selflessness increase unconsciousness by repressing and disguising self-centered motives. The East's glorifi-

---

[2]See "Love and Control."

cation of surrender, detachment, and selflessness hides the unconscious attachments and collusions at the core of the guru /disciple relationship. Disciples are attached to having their idealized projections fulfilled by the guru; the guru is attached to the power that fulfilling them brings. When disciples become gurus, they are ill-prepared to deal with their new power other than by doing what their guru did. Dealing awarely with power involves guarding against its corruptions, instead of denying that one is corruptible. The standards of purity necessary for the role of guru must bring unconscious repression and filtering mechanisms that ensure deceit and hypocrisy around self-interest.[3]

Anyone who denies having an unconscious stops an essential process of awareness which involves being very alert to the workings of one's own filtering mechanisms. This denial can only increase the power of the unconscious. Because a spiritual authority cannot compete well from a position of fallibility, gurus are caught on the horns of a dilemma: by denying the unconscious they become more unconscious; but if they acknowledge its possibility in themselves, they can no longer be infallible.

---

[3]See "The Traps of Being a Guru."

The Traps of Being a Guru

The person most at risk of being strangled by the images demanded by the role of guru is the guru. This includes the great danger of emotional isolation. The literature of Eastern spirituality is rife with warnings about the dangers of the spiritual path. There is good reason for this. Ironically, contributing to these dangers is the common and mistaken notion that the further along "the path" one gets, the less one is likely to succumb to temptations—until one is fully realized, at which point one is no longer subject to the hazards of self-delusion. But in actuality the reverse is more often true, as the temptations get more insidious, powerful, and harder to resist. Seeing more deeply contains no guarantee against one's mind becoming concomitantly more clever at fooling itself. Moreover, when anyone is treated as an "arrived" human being, the potential for self-delusion is far greater than in any other context.

At the heart of the ultimate trap is building and becoming attached to an image of oneself as having arrived at a state where self-delusion is no longer possible. This is the most treacherous form of self-delusion and a veritable breeding ground of hypocrisy and deception. It creates a feedback-proof system where the guru always needs to be right and cannot be open to being shown wrong—which is where learning comes from.[1]

---

[1] See "Gurus, Psychotherapy, and the Unconscious" on one of the greatest self-delusions: that once one becomes fully conscious, then one no longer has or is moved by the unconscious.

107

When people portray themselves as beyond illusion—and therefore no longer subject to ego, mistakes, subjectivities, the unconscious, or creating delusional systems that are self-aggrandizing—what is actually being claimed? Is it that they have never been deluded? Or that they aren't deluding themselves now? Or that they can never be deluded again? For the claim of freedom from self-delusion to have any force, it must also be a claim about the future. Who would go to a guru who said, "I'm free of self-delusion now, but might not be tomorrow"? No matter how much evidence casts doubt on this stance of unchallengeable certainty, it is always possible to maintain that the place of such exalted knowledge is not subject to the proofs and judgments of ordinary people. But whether being beyond self-delusion is possible or not, presenting oneself to others in this fashion sets up an inevitable pattern of interaction. If a person believes another is so realized, it automatically creates not only awe and worship, but the belief that this person "knows better." Why would even the most realized of beings want people to become reliant on his wisdom instead of their own? Whether anyone actually achieves this state can be debated; what ought to be obvious to us is that this mode is authoritarian.

To project that one will be a certain way in the future is to build an image of oneself that has within it the want and need to believe (or for others to believe) one will in fact be that way. This image of the guru as beyond self-delusion cuts off real awareness in both gurus and disciples. A crucial element in being self-aware involves being alert to when one is "putting oneself on"—meaning, telling oneself what one wants to hear.

Let's suppose a person has touched into something that might be called a basic or universal reality (or at least a level of understanding deeper than previously experienced). Doing so could have cut through previous illusions and self-delusions. In the moment, one's clarity can feel so powerful that it is not hard to believe one will never be deluded again (at least not in the same way). But any projection of oneself into the future necessarily comes from images created out of the past; the more absolute they are, the more one ignores what contradicts them. This is one of the greatest occupational hazards of being a guru.

There is a tendency within the human mind to construct a universe with itself at the center. This is one place subjectivity comes from. Sanity is the realization that one is not alone in doing this. Sanity is also the capacity to change through being open to feedback, to new information. The idea that any one mind has a corner on the truth creates isolation that is extraordinary. This easily leads to deterioration of physical or mental health. So, another great danger for gurus is emotional isolation.

Emotional connection is certainly necessary for mental health, and at least beneficial in maintaining physical health. Psychosomatic medicine has found that many physical and psychological problems have their roots in alienation. The guru offers others an escape from alienation through the quick bonding that becoming a member of his group brings, but ironically this eventually causes extreme alienation in him. It is no wonder then that gurus display a spectrum of self-destructive behaviors from drunkenness to ulcers. This is not because they are taking on the karma of their disciples or of the world (a prevalent rationalization). Rather, they are involved in the very human activity of somatizing their conflicts. One guru even alienated himself to the extent that he was literally allergic to people. Everyone had to go through extreme cleansing measures in order to be allowed in his presence.

Being a "knower," as opposed to a seeker, is part of being a guru. This implies an essential division between the guru and others. The guru in effect says, "I'm here, and you're there; and not only can I help you move from here to there, but that's what I'm here for." Being different (or rather, being perceived as different) is the foundation of the guru's dominance. Relations of dominance and submission often contain extreme emotions. But if dominance and submission are the essential ingredients in the glue holding the bond together, the connection is not really personal. Gurus and disciples need each other, but as roles, not as individuals, which makes real human connection almost impossible. So gurus must create other ways of turning themselves on besides intimacy, the most usual ones being adulation, material wealth, impersonal sexuality, and power.

Nor can gurus have any real connection with other supposed "super-humans" (other gurus) because of the inherent competition among them. Years ago, when we first became interested in gurus and Eastern concepts such as enlightenment, it initially seemed an oddity that all these supposedly enlightened beings did not seek out each other's company. With each other they presumably could find deep and real understanding, and respite from always having to deal with minds at a lower level. But since disciples view their guru as a vehicle for their own salvation, they must believe that he can do the best for them. Consequently, the meeting of gurus, when it occurs (it rarely does), is always laden with heavy meaning, as the disciples watch very carefully to see who comes out best. Even the simplest acts (who goes to see whom) have implications of dominance. The fact is that gurus do not "hang out" together because the structure of the role makes it nigh impossible. Thus even intimacy with peers is denied them.

Narcissism and Adulation

A person may touch into a sense of connectedness that feels eternal, and in that moment, be one with it. This experience, for lack of a better word, is called mystical, and as is attested by those who have had it, it cannot be captured by words. This, however, does not stop the human mind from attempting to place the memory of it into some framework. Such experiences that "blow people's minds" (meaning temporarily shatter their boundaries and structures of integration) do not really create a blank slate. Instead they are integrated into some mental structure. Either one has a framework that can handle them, or one looks for a framework that can. The East has put more attention into creating worldviews that take mystical experiences into account.[2]

---

[2]See "Oneness, Enlightenment, and the Mystical Experience."

Attempting to communicate the wonder of such experiences to others is natural and understandable. The problem is that others who have not had similar experiences are prone to give such a person deference and special treatment. It is very difficult not to enjoy this, and thus subtly to reinforce whatever images others have of one's specialness—particularly since it makes people more apt to listen. Gurus can justify this by saying they are using adulation as a tool to help people learn, grow, and free themselves. Unfortunately, the usual structure in which worship occurs involves putting on a pedestal someone who appears to be essentially different from and superior to oneself. Worship creates an "Other," and to sustain such worship, the guru must continually reinforce images of his difference and superiority.

Given that adulation is built into the guru/disciple relationship, another trap for gurus is narcissism. The popular definition of narcissism is being overly enamored with oneself. The psychoanalytic definition involves development having been arrested at the infantile stage of auto-eroticism. What this boils down to is being one's own primary sex object. This view usually sees narcissism as a pathology constructed primarily in infancy.

Rather than placing the sole cause of narcissism in the distant past, our conception views it as an amplification of a normal human tendency to be turned on when someone is turned on to you. This, of course, can and does happen to all of us. It only becomes pathological when it is the sole or primary way one "gets off." This means one only really feels alive when one is the center of another's attention. Narcissists are often very charismatic, as their power is derived from attracting. Intelligent ones are very seductive and skilled at captivating others. Their antennae are always alert for when people are interested in or turned on to them. When what is most important is being the center of importance for others, adoring admirers become fairly interchangeable. Extreme narcissists need to be adored but cannot adore; they do not really experience deep passion. Narcissism creates a piggyback form of passion, as it feeds off others' passion for oneself. Consequently, no matter how much adulation narcissists receive, it is never enough; they always need more.

Most people enjoy feeling special. One may be uncomfortable with this or dislike it, but that's a different issue. Adulation, the ultimate form of special treatment, has an addictive quality difficult to resist. Being the focus of such attention would activate the excitation levels of any sentient being on the receiving end of it. Whether for a guru or a rock star, this can be a more powerful experience than the strongest drug. It is also one of the great seductions of power.

Successful gurus, rock stars, charismatic leaders of any sort, experience the intensity of adulation amplified beyond most people's ken. This can make ordinary relationships pale by comparison. Being the recipient of such adulation and devotion is exceedingly addictive. Here addiction is used in its loose sense to mean mechanically needing an on-going "fix" of adulation to where it becomes the central focus of one's life. Adulation has powerful emotions for the sender as well, and can be easily mistaken for love. It is likewise addicting for the sender, as it is an easy route to feelings of passion. Since adulation is totally a function of image, should the images crack, adulation disappears, demonstrating that it is essentially empty of real care.[3]

Psychoanalytic theory would say that adulation is the emotional experience a narcissist most craves. What better profession for a narcissist than being a guru? Narcissists may become gurus because they crave adulation; but we believe it possible that extreme adulation can also move people into narcissism. We do not doubt that one's past history can contribute to relying on narcissism as a major relational mode. This would include being born with extreme beauty. And of course, people could be more prone to narcissism due to childhood lacks. But intense and continuing adulation alone can bring about narcissism because it is addictive, offering easy access to power. For a guru,

---

[3]"Who Is in Control? The Authoritarian Roots of Addiction" presents a different model of addiction, going into its dynamics in depth.

adulation and power are intricately connected since the disciples' surrender is the ultimate source of his power, and adulation is the prerequisite for surrender. A guru is made to feel he is the center of the universe by his disciples. It is difficult to not be "in love" with that image of oneself.

Deceit and Corruption

Some seem to thrive in the role of spiritual authority. After all, to be more interested in power and position than truth and growth is to be congruent with the actual (rather than professed) values of much of the world and its institutions. Another irony is that although gurus preach detachment, and seekers look to them to learn how to be unattached, gurus become totally attached to the power and privileges of their elevated position. But since their power requires appearing the most non-attached and selfless, this automatically makes gurus either unconsciously or consciously deceitful.

If the guru's message of being personally free of all self-interest is false, is it knowingly false? It is of course possible for the guru to believe it himself, especially because the guru role is both detached and opulent. Thus it is easy to believe one really doesn't need anything or anybody. (Belief and self-interest usually go hand-in-hand.) Also, people who dissemble and lie in order to make others believe in them often believe this is justified because it is ultimately for everyone's good—only coincidentally including their own.

This brings up another major danger of being a spiritual authority. There is nothing within the role to guard against the corruptions of power, because the very notion of corruption is taboo. By denying that self-interest is or can be operative in a guru, there is no way to mitigate against its effects. Using lofty ideals to mask self-interest is common, but when this is melded to images of purity, corruption is guaranteed. The myriad scandals around sex, money, and power that have tainted so many gurus are not surprising, given the structural corruptibility of the role.

In political realms, where the corrupting tendencies of power are legend, we are often warned that constant vigilance is needed to ensure freedom. Authoritarian ways of relating undermine vigilance so that both sides have unconscious vested interests in the unquestioned power of the leader. In spiritual realms, the power is so absolute that it can lead to extreme excesses.

There are few, if any, relationships where the possibilities of personal power match the guru's. If human beings believe a leader can save them, they will obey and follow him anywhere; they are capable of following any order—including killing others and even themselves. Disciples can and do become disillusioned with a guru. It is far more difficult for gurus to become disillusioned with themselves. They can always rationalize anything they do, no matter how mistaken or even sleazy, and find at least a few people willing to support and idolize them. So the guru role makes it extremely difficult to escape the traps of power—the ultimate trap being that in the end, gurus lose their humanity.

Jim Jones and the Jonestown Mass Suicide

Jim Jones, the cult leader of the People's Temple, shocked the world by killing himself and Congressional investigators. What was most disturbing is that he somehow convinced hundreds of his followers to kill themselves and others. In total 914 persons died, including more than 216 children who were poisoned first by the older members. Most people were reputed to have willingly drunk poison without needing to be coerced.

In a review by Jim Miller of four books about Jim Jones (*Newsweek*, June 1, 1981), Jones was quoted as having said the following:

1. "Ever since as a child I saw a dog die, I wanted to kill myself."

2. "If you can't understand the willingness to die ... you will never understand the integrity, honesty, and bravery of the People's Temple."

3. "All you who are in love are in trouble."

4. "I was the master of revolutionary sex, able to copulate fifteen times a day, but now all I want is the orgasm of the grave."[1]

---

[1]This piece is a rational reconstruction based on these four statements made by Jones. It is conjectural and does not purport to be the only possible explanation.

These four statements seemed to have a strange kind of internal consistency and aroused our curiosity. We asked, where in the world does one have to be emotionally and mentally to say such things and really believe them? And why were people willing to follow such a leader, even to death?

The Jonestown events shocked and deeply disturbed many people—a disturbance that went beyond their obvious sordidness. It was as if Jim Jones, as a symbol, touched a dark place in our collective psyche. There is, perhaps, a lesson to be gleaned from so many people denying life in that ultimate way. So the following is an attempt to construct a possible psychological field out of which Jones' four quotes and the actual events surrounding the People's Temple become understandable, making a certain kind of sense—twisted though it be.

When as a child Jones first confronted the reality of death, could it be that he felt ultimately betrayed by God or the universe? If so, life for him became a sham, a lie, and a hypocrisy of cosmic dimensions. For if life ultimately leads to death—its total negation—what good is it and what meaning can it possibly have?

Two interwoven universal processes are buildup, the creation of forms, and breakdown, their dissolution. Buildup and breakdown are embedded in each other. In order to break down, something must have been built up. But, more than that, the process itself of building up and continuing (aging) has the seeds of breakdown within it. As far as is known, every individual structure—whether a galaxy, solar system, or person—forms, endures, and dissolves. Every self-reflecting person at some time faces integrating aging, decay, and death. The two basic ways of doing so are by denying their ultimate reality via systems that propose immortality, or by finding a way to love and appreciate the life one is given without the certainty of endless continuance. We suspect Jones was able to do neither.

If death and decay are all one focuses on, this knowledge can sap all joy from life, casting a shadow that makes everything seem inconsequential and meaningless. Jones perhaps saw that most people placed their ultimate meaning on the hope of immortality, which he looked upon as self-delusion. Here his second quote equating honesty and bravery with the willingness to die becomes understandable.

It is possible that on seeing a dog die, this early confrontation with death produced in Jones a loathing and fear of it so great that the only way he could survive was to try to conquer that fear through "a willingness to die." And the way he attempted to do this was to convince himself he could emotionally welcome death and even worship it. It is true that to be caught in fear inhibits freedom; and much fear has its roots in the fear of death. There are only three ways people handle this fear: by denying it, accepting it, or embracing it. Each way has its own structure and inner dynamic.

Jones chose to embrace death, a path few people overtly take but which has much historical precedence in the worship of our so-called dark side. Satanism involves the worship of the forbidden. The power and charisma it offers are derived from worshipping what others fear.[2] Jones could have believed embracing death to be the ultimate honesty and deepest manifestation of courage. It is here that Jones' third quote (his admonition against love—"All you who are in love are in trouble") becomes understandable.

Worshiping death is different from accepting it: true acceptance does not negate life, while worshipping death must. This is because with such worship, one must be very careful not to become attached to any aspect of life. Loving others automatically ensnares one in caring about life. For example, loving one's children means, among other things, not wanting them to die. Thus with love one can get caught again in fearing death. The stance of protecting oneself against the fear of death through not caring about life is difficult to maintain. Even before attempting to isolate his group in Jonestown, Jones was known to be very para-

---

[2]See "Satanism and the Worship of the Forbidden: Why it Feels Good to Be Bad."

noid, suffering from a variety of persecution fantasies. This means he did not truly conquer fear through negating life. For if he did, what difference would any of it make, including others wanting him dead?

That Jones as a cult leader without constraints sexually used and abused his followers is not unique. However, the extreme nature of public abuse and humiliation that often accompanied the sex are but another indication of how far people can go if surrendered to a leader. If Jones' self-aggrandizing accounts of his sexual exploits have any truth, the sexual frenzies mentioned in the fourth quote could also have been a compulsive attempt momentarily to escape the disconnection and feelings of impotency such a bleak and joyless perspective engenders. We are all impotent before the specter of death. Jones turned his back on the only intelligent solution to one's helplessness in the face of death, which is to live life as fully and caringly as possible. Seeking the "orgasm of the grave" is, of course, seeking the final release. Here is a very concrete example of the Freudian death wish, the idealization of thanatos. We cannot but wonder whether many of our historical atrocities and human shames contain an element of death worship. Inflicting death and pain on the "Other" who "deserves" it is far easier than dealing with one's own pain and death.

Most of the people who joined Jones were folks who hadn't had too many good feelings in life. With them, Jones was able to take his anti-life stance and parlay it into power. By making the unhappy and downtrodden totally justified in feeling that life is misery, decay, pain, etc., Jones gave his followers a momentary sense of specialness. Out of all the world, they alone were not self-deluded. This allowed them to view themselves as a strange kind of elite—winners at last.

In the group they doubtless found a sense of specialness, of connection, and of care for each other that had eluded them all their lives. The group was their family, and Jones their father. (They wrote him confessional "letters to Dad.") The glue that held them all together was submission to Jones and to whatever beliefs he put forth. Not to follow Jones down the path of death meant a return to their empty lives and a negation of the elitist feelings of specialness Jones induced in them—as long as they were "his." In the fifties, popular existentialism equated ultimate freedom with the ability to kill oneself—an escape from the intrinsic absurdity of life. So, too, did the People's Temple, but unlike existentialists, this became the core of their meaning. Jones called suicide a revolutionary act. Although some were coerced, most killed themselves obediently when ordered to.

The Jonestown tragedy is but one more example, albeit a particularly gruesome one, of the inherent risks in surrendering to any authority. Once any person takes on an authoritarian mantle that assumes knowing what's best for others, this delusion inevitably leads to greater delusions. Jones would have been more consistent had he merely killed himself. The fact that he needed a larger, more showy stage for his exit is a seeming paradox. That he needed to assert his power and take many with him is a statement ... but to whom? Who would be left to marvel that could matter to him? Could it be the bloody drama that was played out was his desperate, pathological way of reaching for connection, meaning, and even a perversely achieved immortality?

That a Jim Jones could exist, and lead others to mass suicide which included killing children, is important to examine. The deep discomfort such actions bring points to ... to what? Perhaps what is really being pointed to is something that we would prefer to keep hidden even from ourselves. How much do each of us hold back in life out of not only the fear of death, which is often repressed, but as in Jones' case, the fear of the fear of death?

Fearing death is thought projecting through time, constructing an idea of not being—not being "me" anymore. It is fearing the unknown and perhaps the unknowable. Fearing the fear of death, however, is fearing a psycho-physical state that one can know all too well, a state that can become unbearable in its helplessness and anxiety. In this historical moment, the human species is facing the possibility of mass, perhaps total suicide, by destroying the life-support systems of the planet. Jim Jones's response to fear, though extreme, was uniquely human. To the extent that each of us contains all the potentials of humanity within us, we must look deeply within ourselves lest our own "death wish" prevail.

On Channeling
Disembodied Authorities

Channels, channeled writings, and the spirit entities that supposedly speak through them are part of a trend that includes giving credence to different kinds of otherworldly, non-material, or other-dimensional, super-human intelligences. These presumed entities all function in a similar way in that they make themselves manifest by talking to or through someone they choose, who then becomes their channel. Why the entity chooses a particular person remains mysterious, as is the process of channeling itself. Becoming a channel is also a new frontier of esoteric activity. Anyone who hears a voice inside that is not consciously willed can assume something external is doing the talking and thereby take on the identity of channel.

Turning to disembodied experts is not a surprising progression. In recent years, the godlike stature of many gurus evaporated in a mire of corruption, deceit, and abuse of power. In contrast, incorporeal entities seem free of corruption, as corruption makes little sense without a body to profit from its results. Also, these spirit authorities do not take their followers over in the total way that gurus do by demanding their prime emotional allegiance. This makes involvement with the teachings safer.

The assumption that the spirit and channel are separate entities means incongruities between the channel's behavior and the channeled words are not seen as significant or relevant. A channeled message can never be questioned or challenged because of the impurity of messenger. "Spirits" are assumed to be pure, or at least the purveyors of pure truth, whereas their vessels for this truth are "only human" and do not need to claim or manifest infallibility or purity. Thus being a channel for otherworldly wisdom is less dangerous and confining than being its source, as with gurus. The channel can get drunk even if the "spirit" disapproves, while a guru would at least have to hide or justify the discrepancy between words and actions. The channel is not necessarily even supposed to be the entity's best student or exemplar, unlike those in the guru's inner circle.

Of course, many are exploring these hermetic realms out of an understandable curiosity. Some approach channeling as potentially useful information that emanates from the channel's unconscious, involving possibly some form of extra-sensory perception, or a particular kind of sensitivity or gift of insight. They are more concerned with how astute the information is than with the nature of its source, utilizing only what makes sense to them. In contrast, regarding a channel as merely a passive vehicle enabling a superior, otherworldly intelligence to expound makes it difficult not to be swayed by the channel's input.

Assumptions about Channeling

There is no way ultimately to prove to everyone's satisfaction where a given voice comes from. So, the most revealing and also resolvable questions on channeling involve what the voice is actually saying; the implications of what is said; and whether the voice is assumed to have a direct line to the truth, making it unchallengeable and therefore authoritarian. What mainly interests us are why people consult channels, and the assumptions made about the presumed entities and their channeled messages. Some who call themselves channels may be merely milking the gullible; but we assume that many who channel believe in what they are doing. It is only the latter who interest us.

Those who believe an external intelligence is the source of the voice or writings make at least some of the following assumptions:

1. Being disembodied makes the entity a pure (or purer) voice of cosmic wisdom and spirituality.

2. The entity not only knows more, but can access information otherwise inaccessible, or at least exceedingly difficult to get on one's own.

3. The entity tells the truth.

4. People's well-being is the entity's basic interest.

5. The entity knows what's best for a given human or humans in general.

6. These entities would not be motivated by power or wrongly manipulate those who come to them. In short, they have no self-interest.

7. One is better off getting the information than not.

8. The fact that most channels put forth a similar message and share a similar worldview is sufficient proof that what they say must be for the most part true.

The thread running through these assumptions is that disembodied entities are reliable, trustworthy, benevolent authorities with a deeper understanding of the nature of things. Here channeling, like gurus, creates a context of privileged knowledge that essentially cannot be challenged.

Though therapists are also assumed to know more, good therapists are knowledgeable and careful around transference issues, meaning they are alert to the dangers of becoming an unconscious parental authority for their clients. They also know that even if they see something about a client they're fairly sure of, clients are far better off finding it out for themselves than being told. Channeled "spirits" (or the channels themselves) are also subject to transference, as are gurus. Imputing a different and higher order of existence to be the source of information makes such projections inevitable.[1]

---

[1]See "Gurus, Psychotherapy, and the Unconscious" for more on transference.

Should one give disembodied entities any credence at all, the drama and excitement of a supposed spirit entering a mortal to reveal deep, hidden truths evokes a seductive, magical aura of seemingly ultimate cosmic portent. Wanting to believe that spirits have a direct line to the truth ties into a deep yearning for something truly pure one can trust. When values of purity have been implanted, it becomes difficult to trust oneself as one is never pure enough. So looking for someone or something more pure fits neatly into people's deepest "pure-itanical" conditioning, which instills self-mistrust.[2]

Hearing an inner voice or voices that seem to be coming from outside oneself is neither new nor historically unusual. When the voice urged doing something considered bad or hurtful, it was attributed to possession by evil spirits or the devil; when it voiced values of purity and selflessness, the spirit was assumed to be a messenger of the sacred. Attributing purity to another realm and to the information that supposedly comes from it is part of the age-old split between the sacred and secular created by renunciate religions.[3]

Channeling is an ancient phenomenon necessary for any revealed religion whose unchallengeable dictates have to come from God. God's wishes can only be known in three ways: either God has to speak through a person or assume a human form, or a person has to become godlike (the East's enlightenment paradigm). Thus many writings that are the foundation of traditional renunciate religions, such as the Koran and much of the Old Testament, were considered to be channeled from God by prophets and holy men. They contain the rules for staying in God's good graces. Most sacred texts from all religions are considered to be channeled (divinely revealed).

---

[2]See "Who Is in Control? The Authoritarian Roots of Addiction" on the nature of this conditioning.

[3]See "The Power of Abstraction: The Sacred Word and the Evolution of Morality" on the origin and nature of this split.

Eastern religious worldviews are more generous than Western ones in bestowing infallibility through mastery. It is then not surprising that most modern channels espouse a worldview containing elements of Eastern mysticism, usually including the Oneness perspective, with karma/rebirth presented as a given. Not insignificantly, the alignment with Eastern tradition is used as validation. There are other enticing messages: "If you only knew enough, you would see you are perfect." "All limits are in the mind and can be transcended." These temporarily empowering beliefs are very seductive. What is channeled largely accentuates the positive: beauty, transcending fear, loving yourself, and intimations of immortality within an unlimited universe of plenty. Many channels, either directly or indirectly, put forth the appealing notion that "You create your own reality." What this means, or is taken to mean, is that if you do it right you can create anything; conversely, everything negative that occurs you have really chosen in order to learn a needed lesson. To make this belief work, a theory of karma/rebirth is necessary, for without past lives and karma, it would be hard to explain why one "chose" the particular painful lessons one needed to learn, and why one needed to learn them.[4]

An Example of Channeled Writing: A Course in Miracles

Modern channels bolster credibility by using imagery, values, and archetypes from both Eastern and Western religions. A book that exemplifies this is *A Course in Miracles*. We use it as an example because it purports to be non-authoritarian, while claiming to be channeled by no less an authority than the spirit of Jesus Christ. Also, the *Course* more than intimates that through

---

[4]"Do You Create Your Own Reality?" describes this New Age adaptation of karma.

the proper practice (doing its lessons), anyone can become a channel for the spirit of Christ.

All channeled information, including religions, creates a closed system that is entirely self-referential. Any challenges from outside can be deflected by calling them limited understanding. So there is little to be gained from debating the validity of the *Course's* worldview. Rather, we want to show that its worldview is renunciate, and contrary to its posture that people must rely on themselves, *A Course in Miracles* is authoritarian. We single it out because it is a classic example of programming thought to renunciate beliefs.[5]

Although the *Course* calls itself essentially Christian, it does away with Christianity's more unpalatable dogmas, such as sin, a judgmental God, and damnation. Instead, like the Eastern Oneness perspective, it calls the world we live in an illusion to be transcended and is specific about calling all separation an illusion. It likewise denigrates the self and self-centeredness with such statements as "Either God or ego is insane." Its central message is that through surrendering to God's will, which is pure love, illusions will evaporate and one will be eternally at one with God. The essential methodology used to achieve this is forgiveness. Instead of being forgiven for sin through Christ, however, the new message is that through forgiving one can transform one's life and become Christ-like.

Forgiving consists of letting go of all judgments and grievances toward others and toward the circumstances of the world at large. The ideal is to forgive unconditionally.[6] The very doing

---

[5]"Religion, Cults, and the Spiritual Vacuum" and Part Two discuss in depth the nature and problems of moral systems that promulgate renunciation.

[6]"Love and Control: The Conditions Underlying Unconditional Love" describes how the ideal of unconditional love is a prescription of a renunciate moral order that insidiously impacts emotions and relationships, distorting the experience and expression of love. Its sections "Forgiving and Letting Go" and "The Religious Foundation of Unconditional Love" show how these ideals mask their underlying authoritarianism and why they are

of this is said to loosen the bonds of ego that keep people from their birthright, which is experiencing eternal love without fear. Sin is redefined as lack of love, so forgiveness is not of sin, but instead of error, or rather of one's own and others' illusions. Illusions are presented as the cause of all enmity and suffering, which is similar to certain Hindu and Buddhist perspectives. Letting go of past pains can have psychological benefits; but to turn this into a prescription for salvation ensures doing so becomes an idealized mold that denies and represses vital aspects of being human. This is a real danger of the *Course*, and of re-nunciate religion in general.

A Course in Miracles presents itself as a manual that only needs to be practiced daily to achieve what it calls the necessary "complete reversal of ordinary perception." The *Course's* introduction states that the teachings were channeled through a woman who was compelled to write down the unasked-for words that came to her over a seven-year period, starting sometime in the late sixties. The voice purportedly identified itself as the spirit of the historical Jesus Christ. The *Course* is separated into three sections: a 622-page text that contains its worldview; a workbook for students consisting of 365 daily lessons whose stated purpose is to "train your mind to think along the lines the text sets forth"; and a 69-page manual for teachers.

What is not noteworthy about the *Course* is its worldview, which is not essentially new, but a mixture of Eastern mysticism with Christian love and forgiveness. Of more interest to us is its claim of not being authoritarian. It is overtly stated that it is not necessary to believe any of the *Course's* assertions to experience the promised transformations:

> You need not believe the ideas ... accept them ... [nor] even welcome them. Some of them you may actively resist. None of this will matter, or decrease their efficacy.

---

unlivable. Ideals of unconditional forgiveness or unconditional compassion (the Buddhist version) are variations on the same theme that create unlivable standards of emotional purity.

ON CHANNELING DISEMBODIED AUTHORITIES

All that is required is conscientious daily practice of the lessons.

Daily repetition of the lessons is said to eventually bring forth one's own "Internal Teacher" which in turn, without any external authorities, will lead one to truth. It is assumed that everyone's Inner Teacher will say pretty much the same thing as the channeled voice of the *Course*. This claim is worth examining because under the guise of presenting objective truth that any seeker can find, what is actually going on is the age-old ploy of authoritarian indoctrination: A worldview is presented by an unchallengeable authority as the truth to be found. Then practices are given that reprogram and condition the mind to that viewpoint. To quote from the introduction:

> Our internal beliefs create what is perceived as reality, and we are imprisoned by the cage of our wrong beliefs. Since these beliefs are the problem, the basic solution is to replace these unconscious beliefs by different ones, through affirming new beliefs.

To see how this is done one must look at the nature of the lessons.

The *Course* operates through giving a lesson each day consisting of a statement to be repeated like an affirmation, mantra, or prayer. It unabashedly states that the functions of the lessons are first, "the undoing of the way you see now," and next, "the acquisition of true perception." These two steps—undermining a person's framework for integration, and then programming in so-called truth—are basic to all mind control. We find absurd the idea that truth, true perception, or any kind of wisdom can be instilled first by inculcating self-mistrust and then programming the so-called truth through repetition.

The lessons can be roughly divided into three categories:

1. promulgating detachment from the world by denying its reality;
2. decreeing forgiveness and the letting go of grievances to be the only route to love and salvation;

3. promising immortality and the elimination of all negativity through identifying only with what is delineated as the god aspect within oneself.

A few examples of each category suffice to show what's involved:

Category 1: The world is not real—everything is the opposite of what it seems.

Lesson #1: "Nothing I see ... [in this room, on this street, from this window, in this place] means anything." One is asked to look around and practice this idea on everything in sight. For example, "This table does not mean anything," or "This hand does not mean anything," etc. #3: "I do not understand anything I see in this room (on this street, from this window, in this place)." #5: "I am never upset for the reason I think." #10: "My thoughts do not mean anything." #16: "I have no neutral thoughts." Here one is asked to fill in the blank with anything: "This thought about _____ is not a neutral thought because I have no neutral thoughts." #24: "I do not perceive my own best interests." #25: "I do not know what anything is for." #32: "I have invented the world I see." #128: "The world I see holds nothing I want." #129: "Beyond this world there is a world I want." #132: "I loose the world from all I thought it was."

The above affirmations (or rather negations) are all geared at undermining trust in one's own experience, thoughts, reason, and even in the reality of the world. Lessons #128 and 129 are classical statements of the renunciate perspective.

Category 2: Forgiveness.

Lesson #62: "Forgiveness is my function as the light of the world." #66: "My happiness and my function are one." #69: "My grievances hide the light of the world in me." #72: "Holding grievances is an attack on God's plan for salvation." #77: "I am entitled to miracles." #78: "Let miracles replace all grievances." #342: "I let forgiveness rest upon all things, For thus forgiveness will be given me."

Category 3: God is, or is in everything.

Lesson #29: "God is in everything I see." #93: "Light and joy and peace." #95: "I am one Self united with my Creator." #67: "Love created me like Itself." #99: "Salvation is my only function here." #101: "God's will for me is perfect happiness." #127: "There is no love but God's." #138: "Heaven is the decision I must make." #156: "I walk with God in perfect holiness." #163: "There is no death. The Son of God is free." #170: "There is no cruelty in God and none in me." #186: "Salvation of the world depends on me." #191: "I am the holy Son of God Himself." #199: "I am not a body. I am free." #223: "God is my life. I have no life but His." #248: "Whatever suffers is not part of me." #330 asks, What "is the Ego?" then answers, "The ego is idolatry; ... doomed to suffer...."#340: "I can be free of suffering today."

Finally #350 asks the question "What am I?" and then proceeds to answer,

I am God's Son, complete and healed and whole, shining in the reflection of His love. In me His creation sanctified and guaranteed eternal life. In me is love perfected, fear impossible, and joy established without opposite. I am the holy home of God Himself. I am the Heaven where His Love resides. I am His holy Sinlessness Itself, for in my purity abides His Own.

The *Course in Miracles* is a strange amalgam of *nouveau* sinless, guiltless Christianity with a transcendent, separate creator-protector God; and of Eastern Oneness with an immanent, inclusive God-force. This generates many internal inconsistencies, but then consistency is not a value of channeled "spirits." Cataloging all the inconsistencies would be tedious, but here are a few worth mentioning:

1. Forgive others for your own sake—but you're supposed to be selfless when doing so.

2. God is ultimately responsible for everything—yet people are individually responsible, too. But responsible for what? If God is only love and other virtues, is God also respon-

sible for the suffering caused by the illusion of separateness? The *Course* does not even attempt to deal with the problem of evil, except to dump it into the category of illusion. Illusion is the great garbage can of Eastern religion where one can get rid of anything one doesn't like by making it unreal. The question of why there is illusion at all is beyond the scope of the *Course*.

3. God's plan is to heal everybody, but there is no mention of why God created people so in need of healing. God's master plan gives total freedom to heal oneself. People want total freedom, but also want their personal drama to have a guaranteed (predetermined) happy ending.

The *Course* is but another revealed (by an unchallengeable authority) renunciate ideology that separates the spiritual from the mundane, the pure from the impure, the selfless from the self-centered.[7] It says listen to your own voice, but programs what your voice will say by taking away the validity of experience, reason, thoughts, and disapproved of emotions. Like gurus, it then fills the vacuum it creates with its own renunciate worldview offering the same old coin of eternal bliss. Nothing could be more authoritarian, for who could argue against a disembodied spirit with the credentials of a traditional God? If one were to say (as we do) that one's inner voice says something quite different, then what?

When challenged, adherents often cavalierly reply, "Do the lessons and you'll see for yourself. Besides, you can't know the *Course* or criticize it until you try it." From our perspective, this confidence merely shows that those willing to be programmed get programmed. To understand why this is so, one must not only examine the exercises, but also the nature of the mind that is willing and able to do them daily for an extended time.

---

[7]See "Satanism and the Worship of the Forbidden: Why It Feels Good to Be Bad" and "Who Is in Control?" on the way this split divides a person, causing internal conflict.

As an example we will paraphrase and quote an enthusiast and teacher of the *Course*. We use this person's words only to represent a position which we (and he, too) believe is similar to that of many others. Consequently, we do not think the identity of the person matters. He initially states that before doing the *Course,* he was very disappointed in life because he saw that ideals important to him would not or could not be achieved in this world. "The more I faced the 'real world,' the less real I felt." He had "a divided sense of self that didn't measure up to any-thing"; and his "fragmented idealism" was "contaminated by conflicting ambitions."

Here is a person who wanted the world to fit into what were most probably ideals of purity, where non-violence, compassion, selflessness, and love would reign supreme. It is not surprising this man would gravitate toward a worldview that presented these four items as in fact reigning supreme, this being done by denying the reality of the world where they do not reign supreme. This same person went on to say,

> After years of thrashing about in a senseless world that seemed to oppose my highest aspirations, I have simply forgiven that world ... I'm no longer concerned with defining what the 'real world' is—perhaps, as the *Course* asserts, there is no world at all, but I do know I have gained a personal sense of authenticity.

He then concluded that he now feels better than he ever felt before.

Truth or falsity aside, what's wrong with this? Why shouldn't people do whatever they need to do to feel as good as they can, in a world that doesn't make it easy? It is not a question of whether people should or shouldn't adopt a worldview that fits their ideals in order to feel better—people do what they do. Adopting authoritarian renunciate worldviews in order to feel better has been going on for thousands of years. This is not new. The *Course* is a typical programming system that conditions mistrust for all one's accesses to this world—mind, emotions, senses, and over-all experience. Having been programmed to dis-identify with them and negate them, what is left to trust? All that remains are the "truths" of the *Course in Miracles.*

Denying the reality of what one doesn't like or feel comfortable with can allow a given person to feel better. The real question is, does this bring about a viable world? So much of the *Course* waxes eloquently about the beauty of creation. It totally denies the reality and necessity of destruction. But if destruction is just as real as creation, one's destructive tendencies are not truly dealt with by pretending they are not real. This is the ultimate tragedy of any renunciate paradigm that asks people to renounce (deny) either the reality of destruction or the reality of self-centeredness, as *A Course in Miracles* does. This creates what we consider the real illusion: that denial will ultimately make things right.[8]

Many religions have attempted to placate fear and make people feel better about their lives through denying the importance of this world. Existential fears range from fear of death and pain, to fear of being loveless and unfulfilled. The great illusion is that through denial one can transcend what one is afraid of, whether it be death or isolation. Fear cannot be conquered in this fashion, for it still lives in the structure of the illusions one builds to attempt to contain or eliminate it. And ultimately, if one fears one's destructive side, then one must be constantly watchful lest in an unguarded moment it explode. Trying to keep control of what is denied is itself fear.

What all renunciate worldviews such as *A Course in Miracles* really create are internally divided people who need an external authority to help keep control of their unwanted parts. When inner division is handled by adopting a belief system that further denies the reality of that which one is uncomfortable with, people conclude (wrongly in our view) that they have touched into a deeper, more real part of themselves. In our interpretation, what's really occurring is they become convinced their so-

---

[8]"Oneness, Enlightenment, and the Mystical Experience" critiques in depth the worldview that denies the reality of ordinary experience.

called higher self is the only reality, which initially alleviates conflict. This results in strengthening an inner authoritarian that tries to repress important parts of the self it judges as bad (the self-centered or carnal aspects).[9]

What Are Channels Channeling?

In channeling, where a given voice really comes from can be explained in many ways, with no way to prove to everyone's satisfaction who or what is doing the speaking. This is compounded by the known capacity of the mind to compartmentalize itself to the extent that information in one compartment is blocked off from another. How can one be sure the voice of the "spirit" is not emanating from the part of oneself that yearns to be pure, powerful, and immortal? To the extent that the voice mouths old renunciate paradigms emulating ideals of purity, perfection, and selflessness, there's good reason to suspect that the voice is actually the channel's conditioned, compartmentalized "higher" self.

One common argument for the voice being external is that channels could not have accessed the channeled information on their own. This, coupled with the similarity of most channeled worldviews, is given as evidence that the information comes from a different source than the person doing the channeling. But other explanations for this are possible. For example, in times of crisis, when humanity is facing the possibility of extinction, there is a great and understandable need for reassurance and hope. Some psychologists have asserted that the idea of a group unconscious best explains how people operate in groups. They postulate that groups of people create a context or ambiance that has a life and influence which is more than merely the sum of the individuals involved. So, the appearance and popularity of channels in this historical period of crisis, pain, and spiritual emptiness could be an expression of our group or collective un-

---

[9]See "Who Is in Control?" on the divided psyche and how the higher or ideal self is really an inner authoritarian.

conscious needing to allay enormous fears. Yearnings for per-fection, immortality, and a guarantee that some force out there will take care of everything have been part of the collective desires of humanity for millennia. Naturally this tendency greatly increases in times of breakdown.

Still other explanations are possible. Some might say these voices come from other living minds (ESP), or are the residue of unfulfilled dreams. Whether the true source of a given voice comes from oneself, a collective unconscious, other living minds, disembodied human or non-human spirits, or anything else is not subject to universally accepted verification. Every explanation of channeling phenomena has behind it a worldview that can be challenged by a different worldview. But what we find indis-putable is that for thousands of years, people have been seeking external authorities, whether they be leaders, gods, extra-ter-restrials, oracles, or channels, to reveal the truth and make things all right. From our perspective, this very mentality is a large part of what has brought the world to where it is today.

If maturing as a species has any meaning at all, it must mean that since collective humanity, for whatever reasons, has been instrumental in bringing about the crisis it finds itself in, only humanity—people, all of us—can find the collective solution within ourselves and each other. Putting hope in anything exter-nal deflects from realizing that viable solutions to make things right, or more right, must come from embodied people. So, putting aside whether supposed spirits actually exist or not, the very looking to external authorities to make life right is merely recapitulating an age-old drama. Looking for a savior (or to be one) is the old solution that now has become part of the problem. Our reasons for writing this book stem from a conviction that new and viable solutions involve realizing "The buck stops here," with each of us.

Do You Create Your Own Reality?

Some years ago at a conference examining the spiritual dimension of existence, the keynote speaker, a famous psychologist, in talking about how we all create our own realities, said, "I cannot prove this to you, but I firmly believe that I chose my parents." Presumably this meant he believed that not only he, but each of us, too, create our own reality to the extent that we all choose which parents to be born to. The implications about the nature of existence contained in that remark are vast and include:

1. That he, or something, existed before his birth that did the choosing.
2. That he could have chosen some other way of being born, otherwise there is no real choice. Perhaps he could have even chosen not to be born at all.

To be consistent he would have to acknowledge that his parents, who were also presumably creating their own realities, each chose him. How was this agreement reached? Did these three gather on a different plane of existence and work it out? Or did they each arrive at the same choice independently? Here the problem is how all these independently created universes interact without one being able to essentially influence (change) the outcome for another. If one says the choices of each independent actor always conveniently dovetail (I chose my parents and they chose me, and by extrapolation this is so for all parents and children), what is called choice appears more like an elaborately choreographed dance full of isolated entities acting out their parts with no real freedom at all.

Was it coincidence, accident, or considered forethought that these three entities should arrive upon the same mutual choice; or was it a function of some greater plan that arranged them to be together in this unique way? Did they meet at some other level of reality they later forgot about to see if they would choose each other? But what if one said, "I choose you," and the other replied, "No thanks"? The idea that each of these three people should arbitrarily choose the same event stretches credulity to the breaking point; on the other hand, if there were some higher order or force involved, even if it be that they deserved each other, then what meaning does choice have?

At this point, a bemused reader might wonder why this psychologist found it necessary to make such an extreme claim and why we are devoting time and space to it. The reason is that to maintain a "You create your own reality" perspective, it must be absolute and cannot allow any external influences to be a real factor. For if something outside of me is helping create the reality I'm experiencing, then I am not doing it alone. (Perhaps I do not even have the majority vote.) What is important to see is why this position must be extreme. Elsewhere we show why letting in even a little bit of freedom changes everything.[1] Here to let in just a little bit of determinism or causality that is not self-generated likewise changes everything. For if there is any, even the slightest, separate or accidental external factor contributing to the "reality" that you are experiencing, then you haven't created it all. If you haven't created it all, how much and what part of it have you created? In this framework it has to be all, or it doesn't work.

---

[1]"Am I For Real or Am I On Tape? Free Will and Determinism in Karma" in *Control* shows that the ambiguities between the two are largely a function of a moral agenda.

Our interest in examining the "You create your own reality" framework stems from the irony that it appears the antithesis of authoritarian control, yet the groups that promulgate it are authoritarian. This is because, as we will show, it can neither be proved nor disproved and must be taken on faith. It is important first to clarify why those who have adopted this belief have done so. In querying many of this persuasion, a usual reply is that upon having taken total responsibility for their lives (an extension of the self-created reality point of view), a dramatic shift occurred in which they experienced themselves as self-actualizing, and life itself became richer in every way. This viewpoint can also initially bring:

1. A sense of real power (or empowerment, to use the vernacular). This is especially potent if one had previously felt either victimized or saw oneself largely moved by forces over which one had little or no control.

2. An expansion of the field of possibility by removing previously limiting attitudes, whereby one's vistas enlarge and a new sense of great potential beckons.

3. A letting go (at least on the surface) of blaming others. This can shift the context of relationships, making it easier to connect with people—few enjoy being blamed.

4. A powerful mental alignment with others who share the same belief, bringing a sense of community. Alignment not only reinforces belief, but also opens boundaries, which can bring more energy and newness into life.

Within the self-created reality world view there are serious issues of control and responsibility that this theory tries to simplify under one universal precept. This issue warrants examination not only because many channels, spiritual teachers, prosperity workshops, and "responsibility" seminars are promulgating it, but also because it is interesting and droll to see how the East's somewhat fatalistic beliefs have been turned on their head to meet Western predilections for freedom, self-reliance, control, and personal responsibility. We wish to show why we think operating under this precept in the long run makes people less free and effective, not more so.

Wanting to take charge of one's life is understandable. But the desire for such omnipotence, to be totally in charge to the extent of creating all of one's reality, has deep and unexamined implications about the nature of reality in general. This includes the need for a karma/rebirth theory to make it work. Although it is not usually presented as totally deterministic, in the East the concept of karma has a pronounced deterministic flavor. Since Westerners largely do not have a taste for extreme austerity, undue renunciation, or too much passive acceptance, it is interesting to see the way some Westerners have utilized this concept to give themselves freedom without external constraints.

We will assume the reader has at least a passing familiarity with the idea of karma. Briefly, it states that as you sow in this life, so you shall reap in a future life; and that what you are reaping now, you sowed in some previous lifetime. Karma is presented as a cosmic, impersonal moral principle, law, or force that ensures everyone gets what they deserve. Its essential function is to guarantee the universe is fair and just. Should this idea be given any credence, the questions then involve how it all works. Karma is the moral equivalent of a monotheistic, omnipotent, omniscient God in that it, too, has unbending rules for how to be, with inbuilt rewards and retributions. Karma, like the monotheistic God, cannot be escaped. Although the basic rules of karma are structural, not specific, still, generating "bad karma" is the moral equivalent of sinning.

The theory of karmic causality views all consequences (karma) as generated by the attachments of ego. Karma is more sophisticated than sin for although it is the obstacle to spiritual realization; yet it is also the means by which realization is obtained, for it is part of the chain of progression. So two basic, complementary stances are proposed: Do not resist the karma you have previously generated; and through detaching from ego, generate less, and eventually none. Karma/rebirth theories in the East are thus essentially renunciate in that they mandate renouncing self-centered activity.[2]

The New Age extrapolation of karma theory goes beyond merely saying that one has created karma to live out. It states that at every moment one is creating the whole of whatever it is one is experiencing. It reasons as follows: Where you find yourself now is a function of your past actions and attitudes (karma), and where you will find yourself in the future is determined by what you are doing now. Why not extend this to its extreme limit and say people totally create, and are therefore totally responsible for, their own reality?

Even the most absolute view of "You create your own reality," no matter how bizarre to common sense, cannot be disproved by logic—in the same way that solipsism cannot. In fact, these two views share much in common. Solipsism is the philosophical position that I alone exist and am thus the entire cosmos. Everything that appears to be not-me I am merely fabricating (presumably for my own amusement). Nothing can be presented to a firm solipsist that could logically dissuade this belief or prove it wrong. A difference between solipsism and believing "You create your own reality" is that the latter has a universe populated with many entities each creating their own realities, instead of merely one.

Subjective idealism is the philosophy that starts out by postulating the only thing anyone can know for sure is their own internal experience. The 18th-century thinker Bishop Berkeley is an example of this, as are some forms of Buddhism. This position when pushed to its extreme leads to solipsism, because ultimately your own private world is all you are left with. Solipsism is presented in philosophy classes as an absurdity that

---

[2]The section on "Oneness" in "The Power of Abstraction" shows how karma is the moral underpinning of the Eastern Oneness worldview. An entire section on karma/rebirth (of which this chapter is a part) in *Control* is devoted to showing the hidden authoritarianism within the way karma is conceived and presented.

results from taking the logic of a position to an extreme without regard for reasonableness. No one takes it seriously. Thinkers try to influence other thinkers, but if there are no other thinkers, why bother?

In our view, "You create your own reality" takes karmic theory to the same kind of extreme as solipsism does with subjective idealism. In other words, it is also a logical extension, but pushed to the extreme of multiple omnipotence. It takes the appealing self-creating part of karmic theory and ignores its deterministic and retributive side. The problem that any serious essentially subjective view of reality faces is explaining how and why all the subjective realities seem to dovetail and be facing similar problems in a similar world. Bishop Berkeley was forced to invoke God's subjectivity (the mind and will of God) as a protection from solipsism, and as a constraint that keeps everyone else's subjectivity somewhat in line.

Many who have tried to live in the "You create your own reality" worldview eventually become uncomfortable with its absoluteness. To accommodate this, some have adopted a "multi-leveled" explanation, wherein on one level (the worldly or secular), total self-creation isn't true; but on a supposedly higher, more spiritual level it is. How these different levels of reality interact or create the larger context of reality is left obscure. Other exponents do another kind of levels shift, saying the "I" (in "I create my own reality") they are referring to is an expression of the unity of all being (Oneness).[3] This, in the idiom of the sixties, is a cop-out because to identify the "I" with the unity of all being in this fashion is to give up personal choice. If the whole is directing things and choreographing it all, what does choice mean? When levels are shifted paradox is often invoked to account for contradictions, which from our point of view is an indication of the limitation of a framework, and is not a satisfactory end to inquiry.[4]

---

[3]See "Oneness, Enlightenment, and the Mystical Experience."
[4]Paradox as a way of short-circuiting conceptual frameworks is covered in

If individual choice is so powerful that people even choose their parents, then why not create a reality where one receives great admiration and respect, a lengthy life full of love, delight, and discovery, and great sex on request? The typical answer to this is that people create for themselves the reality they do in order to learn the lessons they need to move on. But who created the lessons that need to be learned, and who decides where to move on to? To say that I created it all for myself paints a picture of people who give themselves a lot of painful lessons to reach a goal they also created for themselves. If something else created the need for the lessons and the goal the lessons bring, then one is not totally creating it all.

This genre of statement is representative of the self-created reality worldview: "I gave myself a flat tire today." Inattention to a worn tire can "cause" a flat, but how and why did one create the nails on the road that punctured the tire? Also, new tires get punctured, or are bought faulty, etc. From here only the "lessons to be learned" rationale can explain why one gave oneself this or any unpleasant reality. "Lessons that need to be learned" is the way karma has been translated by those who have distaste for its retributive and fatalistic aspects.

Similar to the way theories of karma need past lives to justify a particular view of morality, theories of self-created reality need past lives to justify a particular view of responsibility. For underneath the idea that I create my own reality is the corollary that I am therefore totally responsible for everything that happens to me. The psychologist initially mentioned knew that parents contribute to shaping their children, as does the rest of the environment. So to be totally serious about creating reality, one would have to include everything in it.

When asked why thousands of Vietnamese children killed by napalm created that reality for themselves, and what lesson they

---

"The Assault on Reason" and "Oneness, Enlightenment, and the Mystical Experience." It is also discussed in the Buddhism section of *Control.*

learned from this, the only viable explanation is that they created the need to do that to themselves in some past life, and the lesson will carry over into their future lives. Here the notion of karma takes on a particular Western flavor, so that presumably the Vietnamese children chose this particular form of death in order to work out the karma (learn a lesson they themselves created a need to learn). In the East, karma is acquired, not chosen, and so the proper attitude to what comes one's way is surrender to it; whereas the "self-creation" belief makes people feel they have the power to create what they will.

The "You create" version of karma must posit that all the individuals in any particular group who suffer a similar fate—be it the Untouchables in India, the tortured Cambodians, AIDS victims, or any underprivileged group—have chosen similar lessons to learn. The implication is that they chose to be born into a given context precisely to suffer in the way they do. None of this can stand up without resorting to past-life justifications. This becomes especially obvious wherever brutality toward children is concerned, for given their relative innocence, it's unimaginable they could have (as children) created some of the horrible realities they find themselves in. Ultimately (though sometimes reluctantly) reincarnation is dragged out to justify all the horrendous realities so many people find themselves in. (That this view can implicitly be used to justify racism or any brutality ought to be obvious.)

Another example of not wanting any constraints are those who believe that at any given moment they are free to create the total context of their lives. A workshop leader glibly said in a lecture, "Since there is no such thing as objective reality, just choose the reality that works best for you." Without going into the many problems that maintaining such an extreme subjective position entails, here is just one example: Is the choice to create whatever reality one is creating always a conscious choice? The intelligible answer here would have to be "No." If I am creating a given reality in order to teach myself a needed lesson, it is only after experiencing the lesson (usually with some pain) that

I can know I needed it. If I had known beforehand what a painful lesson was in store for me, I might well not have chosen it. So the question is: what's that part of me that knows I need a lesson, and what is its relationship to that part of me that needs the lesson? To say the part of me that knows is my "higher self" only confounds the issue. Why is there a lower self at all, or a higher self that needs to give a lower self a lot of painful lessons?

Traditional psychoanalysis has been very deterministic, attributing one's woes to biology and early traumas that cannot be escaped. (Freud, who was not very optimistic about the possibilities for human freedom, felt that at best one could mitigate and adapt to these external shapers of one's personality— that is, learn to live with them through extended therapy.) Psychoanalytic determinism facilitates blaming the fates or one's parents for one's hangups, and thus encourages a victim mentality. The notion of taking complete responsibility for one's life was a reaction against this. It became the therapeutic alternative many humanistic psychologies used to counter psychoanalytical pessimism. A psychology needs a worldview as a foundation to hold it up. Freud used nineteenth-century deterministic science. Many New Age psychologies adopted Eastern models instead to "empower" the individual to be self-actualizing. The self-created reality theory takes self-actualization and personal responsibility the furthest they can go, to where no constraints exist outside oneself.

Just as karma has causal and ethical implications, so do conceptions of responsibility. To be responsible for any occurrence can mean that one was the cause of it, or that one has an obligation to deal with it, or both. The usual assumption is that if one is the cause, one is obligated to deal with the effects. Karma is about merit and demerit, credit and blame; this too is what many people mean by responsibility. If one is the sole cause (I, and I alone create my reality), then the responsibility for the outcome (the credit or blame), as well as dealing with it, rests solely on one's shoulders. Also, often conveniently, whatever happens to someone else rests completely on theirs.

Believing that you omnipotently create (choose) your universe, and that anything that's happening to you is happening because you're making it happen, can have enormous appeal. It means that if you "do it right" you can get anything you want. This is a pendulum-swing reaction against the powerlessness of the victim mentality where the world is doing it to you. If I am actually doing it, then I can change it; whereas if the world is doing it to me, I probably can't, because it's obviously much harder to change the world. The thought that I am doing it all to myself has a sense of freedom and power in it, and of course one is also totally in control.

As an example of how much control one really has, this cliché is commonly given: "You are creating whatever feelings you are feeling, and are consequently totally responsible for them." This is presented as true by definition; if you're feeling it, you're creating it. This means no one can make me angry. I create the feelings of anger in myself and I am totally responsible for them. There is a difference between acknowledging that attitudes and beliefs shape or influence one's feelings and making them the absolute determinants. If a drunk driver runs over my child, am I the total cause of my anger? This position, when carried to an extreme, blames oneself not only for how one feels, but even for the event that brought about the feelings.

Although this belief has some credibility on the psychological level, it lessens considerably if extended to the physical level where causality is more concrete and visible. This would allow anyone to hit you and then deny responsibility by noting that you are totally responsible for creating the pain you are allowing the cells of your body to register. And that it is also your task to wonder why you created a reality that involves someone hitting you. Though absurd on the physical level, this argument is used to deny contributing to another's psychological pain. It is true a victim mentality that blames only external factors limits possibility. However, to take full responsibility for every occurrence and vicissitude can be just as binding since it can engender guilt, inadequacy, and self-doubt. ("Why am I doing this to myself?")

If you made it happen, then obviously you deserve it; and the responsibility of dealing with it is yours and yours alone. As with traditional karmic theory, cosmic justice is built in. All theories of karma/rebirth have difficulty drawing a line between free will and determinism.[5] But here there is an added difficulty in explaining how it is that on the one hand, past lives create needed lessons to be learned, yet at any moment one is nevertheless free to choose the reality one is experiencing (or any other).

Are there as many realities as there are people? Should we include animals in this? Possible extra-terrestrials? There is a real difference between saying that every subject creates subjectivity, and saying that every subject creates its total reality. How do these separate realities coordinate, or are they not really separate? If on some other level people and their realities are not separate, then something else besides the individual is defining reality. Any common or shared reality would have to be somehow coordinated, but by whom or what? What level of reality is doing the coordinating? Who is really in control? Right now there seem to be billions of people creating painful and frightening realities for themselves. Does each individual facing starvation, disease, and the threat of death need this as a lesson? To say that the species needs this as a lesson just will not do. Such a leap from singular to collective self-creation does away with individual omnipotence and individual responsibility, too.

The point of this discussion is to show the difficulties in maintaining such a framework without creating deep inconsistencies or making assertions about reality that strain credulity. The assertion that reality consists of a multitude of subjectively manufactured realities independent of each other is a viewpoint about reality—a viewpoint that either describes with some accuracy the way things work, or it does not. When a framework is a

---

[5]"Am I For Real or Am I On Tape?" in *Control* examines in depth the complexities involved and presents a dialectical view of the interplay among them.

closed system fraught with inconsistencies, convoluted justifications, and self-affirming explanations that are true by definition (tautologies), then there is good reason to suspect that what is involved is something quite other than a quest for truth. Instead, there's an excellent likelihood that what is really involved is justifying deep personal preferences.

The relationship between control (taking charge) and surrender (letting go) presents one of the deepest existential quandaries humans face. Different worldviews emphasize one over the other. Taoism, which promulgates flowing with the river of life, is strong on the letting go side, as are most Eastern karma/rebirth theories. Surrendering to one's karma, to duty, and to a spiritual authority are deeply embedded in the traditional views of karma.[6] In contrast, the self-created reality theories push control to the hilt. Behind this need for ultimate control is the fear that someone, or something (perhaps an indifferent universe), can come in at any moment and make me feel some way I do not want to, or take away what I cherish most (even my life). So I choose my feelings, choose my time of death, and choose what parents to be reborn to. Here Western preferences for control and unrestricted possibilities create a worldview that also builds an emotional shield of invulnerability to external events. We suspect that feelings of impotence when facing the juggernaut of these changing, unstable times are behind many people adopting this extreme position.

We do think that all of us are participants in creating not only our own reality, but a mutually shared reality. In our view everyone affects and is affected by the context. At times the context is so overpowering (an earthquake or repressive political system) that there is little one can immediately do. At other times an individual can exert real leverage in shaping the context. Within this dialectical perspective, the issue of who or what is in

---

[6]The dialectical relation between control and surrender is discussed in greater depth in "The Seductions of Surrender" (and also in "Buddhism and the Abuse of Detachment" in *Control.*)

control is fluid and ever-changing. We believe the real reason people adopt the self-created reality framework is wanting to have the final say (bottom-line control) over their lives.

In all of us, our nervous systems shape incoming data; our conditioning patterns program responses; our preferences and predilections uniquely filter our experience; and our capacities for self-awareness can bring change. Thus in our view, we do have the freedom to partake in creating tomorrow. But to deny that reality (including one's own) is also at every moment being co-created not only by everyone but by everything ignores the other side of the dialectic. For as I am busy creating reality, reality is busy creating me. To confound this dialectical relationship blurs the task of true awareness, which realizes that to be human involves being both in control and out of control. When to take charge, and when to let go, are at the crux of every existential dilemma. Here no formulas can give the proper resolution. "You create your own reality" is a formula that gives people the illusion of absolute power. Not to acknowledge the interplay of being in and out of control eventually isolates people from the very reality they think they're creating by distorting their perception of it.

Converting to this belief initially can give people energy, confidence, and inspiration to change their lives, but it eventually generates guilt and feelings of failure when reality obstinately resists the hoped-for omnipotence. Probably those who take on this worldview do so out of a deep intuition that there is something basically true and important about one's reality being self-created. We agree. But that each of us creates our own reality is only a partial truth, which if treated like a total truth, is a lie. This belief implies people are totally disconnected units, each creating a separate reality that neither affects nor is affected by others. This is not the consciousness needed to survive.

Healing
Crippled Self-Trust

Many people who give themselves to authoritarian groups and later become disillusioned end up deeply mistrusting themselves. In order to surrender to an external authority, some self-mistrust already has to be present. This includes not believing one could get "it" (whatever "it" is) on one's own. Ironically, people usually implicitly trust their capacity to recognize the authority who can lead them to what they want. But unfortunately, given how easy fear and desire are to manipulate, this is possibly the last thing that should be exempted from mistrust.

The deeper one surrenders to an authoritarian structure, the harder it is to detach from it because one's very identity becomes wrapped around that context—one's emotions, beliefs, images, worldview, relationships, etc. In fact, the group, with the authority figure at the center, becomes the foundation of all meaning, intimacy, and even possibility for the future. Those in the inner circle or high on the organization's rungs have an even more difficult time unhooking. Most have achieved more power and feelings of specialness than they ever had before or could on their own. Each becomes a minor authority to those below.

Leaving a group after having surrendered to it often puts one back into the confusions and lacks that initially made the group appealing. In addition, another sometimes paralyzing form of self-doubt may occur—doubting one's capacity to find a way out of the confusion. One's sense of reality is delicate because many things previously believed now seem the opposite of what they were. What seemed right and good then appears wrong and malevolent now. The guru's seeming unconditional love was really about wanting unconditional power; his selflessness was egomania in disguise; his purity was corrupt. The burning questions in one's mind are: "How could I have been so taken in?" "How can I trust myself to know what's real or good for me?" The difficulty of leaving is compounded by the reality that doing so rarely feels good initially. Instead there's bewilderment, anger mixed with depression, and self-blame.

Fear is a large part of what keeps many in these groups—not only a fear of returning to the uncertainties of being on one's own, but a deep fear of being awash without being able to trust one's own judgment at all. This also impacts trusting others, for disillusionment around basic beliefs often breeds a generalized cynicism. So the stakes in believing or not believing in the authority are very high. The followers' fears of going back to a life that could be even worse than before give the guru more power over them. This is similar to an addict's fear of returning to the drab, dull life the addiction was trying to alleviate. Dependency on an authoritarian group displays many similarities to addiction.[1]

Leaving such a group creates more than an identity crisis, for it involves mistrusting one's deepest emotions and basic perceptions of self, others, and the universe. In addition, one doubts the wisdom of following one's passion. Whereas passion about a cause used to be a sign of authenticity, it, too, can no longer be trusted. The ex-disciple's world has turned on its head: What the guru and group presented as unconditional love was conditional upon accepting their authority; the egoless guru was found to be on a manipulative, even crass, power trip. For people who surrendered totally to a guru and thus experienced passion more deeply than ever before, seeing "The emperor wears

---

[1]See "Who Is in Control? The Authoritarian Roots of Addiction."

no clothes" can be devastating. So it's no wonder people have tremendous resistance to anything that causes them to doubt the veracity of the authority.

Surrendering to an authority makes it easy to overlook or rationalize what would ordinarily be considered unethical. Even more unsettling, one might have found oneself doing, or willing to do, very hurtful things to others. Some ex-cult[2] members later admitted with shame and embarrassment that they would even have killed if the authority had ordered it. Having seen the extent of their capacity for self-delusion and for being so under the sway of another, it is not surprising that many upon leaving the group not only fear themselves, but the world in general. They saw others who were also willing to follow the leader's dictates no matter what; so they realize people are capable of doing most anything, which makes the world a much scarier place.

Ex-cult members often describe themselves as crippled, sometimes even a decade or more later. What is crippled is the capacity to trust oneself which, when lost, is difficult to regain. This is the serious challenge those who leave authoritarian groups face. People usually try to overcome this through a determination never to be duped again. Unfortunately, this stance brings about defensive postures that leave the person cynical and closed. Underneath such cynicism is fear of commitment and openness—both of which previously brought considerable pain. Behind most cynicism there is a disillusioned idealist. This protective posture can make people more functional, but with it they become guarded, rigid, emotionally cut off, and vulnerable to depression because of a deep reservoir of fear and anger. Depression commonly coats fear and anger.

It's difficult to make a deep connection with the world when one is afraid to be conned, deceived, or to follow one's passion. This mistrust can also affect one's personal emotional life. In

---

[2]See "Religion, Cults, and the Spiritual Vacuum" for how we define "cult."

some cases, people become afraid to involve themselves in real intimacy. Becoming disillusioned with the nature of surrender and passion can limit one's capacity to love, because what was previously thought of as love was found to be only image, and essentially a lie. Defending against involvement often leaves ex-cult members with greater boundaries and limits than they had before their cult experience.

What real healing must involve is rebuilding self-trust. This is not an easy task, for having been seduced by the cult experience gives one little reason to trust oneself. Of course, it is possible another person's love or care could break through the deep misgivings, enabling some openness and trust to come. However, being open to one person does not necessarily remove the fear of susceptibility to being taken in by charismatic people, groups and causes, or any other kind of involvement. One can still be basically afraid of oneself.

The most extreme form of mental control occurs when the authority is trusted completely and becomes the center of one's identity. Sadly, society and parents insidiously put out messages from childhood on that others know what's best. Many people are deeply conditioned to expect and hope some outside agency, power, or person will solve their problems. Letting go of expecting or even wanting this is difficult, partially because what one is left with is oneself, and all of one's limitations. But moving past the often great disappointment that there is no ultimate authority who knows what's best for others can allow one to be open to what others offer without fear of being taken over by them. The very ability to do this, however, is linked with self-trust. The capacity to trust oneself has a feedback loop in it: the more you can do it, the more of it you build; likewise, self-doubt breeds self-doubt. Once a person has been hurt and crippled in a way that deeply damages self-trust, the question is how to turn this around?

True healing can be accelerated by understanding the deep mechanisms of what happened, and of authoritarian dynamics in general. Then people can be more confident they won't be taken in again. Part of maturation is realizing that no other person can know with certainty what is appropriate for others. By remaining the ultimate judge of what's right for oneself, one can receive and integrate what others offer without fearing dependency.

One motive for writing this book is our belief that a deeper understanding of the dynamics and pervasiveness of authoritarianism enables people to be less susceptible to it. This does involve becoming more aware, for a real correlation exists between self-trust and awareness. The person who entered the cult had great illusions that were later shattered; the person who left the cult was disillusioned, but did not fully understand or integrate what really happened. Self-deception, in varying degrees, is part of the human condition. Awareness of how easily fear, need, and desire can be manipulated enhances critical intelligence.

Disillusionment in itself is not the real problem. Awareness involves breaking through illusions, which, of course, is disillusioning. Often the real obstacle is being so attached to whatever emotions or meaning the illusions were feeding that letting go of illusions feels like a loss instead of a gain. To see how one's previous good feelings contained illusion can be a bitter pill at first. But even though the caring and sharing in the authoritarian context were found to be mechanical and ephemeral, real caring and sharing are a needed aspect of life. The illusion lay in believing in the authenticity of blind surrender and in the instant intimacy doing so offers.

Part of self-awareness is also seeing the poison and ultimate isolation of the self-defensive posture. The little voice inside that warns not to trust others is deadly. It's the same voice that often comes after being deeply hurt in a love relationship. Its purpose is to ensure that "This will never happen again." Rigidly controlling against further hurt and disillusionment not only closes the door to passion, but also to the possibility of living without fear of oneself. The fear is that without self-control, one would again succumb to being taken over. Such control brings conflict and internal division because something basic is being denied.

A whole person is open to love, which means risking the possibility of again being taken in and hurt.[3]

If one has been truly dis-illusioned about authoritarian relationships (that is, lost one's illusions, rather than merely being disappointed), there is far less likelihood of falling into the same traps or becoming cynical. Cynicism indicates one has not totally given up the illusions, but still blames others or the world for being let down. Often what is held onto are the ideals that mask authoritarianism, even though one has been disillusioned by a given leader. This is why people feel susceptible and do not trust themselves, for as long as they have unlivable ideals, they are manipulable. It is the ideals that are the illusion, not the failures of others or oneself to live up to them.[4] Letting go of illusions is just that—letting go of all of it, including the emotions and expectations they and their loss generate. Then one can be open to the kind of love that is not an illusion.

---

[3]"Who Is in Control?" contains an in-depth analysis of the causes and ramifications of being internally divided, which leads to self-mistrust. It discusses becoming whole through integrating the basic division in oneself.

[4]The often clandestine nature of authoritarian ideals and their power and appeal are the subjects of Part Two of this book.

Part 2

Ideological Masks

Introduction:
The Morals Wars

The greatest struggle on the planet today is for the minds of people. We call this struggle the morals wars because the conflict is about morality and its foundations. What this involves are basic assumptions on how to live and be, what proper action is, and also (most importantly) how problems are to be solved or not solved.

Morality (the accepted structure in a social order dealing with the way people should and do treat each other) is the glue that holds every society together. And underneath every moral order there is a foundation that justifies it. Whatever else this foundation is, it always involves a point of view about what reality is and isn't. At this time in history, the foundations of the old moral order are breaking down. When this occurs, two predictable and opposing forces accelerate the rift in the old order. They are:

1. Powerful movements that attempt to reestablish the strength of the old moral order. The essential stance here is that our basic problems are a function of having strayed too far from the verities of old. The solution given is the necessity to return to them with even more fervor. The increase in popularity and strength of fundamentalist perspectives, worldwide, is the most obvious example of this.

2. The searching for and experimenting with different forms of human interaction. This involves a recognition that new

ways to problem-solve are needed to deal with the planet-threatening dilemmas brought about by human abuse the old moral order has not been able to contain. Those in this camp would include as paramount issues all or most of the following: overpopulation; ecology and the portent of ecological suicide; the leveraging of the human capacity for violence to where it is species-threatening; the increase in discrepancy between haves and have-nots worldwide; the historic omission of half the species (women) from the construction of the public forms of social power. (Many women theorists rightly argue that institutionalized power today is available to a woman only if she plays by the rules set down by men.) Within this point of view one hears from many different directions the need for a basic paradigm shift.

That this book aligns with the second perspective is obvious. A major thesis of these writings is that it is people's deep conditioning to want either to be or to obey an unchallengeable authority that is keeping the planet from the kind of intelligence needed in problem-solving. It is not within the scope of this book to present a new paradigm, although we do put forth the kind of shifts in perspective we think necessary to allow a new paradigm to emerge. Rather, the emphasis is decoding the authoritarianism within often hidden areas of the social order. Unless people can see clearly the water they are swimming in, there is no way to build a life raft that will float. Since much of the authoritarianism in the old structures and hence in our psyches and daily life is unconscious and veiled, it needs to be decoded and unmasked to free ourselves. Without this it will infiltrate any attempts at new solutions.

A problem with being on the side of the new is that it is more difficult to make pronouncements with the total surety that those who back the old moral order are able to assume. Anything really new lacks a history of articulation that lends strength and credibility to its insights. Those seeking new forms are usually splintered into many factions of somewhat differing points of view. Consequently, it is difficult to get the alignment that traditionalists can muster because they come from an established known that worked (to the extent that it did) for a long period (thousands of years). As a result the forces wanting to revive the old are more certain, self-righteous, and morally accusative; while the forces seeking new solutions are often more tentative, sometimes apologetic, and often find themselves on the moral defensive.

The outcome of what we call the morals wars impacts nothing less than human survival. The old order brought us to where we are today. It is unraveling because it cannot deal with the forces it unleashed. If the old wins out, there is little likelihood we will survive as a species. The fact that the major overt agenda of the old order is not species survival, but rather personal salvation, is not insignificant.

History at this moment is being stretched, made taut by the opposing forces of the old and the new. It is in times like this that a crack in history can allow the new to flower. If humanity is to evolve into a viable relationship with itself and the planet, the morals wars cannot be taken lightly. In the past the tensions between old and new had the luxury of working themselves out in whatever time it took. Now, because there is an ecological time clock, the old can defeat the new merely by impeding the necessary changes—which means in the end, no one wins.[1]

The conundrum humanity faces is this: We are on a sinking ship, but the only materials we have to build a ship that will float come from the ship itself. The problem is that we must tear down the old ship before it sinks, rebuilding it at the same time without destroying the needed parts.

---

[1]See "Fundamentalism and the Need for Certainty" for a more in-depth analysis of the struggle between the old and new—and why there is no time for the usual way this struggle has historically resolved itself.

Fundamentalism and the Need for Certainty

undamentalists and modernists are locked in a world-wide battle for minds. This conflict is between old values and structures and a new reality that doesn't yet have a distinct shape or an appropriate moral structure to fit it. The current rise of fundamentalism over the entire planet is predictable in that when the fabric of society, including its moral underpinnings, begins to break down, the desire to return to the familiar and secure is inevitable. We look at the movement of history as occurring through the creation of tensions that turn into polarities, which eventually make the status quo impossible to maintain. Fundamentalism is the bedrock of one pole.

Human impact has gone beyond specific cultures and localities. What is referred to as the "commons," that is, what impacts all the people in the world—water, atmosphere, waste disposal, radiation levels, etc.—cannot be properly protected or managed without a basic agreement on priorities and values. Until pan-cultural survival values are created there is nothing firm to stand on. Pre-industrial tribal values usually do express the necessity of there being harmony with nature. But they were not constructed to deal with the scale of impact wrought by technology. When tribal people take in technology they, too, have difficulty maintaining harmony.[1]

---

[1]"From Animism to Polytheism" in "The Power of Abstraction: The Sacred Word and the Evolution of Morality" discusses how tribal animistic

163

The concept of harmony with nature is valuable, but the problem is what does harmony really consist of in the modern world and how is it to be achieved? Once technology began greatly to leverage human power, the harmony that came from the balance of power between people and nature was lost. Now a new balance is necessary for survival. But this can only come from humans controlling how they utilize power. This requires an entirely different model because species vulnerability is now more a function of the misuse of control than a lack of it. It is our position that attempting to return to the old will not work. Both the quality and quantity of human impact are far beyond the capacity of past solutions to integrate them—largely because the values and worldviews that generated the old ways are authoritarian, and thus by their nature resistant to change. No consensus has ever come from the clash of authoritarian beliefs. Thus, there is much talk of the need for a paradigm shift.

A true paradigm shift would need to consist of not only a basic shift in values, but in the way values are arrived at, kept, and justified. The old moralities are based on authoritarian transmissions that essentially cannot be challenged because the pronouncements are thought to come from an intelligence that is superhuman. Whether this intelligence is called God or an enlightened being does not essentially matter. Waiting for a messianic figure to straighten things out is a part of the old order. If a paradigm shift is to come, it cannot come by fiat. It can only come via a shared discourse of caring people who sense the urgency of this endeavor.

To understand fundamentalism's power as a worldwide movement it is necessary to examine its appeal. Our aim is not merely to show it to be authoritarian, an easy task. Fundamentalism is essentially about controlling people. It can only operate in author-

---

worldviews were a function of a balance of power between people and the world around them. With relatively little control over and protection against nature, achieving harmony with nature's forces was necessary for survival.

itarian hierarchies because unchallengeability can only be passed down and enforced in this way. Those who are given or take power through its dictates, on any level of the hierarchy, have a vested interest in it. This includes males who are given power in the traditional family. But the appeal of fundamentalism goes even deeper because it offers certainty in a very uncertain world.

Western religions contain the most clear-cut expressions of fundamentalism, for in monotheistic worldviews an omnipotent God lays out the rules for everything and everybody. These rules are stated in texts—the Bible or the Koran. The question then becomes how literally is one to take these texts? Here a division occurs between fundamentalists who want to take the words as literally as possible, and revisionists who use the words as guideposts, while revising and modernizing their meaning. Fundamentalists see clearly that once people take it upon themselves to revise the words of God, authority is undermined. Revisionists see clearly that not to do so leaves one with an antiquated worldview that is no longer relevant or credible to many.

Fundamentalists and revisionists have in common wanting to keep a given religious framework operative. Both are interested in it as a foundation for human interaction. Both are interested in reform: Fundamentalists want to return to the original moral purity that is lost when religions grow more secular and either complacent or corrupt. They do this by adhering to the rules more rigidly. Revisionists want to keep the spirit and meaning of the religion alive (as they see it) by refurbishing the worldview and making the morality more flexible and less literal. The problem for fundamentalists is how to incorporate change; the problem for revisionists is how to keep the basic structure while changing it. There comes a time when the changes necessary are so great that making them no longer leaves the basic structure intact. When the source behind a structure is authoritarian, revising it to make it less authoritarian can only take one so far. If it becomes truly non-authoritarian, the structure crumbles. Because fundamentalism and revisionism are both inherent polarized tendencies within authoritarian religion that play off each other, this chapter will examine the mentalities of each, focusing first on the former.

Different fundamentalist groups have different fundamentals to go back to. But what are these fundamentals, and why is it even necessary to go back to them if they are the powerful verities they claim to be? Fundamentalists all share the same viewpoint that what must be returned to are the unchallengeable and unchanging dictates of a higher power. They all locate the cause of the need to return in the failings of humanity, that is, in people succumbing to evil.[2]

Some religions are more rigidly authoritarian than others. We devote little attention to Islam because it is so obviously authoritarian—the very word Islam means submission. It is an extension of the dualistic Judeo-Christian cosmology whose basic premise is that, above all, people must surrender to the will of God as defined by the Koran. The words of the Koran are not subject to deep questioning. Some Islamic fundamentalists consider all of modernity the devil's workshop, and with the moral righteousness that can only come from certainty, they would destroy it if they could.

Revisionist movements within Islam are deeply constrained in how far they can overtly challenge orthodoxy. Within Sufism (the mystical branch of Islam) the idea of the unity of all existence was put forth in a very hidden fashion. The overt content of the writings had to be couched in a way that did not directly challenge the Koran, which is unabashedly dualistic; so their mystical point of view was covertly expressed in love poems. The need to protect itself from Islamic orthodoxy is to our minds the real reason Sufism was esoteric. Significant elements within Islam have never been shy, even today, of maiming and killing those who disagree with them. Such draconian punishment stands as a stark example of how protecting what is considered sacred is used to justify violence.

---

[2]On the intrinsic problems within the categories of good and evil, see "Satanism and the Worship of the Forbidden: Why It Feels Good to Be Bad."

The Essence of Fundamentalism

Religions are worldviews, a prime function of which is to make the moral order seem non-arbitrary. One of the great fears in the human psyche (sometimes conscious, but often not) is of chaos and anarchy—not merely social, political, and behavioral anarchy, but an inner psychological anarchy as well. The fear underneath much of fundamentalism is that without powerful constraints, people (and oneself, too) would run amuck. Fundamentalism constructs hard categories of good and evil that battle for the souls of people. Evil is presented as so powerful that a person cannot withstand its temptations unless armed with the proper beliefs. Fear and mistrust of oneself are not only promoted, but assuaged only through adopting the given beliefs with certainty.[3]

The great psychological appeal of fundamentalism is that it offers certainty. But what is the appeal of certainty? Certainty can feel better than uncertainty and confusion. It can eliminate internal conflict, or at least suppress and bring relief from it. Religious certainty can only come from surrendering to a higher authority, which like all forms of surrender, releases blocked energy, gives direction, and can bring easy alignment with others who share the same certainty.[4]

Certainty must be able to withstand challenges and counter-evidence—anything that brings doubt. No combination of reason and experience can give the necessary kind of certainty, especially about the future. So faith is the key to religious certainty. Faith really is belief in an ideology, and the simpler and more unambiguous the ideology, the easier to keep the faith. A simple universe with a simple good (those who follow the

---

[3]"Satanism" shows how satanism is the underbelly of monotheism—an extreme reaction against the constraints of a repressive morality.
[4]See "The Seductions of Surrender."

rules), and a simple evil (those who do not), and simple explanations that can never be disproven are necessary for certainty. Everything that occurs is "a test of faith," "a lesson," "the will of God," or "God works in mysterious ways." These are some of the catechisms that keep certainty from being shaken. Religious certainty is about basics—faith in an afterlife, in a higher intelligence that ultimately ensures the universe is fair and just, and faith that if one follows the rules this intelligence personally cares and protects.

The rules serve two basic functions: They program the individual to obey authority and curb unwanted expressions of self-centeredness. We say "curb" purposefully, as absolute rules do not and cannot really eliminate a given activity; rather they operate to keep behaviors within a tolerable spectrum of deviance. One rule from the Ten Commandments, "Thou shalt not kill," is a case in point. Not only has it not stopped killing, but it is our thesis that it was never really meant to. There is a seeming contradiction between the taboo against killing and actual behavior, because fundamentalists as a group (there are exceptions) have often favored the death penalty and have been more "hawkish" when dealing with enemies. To say "If you break the rule against killing, we'll kill you" is inconsistent only at the verbal level. It is totally consistent with authoritarian agendas of doing whatever is necessary to ensure the rules are obeyed. Of course, other rules can be brought up to justify killing a killer—"An eye for an eye...," etc. Christ's crucifixion itself justifies using pain and killing as a means for some higher end. If God has his only son tortured and killed in order to save humanity, this sets a powerful example.

With most fundamentalists, literal consistency that would apply the rule to all facets of behavior is not a value. On the contrary, because the rules come from a source that is unchallengeable, doing whatever it takes to protect them is justified. Anything designated as evil—the rule breakers, the infidel, the evil empire—all can be treated outside the rules in the name of protecting the rules. The inevitable result of putting rules before people we call "ideological uncaringness." Here what one really cares about is keeping certainty and protecting the ideology that gives it. Authoritarian morality contains an inherent double standard: there is the morality itself, and then there is protecting it. Protecting the authoritarian system and its morality always takes precedence over the morality itself. Killing and violence or the threat of them have always been the bottom line of authoritarian power. The more certainty there is that the rules must be obeyed, the easier it is to sacrifice others who differ.

A key social function of morality is to keep aggression within acceptable bounds. This is done by legitimating it in certain places, forbidding it in others. The concept of "rights" accomplishes this. Until fairly recently, husbands had the right to beat wives. The function of such a right is to keep wives in line. The rights of parents over children and of governments to kill when they legislate doing so have a similar function. The more repressive a society is, the more there is bottled-up aggression that needs socially acceptable outlets. War, racism, wife- and child-beating, and socially sanctioned vengeance are examples of traditional outlets. The willingness to protect a belief at all costs has been one of the great sources of violence.

Fundamentalism's moral certainty also allows a double standard of morality between the private and public sectors. The public sector is allowed great latitude in order to "protect" the moral purity of the private sphere. Actually, the ideal of many fundamentalists is not to have a private sector, but to have a theocracy that rules every aspect of life. This double standard also offers an escape clause. Even though lying is considered wrong ("Thou shalt not bear false witness"), it's O.K. to lie if it serves some higher purpose. So parents can lie to their children and government officials to their citizens "for their own good."

The issue for fundamentalism is how to get people to obey absolute rules that cannot be obeyed absolutely. There is of course force and fear. But it is more reliable to have people who want to obey the rules. The easiest way to do this is to make people feel bad about themselves and then offer them a way of feeling better. Fundamentalism does this by creating a world-view of sin and redemption via a moral order whose basic tenets give these easy answers to life:

1. Why am I here? To get better through obeying the rules.

2. Why do I need to get better? Because a part of you is bad (original sin)—you're not good enough.

3. What happens if I break the rules? You get punished by a power that is inescapable. If you have sufficient remorse and resubmit, you may be forgiven.

4. What happens if I keep the rules? You get rewarded by that same power—usually after death.

The old moral order was not originally fundamentalist; it was simply the old order. Fundamentalism is wanting to return to whatever idea one has of its original purity. Its essence lies in the belief that an unassailable higher power laid out not only rules for proper human activity, but also put forth a cosmology, that is, a picture of existence, meaning, and purpose that is true for all times. Certainty within fundamentalism is dependent upon an unchanging core of belief.

The fundamentalist distaste for evolutionary theories is more than the fact that evolution makes the literal interpretation of the Bible difficult. It's doubtful that all anti-evolutionists literally believe the world was created in seven days. Evolution intro-duces the ideas of change and of a continuity within life which gives an entirely different shape to the position of humanity in the cosmos. Evolution not only introduces but is based on the idea of process. Once reality is a process, and humanity is not at the center of it, there is no telling for sure where it is all going to lead. Evolution undermines certainty, so fundamentalists deeply fear it.

Organized religions are the oldest, most static, and past-ori-ented of institutions, geared at keeping their authority intact. Thus they must consider themselves not a part of history, but beyond it. Christianity ends history with God's final judgment. Eastern religions undermine history more subtly by making it cyclical and repetitive, and also by making escape from the wheel of death and rebirth (history) the final reward. The end result in both the East and West is that the truths offered are unchanging truths, not subject to the questionings of different times.

An appeal of fundamentalism in a world out of control is that it offers the promise of control through previously effective authoritarian mechanisms. But if part of the reason the world is out of control is the inability of old ways to keep it in control, then attempting to go back is not only useless, it is highly dangerous. If there were no time pressure on solving the problems of human survival, the predictable rise of fundamentalism could be taken in stride. Until now, the historical tension between the old and the new eventually resolved itself with the old fading, as over generations it became increasingly irrelevant. What is different now is there is not the luxury of waiting.

The Quandaries of Revisionism

Historically all religions undergo revisions that create different sects, each developing in time a new orthodoxy. Revisions are deemed necessary because of dissatisfaction with the prevailing orthodoxy, either owing to its corruption or to the loss of its relevance and hold over people. Within all religions there is a tension between change and the status quo. When traditional forms lose relevance the impetus to change increases, taking two directions: backward in an attempt to recapture the old, and forward to further revisions. To the extent that revisions are variations on the same theme (Christianity or Buddhism, for instance), they must have some commonality and share at least some core beliefs— even with fundamentalists. The more flexible the core beliefs, the more they can be stretched and still keep the basic form. One reason some people are turning to Buddhism is that its core beliefs are more flexible than monotheism's.

The worldwide increase of both fundamentalism and revisionism is a reflection of the stagnation of current orthodoxy. However, unlike previous reforms, Western monotheism is being stretched to where it is no longer keeping the same form. Fundamentalists see this and blame the moral and ideological complacency of mainstream religion for setting a bad example. They wish to go back to their view of an earlier, purer orthodoxy. Fundamentalists are essentially authoritarian, whereas modern revisionists are attempting to infuse old authoritarian structures with non-authoritarian values. Revisionism displays a current existential quandary: can one sufficiently change, and yet still keep some footing that offers stability, familiarity, and comfort in these chaotic times?

Revising religion has two interrelated aspects. Revising the theology involves making it more tenable and palatable to modern minds; revising the institution involves making it more receptive to modern concerns and needs. Often people are not that interested in the intricacies of theological discourse, but rather want a safe haven to be with people, especially for their children. A prime example is what we call consumer-driven churches. Previously churches told people how to live; now people tell churches what they want. These kinds of churches that are rapidly increasing in number and membership have public relations firms, advertising campaigns, and take polls to see what people want and then accommodate them.

What do people want? The denomination often counts far less than what kind of services a church offers. These new churches offer adult education, child care, celebrations, self-improvement groups, organized athletics and gyms, clubs, lectures, singles groups, and marriage enrichment. Some have close to 20,000 members. A wag remarked that the size of the church is limited only by the size of its parking lot. They also offer volunteer programs to help others and a soft Sunday school program to imbue children with Christian virtues of love, cooperation, and compassion without sin or guilt. Sin, guilt, hell, and sermons that tell the congregation how to live or to sacrifice this life for the next are emphatically not wanted. Instead these churches offer an umbrella of loosely shared values that basically say good people try to improve themselves, take care of family and friends, and help others along the way if they can. These churches claim that this is the real message of Christ.

Sin, damnation, and punishment are out; loving and accepting yourself, increasing self-esteem, and taking responsibility are in. Many humanistic precepts have been incorporated into the new Christianity and Judaism, whose major difference seems to be more comfort with one symbol system than another. These days many people feel free to revise their beliefs eclectically to suit their needs and proclivities. For instance, many who call themselves Christians no longer see Christ as God, but rather as a great teacher. Many Catholics divorce, use birth control, and largely ignore the dictates of the pope, whom they consider old-fashioned. Polls found most Americans believed in some kind of afterlife; few believed in hell (*Newsweek,* March 27, 1989). Others who also still think of themselves as Christians or Jews believe in karma/rebirth.

A religion is a worldview and a moral system, with a theology that explains and justifies them. Most people whose religion is part of their identity and relation to community can hold onto their identity as, say, Christians, while being unconcerned about theology. But this cannot continue indefinitely; in order for a religion to survive and pass on from one generation to the next, it must have a theology that gives the worldview some credibility. Even though the Catholic Church discourages its members from theological inquiry (it kept the Mass in Latin until the mid-1960s), it has a whole order, the Jesuits, devoted to it. This is because the Church knows there must be an answer for every question—reassurance for every doubt.

Should one want to remain a Christian and believe in karma/rebirth, eventually one has to reconcile a separate monotheistic God with an impersonal universal force (karma). Did God create karma? It must have, since it creates everything; but having done so, is God then subject to karma or is karma subject to God? And can or does God interfere with or change karma within its creation? If God set up karma and thereafter leaves the world alone, why pay any attention to God? Or if God can interfere with karma, then karma is not the absolute principle it purports to be, so why pay much attention to it? These are some of the problems a theology that wanted to reconcile the two would face. It is possible to reconcile them, because the mind can reconcile any two things if it tries hard enough. However, with some issues reconciling them becomes sufficiently arcane and convoluted that both sides lose their form and force.

There are intrinsic problems in trying to revise an authoritarian worldview unless the revisions themselves become new authoritarian pronouncements, as with the Protestant Reformation. The revisions of a Calvin or Luther were considered God-inspired and not really revisions, but a return to God's intent. Here the Bible is still the ultimate authority, and the line between revisionism and fundamentalism blurs. When the basic tenets of a religious worldview undergo revision, the question is who is doing it, and under what authority?

The impetus behind revisionism is to include social change while preserving as much tradition as possible. In modern times, social change has been accelerated by science and democratic ideals. The worldwide push of women to participate equally in arenas of power is also shaking up the old order. It is through revisions incorporating new knowledge and values that religions evolve. Buddha, Christ, and Mohammed were social reformers whose revisions attempted to reform the corruption and inequities within the prevailing order. Buddha did away with the caste system; Christ brought love to a harsh war-God and did away with old ethnic taboos; Mohammed brought law and moral regularity that curbed abuse. Each of them was considered uniquely inspired and so their words became the basis of the new authority. When revisions go to the core of beliefs, what must emerge is a new religion, as it did with the above three.

When revisions tamper with the basic structure, what occurs is people trying to hold onto their identity without being certain of the foundation of that identity. When do revisions cease being revisions of a basic worldview and instead become a different worldview using the same name? People have said that

174

the essence of Christianity is love, and so if you are loving, you are a Christian. How does Christian love differ from Buddhist compassion or any love? Perhaps it doesn't, but then why call oneself a Christian? At one time, being a Christian involved believing in all or most (or at least some) of the following:

1. Belief in the Trinity of God, which includes a transcendent God who is the creator of it all.

2. That the Old and New Testaments were divinely inspired or revealed, and hence are the ultimate authority behind Christianity. (Catholic traditionalists include the historical body of church pronouncements.)

3. Humans are born with something wrong with them (sin) and thus need to be saved.

4. Christ was literally fathered by God through a virgin. The virgin birth was used to remove Christ and his mother from the contamination of sin (carnality).

5. As the son of God, Christ was uniquely and at least partially divine, and was God's primary messenger of truth.

6. God sent what he loved the most, his son, to earth to be hideously tortured to death to enable people to atone for their sins. He was brought back to life (resurrected) and then ascended to his father's side (heaven). Faith in Christ is the only doorway to salvation (meaning eternal life in heaven). Some sects also add good works and obedience to Christ's dictates.

7. Only the saved go to heaven; others go elsewhere (hell, limbo, purgatory).

There are people who think of themselves as Christians who question the veracity of some, most, or even all of the above, whereas fundamentalists still believe in most or all of these tenets. With few or no points of intersection of belief between them, what similarities are there to warrant using the word Christian for both groups, and why would they want to? Actually, most fundamentalists do not want to.

Arguments about which, if any, of these tenets are necessary for Christianity to remain Christianity, and also how far each can be bent, are in the realm of theology. It is within theology that modern revisionists have difficulties. Certainty (absolute faith) is a key part of what gives a religion its psychological strength. It is much easier to have faith in what one thinks is the word of God than in human revisions of it.

A televised debate between a fundamentalist preacher and a revisionist clergyman specifically addressed issues around Biblical interpretation. A key controversy discussed was whether the Bible is sexist. What struck us was not the nature or quality of their arguments, which were, of course, totally predictable, but rather the demeanor of each participant. The fundamentalist preacher had an unlined face, a happy smile, glib aphorisms such as "Don't try to change God's word; change yours instead," that came effortlessly. In contrast, the other clergyman had an earnest, heartfelt expression. Here was a man aware of deep ambiguities, but not easily able to reconcile them. He pointed to passages that were blatantly sexist, but had a hard time showing that God was not sexist. As a Christian, he could not throw out the baby with the bath water; that is, he could not ultimately deny the authority of the Bible. The problem is that when attempting to revise deep structures, throwing out the bath water is not enough.

The argument the fundamentalist minister used over and over again, which he considered unassailable, was that the Bible is the word of God and any tampering with it is merely the word of man. He then argued that once humans reinterpret God, what remains is human subjectivity, not God's objectivity. The revisionist brought up "facts" and contemporary moral issues to show the need for revisions. The facts involved accepted scientific knowledge, and the moral issues involved modern humanistic and democratic values such as treating women equally. To adapt Christianity to them, he had to call the Bible the metaphoric word of God. The problem is that metaphors can be made to stand for pretty much anything one wants. The fundamentalist radiated certainty, while his opponent had an apologetic and troubled mien.

Though revisions do undermine the certainty of pronouncements, they still bolster the basic worldview by being unable to challenge it directly. This handcuffed the revisionist, who was asked directly by the fundamentalist whether he believed the Bible was the word of God. He sputtered around uncomfortably about it being "divinely inspired," much to the glee of his opponent. But obviously not all of it could be divinely inspired, as he pointed out sections he felt were blatantly sexist and wrong. Yet he could not ask the really hard questions, which are: Can a text like the Bible, some of which is over 3,000 years old, be an appropriate foundation for current interaction? Is it worth revising, and what makes it so?

Catholicism developed mechanisms that allowed for revisions within certain limits, while maintaining certainty. The Church gave itself that power through councils that determined dogma, and by making the pope infallible (having a direct line from God) on matters of faith and morality. Now Catholicism has a serious schism between modernists and traditionalists. The former want the church to revise its position around such issues as marriage and celibacy for the clergy, birth control, abortion, and an overall democratization of the church itself. Traditionalists are not only hardening around old dogma, but are threatening those who disagree in public with excommunication.

We view the movement of the Catholic Church to a more fundamentalist stance as inevitable because the revisions demanded are sufficiently extreme that granting them would undermine the basic authority and credibility of the Church. If one day birth control is a mortal sin, and the next day it's O.K., this could not help but make people wonder how seriously to take the whole thing. Yet, birth control is a crying need worldwide. The Catholic Church's stance on the issue is another tragic illustration of ideological uncaringness, where maintaining power and order through an ideology becomes more important than the effects of the ideology.

Revisionism and the Need for Identity

Why anyone who no longer believes in the special divinity of Christ still wants to remain a Christian involves issues of identity, morality, and relation to community. A primary bond people have to any religion is its moral system. One's values are a large part of one's identity and also how one relates to community. If one is a Christian or Buddhist, then to be in a community that shares basic values is not only comfortable, but brings a basic trust, for one knows what to expect from others and how to negotiate. A moral system affects one's day-to-day life by creating a context in which to operate.

With fundamentalists their moral system is extremely important, but as a means to the end of personal salvation. It is the worldview that guarantees salvation, so they are not tolerant of anything that threatens the certainty of the worldview. This is why the essence of fundamentalism is the need for certainty. Modern revisionists are more interested in who they are in this world. They are willing to revise an old worldview and its morality to keep a sense of identity and ground for stability in what has come to be a very shaky world. When Christ becomes a symbol for universal love, and the Old Testament God becomes an immanent force in everything instead of a transcendent separate entity, what is being held onto is more than roots and ritual—it is a moral identity, a way of structuring one's personality. To say I'm a Christian really means I'm a good person who can be counted on to behave appropriately.

The strength of fundamentalism lies in an authoritarianism that grounds its morality in what it considers absolute truth. The big problem for revisionists is how to show their morality is not merely subjective, and thus arbitrary. This is dealt with in three major ways:

1. Revisionists, too, return to the past and attempt to show historically that they are reviving the original spirit of the teachings. They also try to show that the founders, a Christ or Buddha, cared more about people than their ideologies. The implication here is that much of what is considered fundamental by fundamentalists is really the result of unhealthy early revisions, which sullied the original spirit or truth of the founder.

2. In order to properly understand the founder's or religion's statements, revisionists assert they must be placed in a historical context and reinterpreted in the light of modern findings and perspectives. This includes considering the authority of sacred texts as being allegorical and metaphoric, not literal.

3. Revisionists keep the parts of a religion they can believe in and drop the parts they cannot. (An example is dropping Christ's divinity and viewing him as a great teacher.) This approach is often combined with taking appealing parts from other religions—an activity with much historical precedent that is called syncretism. It occurs when different worldviews come into contact and the absoluteness of each begins to erode, as is increasingly the case now. There are people incorporating into Christianity such diverse elements as the mother-goddess; karma; cosmic unity, which implies God's immanence; and notions of enlightenment, with Christ as an enlightened being.[5]

---

[5]See "On Channeling Disembodied Authorities" for a contemporary example of syncretism: The appeal of a new channeled religious framework, *A Course in Miracles,* is that it attempts to blend Christian love with Eastern Oneness, although it does not adequately reconcile them. Instead, to make itself credible, it relies on the assertion that its "truths" are channeled by an unchallengeable and impeccable authority, the spirit of Jesus Christ.

These approaches all dilute the authority of the original belief system, yet can work short term to keep wanted values intact. But over the long term, a religion must have a worldview strong enough to sustain itself. The problem for the revisionist is, what can establish the necessary credibility? That is, from where does the final word come that validates not only a given worldview, but the system of morality that flows from it? Can an authoritarian worldview be revised in some way that is not authoritarian? What could another way be: an appeal to reason, intuition, common sense, science, philosophy, or the sum total of human experience? These are all legitimate appeals, but can they support sacred pronouncements well enough to keep them sacred?

The question is, what is the bottom-line basis for one's worldview? The essence of all authoritarian religions is the demand for faith in the higher authority they espouse. To move the basis to one's own intelligence or anything else changes everything. Modern attempts to democratize essentially authoritarian worldviews must either fall short or alter them beyond recognition. Do Christians each get to vote on or personally choose which of the above tenets of basic Christianity are needed to qualify as Christian? Can one use archeological findings of the ancient prevalence of mother-goddesses to decree that God is female? Though this can be done, what is left is no longer the absolute word of God, but rather human preference.

It is likewise impossible to eradicate authoritarianism from the religious hierarchy itself. When the foundation of belief is based on the assumption that truth comes from a "higher" intelligence not available to ordinary folk, this necessarily sets up an authoritarian hierarchy. It is immaterial whether the higher intelligence comes from sacred texts or an enlightened master. Are Zen Buddhists to vote for whom their roshi should be? This would politicize the role, removing the sanctity and absoluteness that the authoritarian structure of lineage purports to give.

We are truly sympathetic to those who cannot accept authoritarian pronouncements. Our examination of the inherent problems within revisionism aims not to bolster the fundamentalist position, but rather to show the difficulties in trying to revise essentially authoritarian structures by making them less so. Reinterpreting the old can work as long as the world remains sufficiently similar that revising the essential tenets enables them to remain at least somewhat pertinent. The now-existent world religions were constructed when accumulation via agriculture, authoritarian hierarchy, and patriarchy moved the species into its historical and still current ways of leveraging power. The operative values became accumulating and expanding, using killing and war as the bottom line of power and ultimate method of problem-solving. The authoritarian religions and their moralities that evolved and worked in tandem with the old political orders justified doing whatever it took to maintain power.

What's at Stake?

The struggle between the old order and the budding, unformed new, which we call the morals wars, is really between old cosmologies that separate the spiritual from the worldly, and people reaching for a new worldview that supports infusing the spiritual into life. This rift between the old and the new underlies the controversies between fundamentalists and revisionists, who are both under the umbrella of the same religion. The revisionists are at a basic disadvantage, for they have to tolerate the fundamentalists' moral slurs, while fundamentalists have no need for such tolerance.

Within liberalism there is a tradition of tolerance, especially religious tolerance. While fundamentalists show little tolerance for anything that falls outside their beliefs, the liberal mind is usually compelled to tolerate the fundamentalists who make them immoral or even evil. We agree that people should be able to believe what they will without coercion. But respecting people's right to have differing beliefs does not mean one must respect the beliefs themselves. Unfortunately, the concept of religious tolerance has come to include not being critical of others' beliefs. Tolerance only works well if all the players play by the same rules.

When some try to force their beliefs on others, how tolerant should one be of this? The problem with tolerating viewpoints that are themselves intolerant is their aim is to do away with tolerance altogether.

The cultural taboo against criticizing religion exists partially because religion is looked upon, with good reason, as being beyond reason. In realms of faith, belief, or even intuition, what criteria can there be for criticism? The truth or falsity of a given worldview may not ultimately be provable. But what can be shown is whether it is authoritarian. Authoritarianism is present in much that is taken for granted, often including what is held by some to be sacred. The prescription that what people hold sacred should not be criticized is itself unconsciously authoritarian. The sacred and taboo go together—in particular the taboo against challenging the sacred. In our view, the sacred is formally made sacred precisely to protect it from criticism, because it cannot stand on its own. Tolerance needs to be redefined to encourage discourse that can question the validity and viability of any belief based upon its impact on the world. This is especially needed when the stakes are high. We believe the stakes could not be higher.

Historically, whenever a changing world brought a rift between the old and new, the old eventually faded simply because it could not adequately incorporate the new into its framework. This took time, upheavals, and bloodshed. Ultimately the old could not triumph, simply because it was old. In this particular epoch the game is different. Humanity is not only facing the need to change, it is facing an ecological time clock for its survival. Now the old can win simply by impeding whatever transformations are necessary long enough for the time clock to run out. And although this victory would be Pyrrhic, we suspect that those with an apocalyptical mentality would not care.

To the extent that fundamentalism impedes change, there is good reason to oppose it. To the extent that revisionists are bound by the same authoritarian worldview and moral order, they legitimize the fundamentalists' agenda of going back to moral purity. The focus of fundamentalism is the salvation of the individual after death. Modern revisionists want to broaden their religion to include caring about the present and future of life on this planet. They are constrained by having to refurbish an essentially authoritarian worldview constructed when the species was not at risk. In an overused, overpopulated planet, planetary values must somehow change from quantity to quality, from accumulation to preservation. Growing up as an individual involves facing one's mortality; growing up as a species involves realizing that humanity is mortal, too. Human survival is no longer a given, and it will only be prolonged if people are able to redirect what is destructive to the species and planetary systems. This requires a morality based not only on the mortality of the individual, but also on the mortality of the species. Whether or not one believes in personal immortality, having morality based on this belief instead of on what promotes viable life in this world is an indulgence that is no longer affordable.

Satanism and the Worship of the Forbidden
Why It Feels Good to Be Bad

What is a satanist, and why would anyone want to be one? This question warrants examination not only because devil worship and ritualized abuse have surfaced and become more overt, but also because respected segments of society are using the idea of Satan as an explanation for the world's ills. The Catholic Church has increased its number of exorcists, thus further legitimizing the concept. And a former key U.S. official who headed the "War on Drugs" publicly blamed the spread of crack-cocaine on the devil, rather than on the hopelessness of people's lives (*San Francisco Chronicle*, June 12, 1990). The focus of this chapter is not so much on satanism itself, but rather uses it as an extreme example of the allure and power of the forbidden. Guilt aside, most people have experienced enjoyment doing something they considered wrong, possibly even immoral. The really interesting and relevant question is why it sometimes feels good to be bad.

In worshipping Satan, what is one doing? One is either worshipping an entity, some force or power, or the symbolic representation of a principle. Satanism, then, is worshipping evil as a symbol, manifestation, spirit, archetype, or flat-out metaphysical power. Whichever it is, above all the word "Satan" refers to an abstract idea of pure intentional evil. Simply put, satanism is the worship of evil over good, or else it redefines what is ordinarily considered evil as the good.

185

One must remember Satan as a figure or force comes out of traditional Western religions. Satanism as a framework for activity involves a worldview that is the underbelly of Western religions and their separation of behavior into two distinct moral categories—good and evil. It is a construction of Western monotheism to separate God dualistically from everything else. This worldview splits existence into God and God's creation; from this basic dualism all others flow. Abstracting out the concepts of good and evil from life, then reifying and anthropomorphizing the two abstractions (God and Satan), is a foundation of Western fundamentalist religious cosmology. But an anthropomorphized force of evil is not limited to fundamentalism. The official theologies of Catholicism, as well as many Protestant, Islamic, and Jewish sects, still promulgate belief in a force of evil whose purpose is solely to lead people astray. Satanism is a foil for and counterpoint to the religions that created Satan.

The concept of Satan comes from a context containing an impeccable monotheistic God that is the source and power behind all good. A powerful fallen angel, who spitefully tries to subvert goodness at every turn, is used to explain why earth is less than a paradise. Any success and power gained by those in his clutches is explained by his purported dual role as both tempter and punisher—after death he makes people pay for the pleasures he seduces them into.

Historically, satanism has been associated with black magic, witchcraft, and demonology. The basic underlying assumption is that by associating with, or giving oneself to, the powers of evil, a person could to some extent control and manipulate that power. The rites and rituals for summoning the dark forces were often activities that were morally forbidden and involved breaking taboos around—guess what?—sex and violence. Old fertility rites and shamanistic or pagan healing practices that contradicted the power of organized religions have also been labeled satanic. But this chapter is not about the politics of religion—what religions do to maintain power. Rather our interest is where the allure of the forbidden comes from.

Leaving aside (for now) the issue of whether the evil that satanists worship is really evil, or whether the God others worship is really good, what kind of universe do such conceptualizations imply? To really understand satanism requires taking an excursion into the nature of good and evil.

Good and Evil

The words "good" and "evil" are abstract symbols, each purporting to designate a class of activities that includes not only the consequences of actions, but also the intention behind them. So that if I intend good but evil befalls, I might not be held blameless; but neither would I be called evil. To be evil then is to intend evil. But this is not as obvious or simple as it sounds. What does it mean to intend evil—exactly what is it that one is intending?

According to the Oxford dictionary, "evil" has the same etymological root as the words "up" and "over"; initially the primary meaning of evil was either "exceeding due measure" or "overstepping proper limits." It goes on to define the common usages of the word "evil" in two ways: as the "antithesis of good," or as "willing and doing harm." Defining evil as the opposite of good is easy when the good is an accepted given. So, if an acknowledged higher power lays out the good, then disobedience is evil. But the second definition of evil as willfully doing harm is not so simple, for it raises questions as to how much harm, and to what? Moreover, there is no agreement about what constitutes harm. Is punishment harmful or good? Should other species be included in these moral considerations—is eating them O.K.? Is it worse to eat some species than others, and if so, why? For that matter, is self-destructiveness or suicide a harming that is evil? How about harming the Earth itself? Is vengeance evil? What is proper—"An eye for an eye" or "Turn the other cheek"?

Good and evil as concepts intend to describe, or subsume under their banner of meaning, an endless array of actions and events. Speculations and assumptions about the early history of human experiences are difficult enough to maintain; conjectures about the history of a word and thus a concept are even more speculative. Yet the concepts of good and evil as distinct categories had either to be a part of humanity's earliest linguistic constructions or to have come about sometime later. In our view, the concept of evil began when the discovery of agriculture brought accumulation and early hierarchies of power that made human labor a commodity to use and abuse. Hierarchy brought a brutality toward insiders that did not occur within tribal bands. In early nature worship and polytheism the spirits and gods were neither wholly good nor bad, but capable of causing both good fortune and harm. The two interrelated concepts of good and evil evolved in tandem with the increase of religious abstraction that progressively separated concepts of the spiritual from nature. This split between the sacred and worldly eventually hardened to mutual exclusivity in the West with monotheism; it also hardened the categories of good and evil.[1]

Different cultures have different ideas about what is evil. Some even claim whole cultures can be evil and a tool of Satan, as certain Islamic fundamentalists say of the West. Arguments aside about what's really good and evil, it's safe to say that within a given culture, evil is a grouping of human activities that are morally forbidden. All cultures have taboos, but breaking them is not necessarily considered evil. Ancestral tradition, rather than religion, was most probably the original source of morality. Linking taboo with evil (and the concomitant notion of sin) is the result of religion becoming the foundation of morality.[2]

---

[1] See "The Power of Abstraction: The Sacred Word and the Evolution of Morality" on the evolution of this split and how it gave religion control of morality.

[2] "Religion, Cults, and the Spiritual Vacuum" contains a concise statement on the link between religion and morality; "The Power of Abstraction" traces the four major stages of religious abstraction and their link with morality. "The Roots of Authoritarianism" (a section in *Control*) also describes the gradual ethicizing of religion whereby it became the foundation of morality.

Having good and evil as separate categories made it easier to control people within hierarchies. The external controls of tribalism (group approval or censure, shame, and ostracism) became insufficient for controlling larger groups in which people did not know each other. A dualistic morality where the abstract concepts of good and evil are internalized, coupled with an omniscient God who spies on every act, shifts control to internal mechanisms such as fear and guilt. In the East the relentless and unforgiving law of karma functions in the same way as an omniscient God, rewarding or punishing one's every action. Complex societies need some kind of internal control mechanisms, and religions became their source.

Ever since society became stratified, religion has evolved in the direction of increasing control over people by promulgating renunciation and self-sacrifice. Good and evil as mutually exclusive categories make it easier to have a renunciate religion—when evil is spelled out, there is something clear-cut to renounce. What is less clear is that any renunciate morality must also be dualistic, and must involve some kind of sacrifice; otherwise what's the big deal, why call it renouncing? Renouncing implies two things by definition—one must renounce (give up, sacrifice) one thing for something else that is presumed to have more worth. A renunciate morality is also necessarily authoritarian, since an unchallengeable authority is needed to spell out what is good and bad. Within renunciate religions the sacred and sacrifice are always key concepts. When anything is made sacred (higher), one can always justify sacrificing what is not sacred (lower) to it. The social hierarchies that sacrifice those lower to those higher utilize moralities that justify this through separating the sacred and profane.[3]

What one should sacrifice, and to what, varies in different

---

[3]"Religion" (Part One) and "Dualism and Renunciation" in "Oneness, Enlightenment, and the Mystical Experience" broadly describe the nature of renunciate religion and morality. "The Power of Abstraction" shows the historical links between religion, morality, sacrifice, and social power.

systems, but underneath all of them is a simple structure. Sacrifice involves sacrificing self-interest (which includes pleasure, self-enhancement, and carnal desires) for a perceived higher, more important interest. What's more important could be the revealed dictates of an omniscient God; ideals of spiritual realization that negate the self; loyalty to ruler, country, clan, or family; or even an ethical utilitarian model such as John Stuart Mill's "the greatest good for the greatest number." The issue is really not whether the perceived higher interest is in fact higher, or whether sacrifice in any particular instance is or is not appropriate. The aim here is simply to show how renunciate moralities come to define the good as renouncing self-interest; and furthermore, that the abstract categories of good and evil become internalized in the human psyche as the selfless and the selfish.

Evil is on the far end of the spectrum of self-centeredness, while saintliness is on the far end of being selfless. It is not that all self-centeredness is considered evil, only the extremes. (Catholics do distinguish between mortal and venal sins, as do parents between being really bad and merely naughty.) Evil is usually too extreme a concept to be a useful standard in daily life. Nevertheless, most of us as children have been conditioned to the idea that being bad means disobeying the rules and being selfish, while being good means obeying the rules and putting others first. Even those who eventually either question or change the rules usually keep the basic distinction between the selfless and self-centered. When people judge others to be morally lacking, it almost always involves some perceived aspect of self-centeredness in the other; likewise, when people judge themselves as not being morally good enough, it is because they do not meet their own standards for selfless behavior.

The Problem of Evil

To be credible, all religions have somehow to explain the existence of pain, cruelty, violence, unfairness, and suffering. The concept of an evil force initially offers an easy answer. But once evil is used as an explanation, it contains its own problems that force religious apologists to become both convoluted and arcane. The problem of evil simply put is this: does evil (however defined) exist in the universe, and if so, why is it here and where did it originate? Evil is the bane of all religions, particularly those that want the deity to be both the first cause (the originator of it all) and yet untainted by anything negative. This is especially true of Western transcendent religions.

In any monotheism that sees God as not only the creator of everything, but as all good, wise, and powerful, the problem is this: Is evil an independent power or is it in some fashion a part of God's master plan? If it is part of God's plan, and God is pure goodness, how could evil be pure evil? Or, if evil is independent of God's goodness, where did it come from? Did God create a kind of Frankenstein monster that got out of hand? But this takes away from the power of God. An all-powerful God had to create everything, including evil, by definition. And so to keep God purely good, certain sects (decreed to be heresies) tried limiting God's power. But this, too, puts monotheism in question, for how could a God with limited power have created everything? Gnosticism and Manicheism, like their predecessors Zoroastrianism and Mithraism, saw good and evil on equal footing, with the struggle between the two the cosmic battle at the core of existence. Both good and evil are given autonomous power, and both exist within humanity. Within Christianity, this conceptualization was labeled a heresy and just would not do, since it essentially did away with monotheism. If two cosmic forces are equal, there cannot be just one God.

The difficulty in reconciling God's perfect goodness and omnipotence with evil is that either God wants to eradicate evil but cannot, so is not omnipotent, or God is able to but does not want to. For the latter to be true and God still to be all-good, God must have a good reason for creating and allowing evil. The search for God's motive led to the stock answer to the problem of evil: God created it in order to give humans free will, wherein people could morally choose good over evil. Human existence is thus viewed as a morality play to test and then reward or punish the players. Why God would want to do this also poses the interesting question of whether Satan "fell" of his own free will or was pushed because God wanted and needed a devil?

The "morality play" solution cannot stand up under close examination. Eternity is a long time. To be damned eternally for succumbing to the powerful temptations that God (through his vehicle Satan) put forth as a test again paints a picture of a harsh, vengeful God who gives the ultimate punishment for disobedience. What caring parent would so test and punish a child? Also, to postulate that God created evil (or to be kinder, allowed it) in order to give humanity the freedom to choose does not explain why God made it much easier for some to choose good than others. Why some are given an easier context (loving parents) to choose good in than others (severely emotionally deprived children) is never adequately addressed. This is an especially poignant issue in Christianity because you only have one chance to do it right.

Calvinists pushed the argument further in asking if God knew beforehand the choices one would make. For them, to say no would put a limit on the power and knowledge of God. So, if God knew beforehand what choice one would make, it had to have been predetermined. The problem here was why so many people were predetermined to be bad. The Calvinist solution was to emphasize that mankind is essentially evil (original sin) and could only be saved by the grace of God. What was not properly addressed is why some received grace and some did not; and why God would construct a whole species that was born initially evil, and concern himself with whom to save and whom not to. Being omniscient, there could not even be any mystery in watching the morality play unfold, for God must have known from the get-go who were the few elect he was going to save, and that he was creating a large majority to be damned eternally. This seems like an odd pastime for a God who is all good. From a human standpoint, this does not seem like a very nice thing to do.

One is left, as usual, with the why of God's motives being beyond the ken of humanity. Looking at the workings of God's creation was enough to produce a common stance within atheism, which is: If there were a God who controls the world, it would be the duty of every moral human to despise it—given the success that violence, callousness, and greed bring.

Monotheistic dualism that separates God from everything else presents an almost whimsical picture of a God who is a supreme egoist creating the universe for the express purpose of being worshipped—rewarding those who do it properly (according to his rules) and punishing those who don't. That this is reminiscent of all authoritarian power is no accident, for authoritarian secular power uses an authoritarian religion with its sacred symbolisms and its morality based on duty and sacrifice to justify itself. The question of whether God created the authoritarian form (as fundamentalists believe), or whether the form projected a God to justify itself, is not trivial.

When God is presented as the paragon of goodness, something must be made the paragon of evil, but the idea of there being an evil incarnate brings its own questions: What is Satan's motive for being evil? Is he a mere tool for God's plan or is he evil by choice? Is evil Satan's essential nature or is it a spiteful reaction for being thrown out of heaven? Is Satan being punished for being Satan or is he having a good time, enjoying himself as he messes things up? One can understand why he tempts people, but when successful why does he punish them? Actually, if what the game were really about is a battle for souls, Satan would do far better without the bad press of hell. If in punishing sinners he is doing what God wants, he is not being God's adversary, just his dupe. One argument is that Satan feels so bad about his relation to God that his only pleasures come from making others feel bad, too. So he tempts with forbidden (by God) pleasures, and then "gets off" by torturing those he seduced—he is thus the ultimate sadist. But then one gets back to how an all-good God could create a being of pure evil with no redeeming qualities. Satan is monotheism's attempt to get an all-powerful God off the moral hook. But what cannot be escaped is either Satan is doing God's will or he isn't.

Catholicism's power is linked to forgiving sin and protecting people from evil. To do this, sin must be real, as must be some externalized form of evil. The Catholic Church, in designating official exorcists, acknowledges Satan as a force to be reckoned with; at the same time, it designates itself as the protecting power. Satan functions as monotheism's garbage can into which all the bad things that happen can be thrown. Using Satan as an explanation for the ills of the world stops further probing.

Interestingly, Satan is also blamed for any questioning of faith. Lucifer was so named because he was the "bringer of light," that is, reason. Lucifer is portrayed as the silver-tongued devil who uses reason to seduce people by convincing them either that evil doesn't exist or it's a good thing to do. Every sophisticated closed system of thought constructs ways of disarming challenge. This particular ploy is airtight, stating any argument powerful enough to question faith is by definition a construction of Satan. What is really involved is a circular defense. An authoritarian system of belief is put forth, and then an authoritarian premise from within the system is used to make the system itself impregnable. The premise is that there is a devil who is smarter than human reason, thus human reason cannot be trusted to question the system of belief. Should one buy into this, what results is fearing one's own intelligence.[4]

Eastern beliefs that assert the unity of all being (Oneness), where spirit or God is immanent, frame the nature of evil differently, in a more sophisticated way that avoids many of the

---

[4]See "Guru Ploys" and "The Assault on Reason" on how authoritarian closed systems disarm critical thought.

above problems. Hinduism places evil in the category of *maya* or illusion, the illusion of separateness; Buddhism sees evil as ignorance. It defines ignorance as thinking that one is, or has, a self that continually needs protecting and enhancing. Close analysis shows that the concepts of illusion and ignorance are not essentially different. Both concepts attribute evil to the illusion of being a separate self.

Eastern dualism takes on a subtler form than monotheism, in which the split between good and evil is softened, but not eradicated. Instead of dividing the cosmos into two entities, God and God's creation, the East creates two levels in order to support its own dualistic renunciate morality. This covert dualism consists in constructing a spiritual realm supposedly beyond duality and beyond good and evil, and a realm of illusion or ignorance where good and evil play themselves out. However, spirituality and goodness become identified with the higher level (unity), and evil operates out of the lower level that denies or is unaware of this unity. This is where most Eastern conceptions break down because they do not make unity truly beyond good and evil, but rather make it the source of only goodness. As with monotheism, the world becomes a morality play constructed so that people can learn to be better. But to what purpose? And that is the rub. The big question is why is there illusion and ignorance in the first place?[5]

The basic question for any cosmology remains: why has the whole thing been constructed in this fashion? Christians say it is because we are born in sin. Buddhists say it is because we are born to suffering through ignorance. Hindus say it's because we are born at all (individuated and separate). Throughout all of this, the implication is that people deserve what they get. Whatever else they serve, this is a major function of the concepts of both original sin and karma. To trivialize evil by declaring it illusory and making ultimate reality something beyond it is

---

[5]"Oneness" shows in more detail the ways the Oneness ideology hides its dualism.

soothing only if not properly examined. Human beings still kill, maim, exploit, and abuse each other with exquisite ingenuity and casual justifications.

Satanism as an Avenue to Power

Monotheism views God and nature as essentially different; thus its basic dualism is more conscious and extreme than in the East. This leads to hard dualistic categories such as heaven and hell, God and the devil, salvation and damnation, and of course, good and evil. Satanism is a particularly Western phenomenon precisely because monotheism constructs the most extreme separation between good and evil, which translates into a rigid division of the sanctioned and forbidden. We consider the essence of satanism to be the worship of the forbidden, through worshipping a personified force that sanctions the forbidden. Satanism is a reaction against the moral imperatives of a monotheistic God that define absolute good, and against the demands to repress both sexuality and carnality. When spirit is abstracted from nature and the body, what is denied or denigrated is the fact that a human being is, among other things, an animal. This is ironic, since animals other than humans do not create abominations. Making the body lowly justifies dominating and repressing it, just as making nature lowly justifies exploiting it. Worshipping evil can only take place in a culture that makes "the good" obtainable solely through renouncing a deep part of what it is to be human. Thus temptation is the mirror image of renunciation— the more one renounces an aspect of being human (sexuality for example), the more temptation there is.

Worship involves awe. Significantly, what brings awe is a sense of being in touch with a greater or unknown power. So it is possible to worship nature, beauty, a guru, a ruler, as well as a deity. In worshipping Satan or God, the dynamics are similar. Since worship alone generates the feelings, whether the power actually exists or not does not make much difference. Those worshipping Greek, Aztec, or any gods all received basically the same experience. The object, force, person or abstraction, whatever it is that is being worshipped, is necessarily perceived as having power—the power to, in some fashion, affect one's life. One reason the object of worship is so perceived is that whenever the person either physically or mentally contacts it, emotions change. This is often accompanied by a state of surrender that has its own emotional field.[6]

Worship is not simply a one-directional activity where there is output from the worshiper, and that's it. What loops back are feelings of participating in, and identifying with, a higher power, which translates into feeling more powerful oneself. If worshipping had no effect on how the worshiper felt, worship would not be long-lived. It is in large part the change in emotion that verifies and reinforces the belief that the object or idea being worshipped both exists and deserves it.

Historically monotheism supplanted polytheism because its God was more powerful. It raised God to a higher level of abstraction, giving it more general and thus inclusive powers (omnipotence and omniscience). Religions promote the power of God but downplay the relationship of worship to power by emphasizing God's goodness, justice, or mercy. Yet much of prayer is geared at trying to get God's power on one's side—or giving thanks that it is. In stark contrast, satanists blatantly worship Satan to increase power.[7]

In worshipping God, one is giving allegiance to the image one has of God. One tries to live by the rules believed to be God's dictates for humanity, and of course, one hopes to reap the benefits of doing so. There are many worldly benefits of aligning with an accepted higher power that has specific rules for living flowing from it. Two key ones that are not unrelated are cer-

---

[6]"The Seductions of Surrender" describes how surrender to any authority likewise has its own powerful dynamics, no matter who or what is surrendered to.

[7]"The Power of Abstraction" shows the relationship between power and religious abstraction.

tainty and power. Certainty about what's right and true can be used to direct or manipulate those less certain, and to justify coercion, as well as to eliminate internal conflict.[8]

Worshiping Satan is similar to worshipping God in that one is also aligning with a perceived higher power, except the power represents what is considered evil instead of good. The abstract concept of evil is easily anthropomorphized into a satanic figure because intention is necessary for evil to be evil. Intention implies both will and some form of consciousness. What kind of consciousness does Satan represent? The usual image Satan brings to mind is of an entity or force whose existence involves leading people astray, and gleefully tormenting them when succeeding. Does Satan enjoy being evil, is he having fun; or is he being punished and thus suffering from being evil? This is not to make light of a deep issue, because underneath these conundrums is an ultimately important question: does being bad feel good?

When good and evil are conceptualized in an either/or way creating a dualistic framework for morality, being bad does, or can, feel very good indeed. This is the lynchpin around which satanism revolves. Interestingly, one finds in such colloquial expressions as "you lucky devil," "handsome devil," "devilish grin," and in the outlaw hero, a cultural ambivalence toward not only the devil archetype, but toward being bad or naughty. Being bad has sly appeal and is often viewed with indulgence. This is because what is considered bad, thus forbidden, includes carnal and self-centered aspects of being human. As at least some of what is forbidden is life-enhancing and unhealthy to repress, releasing these stifled aspects of oneself allows people to feel more alive. In satanism, worshipping the forbidden allows these feelings such extreme expression and release that they become associated with power.

It is our contention that what satanism actually involves is a bleak attempt to generate personal power—actually power over those ensnared (often children). People become satanists because

---

[8]See "Religion" and in "Fundamentalism and the Need for Certainty."

they find it more attractive than whatever beliefs or allegiances they previously held. Here is a picture, a scenario, of how this could work—in order to show the appeal of satanism, we will briefly play "devil's advocate."

Take a child brought up to believe the lusts of the body are dirty and wrong; that an omniscient God spies on and judges its every little sneaky mean thought and action; that it is born in sin (original sin) and can only be saved by accepting the dictates of this God's rules. The child, for whatever reasons, cannot sufficiently repress what is labeled bad, and is thus labeled bad. These children are easily made to feel something is deeply wrong with them. In fact, children in general are made to feel bad about themselves for breaking rules they had no say in establishing. It can seem to children that what's fun is forbidden. Often these rules deny them both the legitimacy of their animal feelings and the resentments that come from such a basic denial. In their failed struggle to be good, many children act out in ways that make it difficult to get social rewards.

When people believe they are fundamentally bad, they are vulnerable to satanic beliefs. There are satanists who put forth this kind of message: "You've been sold a bill of goods meant to keep you down. If God rules the world and makes the rules, why is it that those who get ahead are those who break the rules? You were told that if you break the rules you will go to hell. Look around—most people's lives are already hell, including yours. The secret is that it is Satan who really rules the world. So if you want to have power, do well, and succeed, all you have to do is go right to the source—don't fool around—worship evil itself and you'll have the edge."

As proof, all the visible moral contradictions and hypocrisies can be pointed out: how the church extols poverty but lives in splendor; how it's really the "bad guys" who have much of the power in the world through lies, corruption, violence, and generating fear. Satanists can say these have always been the real force underneath business, government, orthodox religion, and organized crime—the four pillars of earthly power. They can further say it is might that makes right in this world; and that contrary to the lies one is fed, it is evil that triumphs in the end. (To paraphrase a line by Bob Dylan—Steal a little and they put you in jail, steal a lot and they make you king.) So where good and evil are polarized, satanists can make a strong empirical case that evil is the real power in the world. Satan, after all, has been traditionally called "the prince of the world."

It must be remembered that satanism as a cult, a belief system, a religion, cannot itself be ultimately divorced from the religious framework that abstractly separated good and evil, and then gave evil a personalized name—Satan. Satanism is worshipping the dark side of this split—"the prince of darkness." This can be seen in satanic rituals, the more conservative of which are structured excursions into what orthodox religion deems blasphemous. The "black mass" is geared at breaking taboos. It reactively reverses and inverts the rituals of the accepted mass. Even in the more extreme cults, the ritualized use of blood sacrifice, torture, nudity, sexual rites, orgies, excrement, and the like are all examples of the worship of the forbidden. The specifics of such grotesqueries and cruelties are not the issue here; rather we are interested in people's attraction to them for that is the real problem.

Belief in satanism spawns cults that display many of the dynamics covered in Part One of this book. Surrendering to the will of Satan as defined by a leader is not too different from surrendering to a guru or to the will of God as defined by a given spiritual authority. The psychological effects of surrender are pretty much the same in each case. There is, however, a real difference between satanic cults and others. Other groups that accept the polarized split between good and evil ostensibly try to eliminate or minimize the negative pole. Many do this by promoting sacrifice of worldly interests and desires.

In contrast, the motives underlying satanism are directly related to power—power in this world. In aligning with evil (the dark side of the pole), what people are doing is aligning with their perception of where real power lies. Satanism tells people that much of what's considered bad is really good to do. The taboos and constraints around "badness" are lifted all of a sudden. Release from that suppression can contain tremendous energy. Satanic practices are geared at creating great emotional release, even frenzy, through breaking taboos. All this is on top of the normal cultic group energy tapped into through ritual, shared belief, and surrender. This energy feels like power—which seems to be a confirmation of the truth of worshipping Satan.

It is the release that comes from acting out the forbidden that is the key to satanism. This is true not only in the more extreme abusive cults, but also in the more sanitized middle-class versions. What is it that is forbidden? It is interesting how many of the rites involve excesses of carnality—of bodily functions. Then too, there is the affirmation of personal greed and the lust for power. Satanism elevates "sin" as the doorway to power. For those whose psyches have been crippled by internalizing harsh conceptions of sin, the reactive pendulum swing from suppressing the forbidden to worshipping it does indeed feel like great power.

The Divided Self: Good and Evil Internalized

The cosmic battleground between good and evil (God and Satan) not only dualistically divides reality, but creates a division within the psyche. Thus the battle continues on an individual basis between the aspect of oneself that is labeled good (the giving, loving, cooperative, compassionate, altruistic elements) and the aspect labeled bad (the different expressions of self-centeredness). Becoming a satanist is one way of ending the battle—an easier way than becoming a saint.[9]

"The devil made me do it." Behind this statement lies a worldview in which an evil spirit (or spirits) can come in and take con-

---

[9]See "Who Is in Control? The Authoritarian Roots of Addiction" for an analysis of the internal split, addiction being another expression of the resulting inner battle.

trol over, or possess, a person. The idea of "possession" involves being under the control of an external, malevolent force that bends you to its will. For those who think they are possessed, it does indeed feel like some alien force has taken over, making them do forbidden things. But possession is just another extreme example of having a rigidly compartmentalized psyche, a divided self.

The statements "The devil made me do it" and "My addiction made me do it" have a similar ring; the latter, in our view, is a secular version of possession. It is not that people consciously adopt such beliefs in order to get away with things. Possession and addiction are structurally similar in that they both allow the suppressed and forbidden aspects of oneself to come out in a way that can be more easily forgiven, both by oneself and others. By externalizing and dis-identifying from the taboo activity (making it "not me"), a doorway opens that permits one to act out the forbidden without interfering with one's self-image of being essentially a "good" person. This occurs when the split is so deep and unconscious that the part of the person doing the "nasties" does feel truly alien. Blame and responsibility are thus externalized and projected onto something else. Then too, there is the tragic explosion where a mild-mannered "nice" person goes berserk, usually killing others and then himself. For us going berserk is another sign of a rigidly compartmentalized and repressed psyche seeking release.

The release that comes from being "bad," breaking the rules, or acting out taboos is not limited to satanism. Satanism is but an extreme example of how a divided human being tries to deal with internal conflict by giving ascendancy to what is defined as bad. This is particularly appealing if being good has not paid off. In our observation, many people live with varying degrees of this split within themselves. Here life becomes a battleground for control between the "good" or so-called higher self, and the "bad" or lower self. The inner war between highly conditioned "good" and "bad" compartments may seem an overly simplistic model, but it is no more simplistic than its source—a universe divided into good and evil, God and the devil.

202

Perhaps the most bizarre example of compartmentalization is the psychopathology referred to as multiple personality disorder, in which one body seems to be carrying around a number of distinct personalities. Some of them are sometimes cognizant of the existence of some of the others. The drama within this person becomes "Who is in control?" Interestingly, one "personality" rarely holds another in high esteem. The one constant in all cases of multiple personality seems to be that the person was severely abused and traumatized as a young child. The severity of abuse was so extreme that the adult or adults involved would be classified as deranged. Children so treated by significant adults cannot help but feel that there is something fundamentally wrong with them, and that they somehow deserve what they are getting. The adults are probably putting out this message as part of the abuse—"I'll beat the devil out of you."

The resulting fragmentation of personality into distinct and separate voices with no overall integration can act as a self-protective survival strategy. It's the way people with multiple personalities learned to safely express different parts of themselves without having to be responsible for any of them. In order to have such extreme fragmentation, the messages given about how to be (that is, how to be "good") had to be not only contradictory, but impossible to achieve. There was nothing these people could do to satisfy their abusers. We look at multiple personalities as yet another way of giving up on trying to be "good"—in this case by letting go of the integrating aspect of the mind that remembers, identifies with, and evaluates what the organism does. Although compartmentalization to this degree is relatively rare, the phenomenon itself is not. It is most likely to occur whenever people internalize values they cannot live up to. Folk wisdom has intuited this, as shown by the adage "Don't tell the right hand what the left hand is doing."

The Dark Side of Monotheism

Satanism and possession by evil spirits are but extreme examples of the underbelly of monotheism's renunciate moral system—a system that asks people not only to sacrifice this life for the next, but puts the highest value on the purity of selfless behavior. The self-centeredness and the carnality that are part of being an animal, if not made out-and-out evil, are made into something to repress and transcend. It is this artificial polarization between spiritual selflessness and carnal self-centeredness that is at the bottom of inner fragmentation.

The great fear, of course, is that if the forbidden were not suppressed, the base nature of humanity (whether original sin, callous social Darwinism, or greedy me-firsters) would reign. It is true that if children are not brought up with love, and if people are not treated well, they are very likely to take it out on those around them unless constrained by fear or coercion. The old authoritarian moralities kept people in line by building self-mistrust. This was done by creating an inner battle between good and evil wherein one could only become good by surrendering to the authority who told you what good is. That this is not working ought to be evident. Try telling a boy in the ghetto whose options are becoming a crack dealer or a shoeshine boy that he better make the right choice or he will go to hell. He may feel like he is already in hell.

The battle between an irreproachable God and an evil Satan creates a symbol system that polarizes thoughts and behavior into moral compartments that people can only fit into by denying essential parts of themselves. The ensuing struggle, as the denied or suppressed aspects seek some kind of expression, necessarily breeds self-mistrust and self-condemnation. From self-mistrust people look to an authority to find out how to be. This makes controlling them easy. Surrendering to an authority is yet another way of attempting to end the inner battle. The sad outcome of all this is that people remain children looking outward for verification—being willing to follow the latest fad, fashion, savior, or charismatic leader in the hope of feeling whole. Satanism is an extreme manifestation of this more general distortion brought about by dividing the self.

The basic crisis on the planet today is moral, involving how people treat each other and the planet. The old symbol systems that polarize good and evil, the sacred and the secular, spirit and nature, the selfless and self-centered, created a division within human beings that led to rigid mental compartments. A truly whole person is one who can integrate the diversities within being human without denying any of them. Just as "good" people attempt to deny the cravings of the animal within them, satanists must deny their empathetic caring aspects.

Mental compartments easily justify hierarchical social compartments—caste and class, haves and have-nots, good guys and bad guys. Communism as a symbol system tried to eliminate only social compartments, but failed. The failure was partially because self-sacrifice was still made the highest good, with the difference being only in what one was sacrificing to. In communism one sacrifices to the abstract idea of the supposed collective good, the state. It at first seemed revolutionary, but it was still stuck in the old morality that made self-sacrifice the highest virtue. Regimes used this ideal to justify their blatant, heartless, and corrupt exercise of power. As a secular ideology, communism did not have the luxury of promising people otherworldly rewards. Thus it was a renunciate experiment whose results could actually be seen. Its failure and the misery it wrought should not be minimized or forgotten, especially because religious renunciate worldviews cannot be so tested given that there is no good test for the afterlife. Religions too historically engendered their own on-going miseries and extreme reactions—satanism being but one.[10]

---

[10]"Communism" in *Control*, analyzes its attempt to build a new social system through politicizing and coercively using the old renunciate morality of self-sacrifice.

The ethical symbol systems of recorded history reflect the essential power structure of recorded history: authoritarian hierarchy. Unchallengeable authorities at the top of the hierarchy make this work by delineating who is to sacrifice what to whom. A different kind of symbol system for morality is necessary that can view the altruistic and the egotistical as not only each being needed to define the other, but each only having meaning in the context of the other. Caring for others is a natural human expression that cannot be ultimately fragmented off from caring for oneself. A morality that does not polarize the two would allow people to be more in touch with and express what is appropriate, without being distorted by a compartmentalized psyche. The perspectives offered in this book do not make sacrifice a virtue in and of itself, and do not categorically divide the self-centered from the selfless. It is because of this division that so often corruption lies behind the face of righteousness, and behind the face of God lurks Satan.

Who Is in Control?

The Authoritarian Roots
of Addiction

The fears surrounding addiction, whether for oneself or others, involve being self-destructively out of control. Fearing addiction in oneself is really fearing oneself. This chapter explains self-destructiveness not as something inherent in the nature of the animal, but rather as a manifestation of a moral order that imposes unlivable values. As it presents a different, somewhat radical framework, this is done as carefully as we know how by first building a foundation for our point of view. Since the struggle for control within addiction is presented here as a product of a divided, conflict-driven self, the origin and nature of this inner division are shown before discussing the dynamics of addiction. We believe that shedding some light on the phenomenon of feeling out of control can significantly impact the way some people conceive of and thus react toward addiction. We hope those willing to take this excursion will glean another point of view about self-destructiveness that offers the possibility of becoming a whole human being who is not internally at war.

What Is Addiction?

Authoritarian systems and structures, wherever they occur, are essentially about maintaining control over people. Not coincidentally, control is also a major issue in addiction. Here, however, the inner experience involves trying to impose control while feeling out of control. From our point of view, a direct link exists between authoritarianism and the so-called addictive personality, particularly around issues of control. Moreover, the current epidemic of addiction points to a society that itself is out of control. We view addiction as symptomatic of the unraveling of age-old authoritarian controls that used to work and no longer do.

Our focus will be three-fold: to make clear the link between authoritarianism and addiction; to present a framework for analyzing the dynamics of addiction that differs from both the prevailing disease model, and what we call "responsibility" models, which currently challenge the disease model; and to present possibilities for ending the inner battle for control.

Showing the connection between authoritarianism and addiction reveals how the authoritarian personality displays itself not only in extreme forms of political or religious fanaticism, but also in banal day-to-day life. In fact, it is a hidden cause of many forms of dysfunctional behavior. Addiction offers a graphic illustration of covert internal mechanisms that reveals how hidden authoritarianism operates in daily life. We demonstrate how authoritarianism is not merely externally imposed, but that there is an inner authoritarian working to maintain control. This interior phenomenon is far more prevalent in people than one would suspect. This chapter aims at providing a framework whereby people can determine for themselves whether they have an inner authoritarian.

Addiction has become such an ubiquitous concern that its meaning has expanded to include all kinds of habits and behaviors that do not necessarily have physiological withdrawal symptoms. Until the disease model came into vogue, the medical definition of addiction was linked only to drugs that caused withdrawal. In the current way the word addiction is used, it can refer to any compulsive, excessive, problematic, or self-destructive habit. Supposedly one can be addicted to love, food, sex, shopping, gambling, power, exercise, work, crime, and even to needing to nurture addicted or dependent people (what is referred to as co-dependency). In short, from this perspective, one can be "addicted" to any aspect of life that brings gratification, be it pornography or romance novels, football or gossip. Countless support groups have sprung up to help people deal with countless so-called addictions.

Since the word addiction is now used so loosely, one could stretch the term still more and consider structures, institutions, and society itself as being addicted to ways of doing things, fixes that are self-destructive over the long term. Business is addicted to a cost-effectiveness that does not factor in pollution, maintenance, and cleanup. The way energy is used exemplifies a focus on immediate "turn-ons" without concern for the ultimate destructiveness of doing so. These are but two symptoms of what could be called an addictive society. One could extend the metaphor further and say that accumulation societies in general are addicted to expansion, which is no longer appropriate as we are now facing a world of limit. This includes the limit of the ozone layer to protect life on this planet.

We view addiction not only as a personal disorder, but as a social disorder as well. Our interest is not to overburden the concept of addiction still further, but rather to make clear why we do not consider addiction merely a personal problem. People reflect the society of which they are a part. Many are left out of the rewards of "the good life." Many others have to sacrifice basic human psychological needs, such as time for friendship, intimacy, children, and leisure, in order to succeed. Given our stressful social context, it ought not be surprising that addictive or self-destructive behavior is rife. In a world engaged in dangerously dysfunctional behavior around such basic and not subtle issues as ecology, overpopulation, allocation of resources, etc., it is no wonder that individuals also allocate their personal resources in self-destructive ways.

Addiction is understandable when people find the life they are leading without the addiction unrewarding, dismal, or hopeless. Addictions offer at least a momentary way out. The life of an addict provides something concrete to be involved in which fixes the person up short term. The "fix," whatever it is—be it a substance, activity, or mode of relating—is both obtainable and delivers a consistent, known result.[1] In a chaotic world, this supplies a strange kind of stability, comfort, and even security. Being addicted seems like the opposite of self-control; yet both at their root involve wanting to control feelings.

Certain drugs bring instant change, instant intensity, an instant shift to another place, another way of being. The power to make this change is literally in one's own hands. Such drugs offer the siren song of enormous control with quick reinforcement at one level, and being out of control (addicted) at another. The "junk" also becomes the focal point for meaning—either trying to get it or get off it. In the shadowy world of the drug addict, it is the hub around which all personal connections spin. And in fact it really does connect people. They depend on each other for supplies of the drug and safety against the law, and they share a sly knowingness about the weakness of the flesh. Just like a shared ideology brings meaning and bonding, so too does a shared addiction. In most instances people get into highly addictive drugs in the first place because their lives previously had little meaning. Giving up the drug with all its self-destructive aspects threatens a return to that dimly remembered place of drab isolation and meaninglessness that the drug replaced.

Tying the meaning of addiction to the occurrence of physiological withdrawal symptoms when the substance is eliminated has concreteness and simplicity. This traditional medical definition does have the advantage of countering the extreme extensions of the term that risk essentially defining its meaning out of existence by claiming anything can be an addiction. But physiological withdrawal in and of itself is not the real problem. Many

---

[1]Contrary to popular conceptions, the dosage of most substances that lead to addiction cannot be endlessly increased, so habitual users eventually arrive at a stable intake.

who are given morphine for pain go through withdrawal when they stop, and then resume their lives without ever seeking it again. The real problem is when the addiction takes control over people's lives. The factors behind this seeming loss of control are our primary focus.

Thus we will not split hairs in trying to draw a firm line between physiological and psychological factors; nor will we concern ourselves with whether what is being called an addiction is really a bad habit, a compulsion, escapism, etc. We are not presenting a theory of addiction that purports to explain all the reasons for it, nor cover all the intricate ways people find themselves in the throes of it. We do not presume that our model (nor any) can address all the varieties of addiction. Rather, we wish to focus on the phenomenon of control and the conflicts the seeming loss of it brings.

The Peruvian laborer who chews coca leaves daily as an aid to grueling work is addicted, but often has no conflict about it. This is likewise true for most people who use caffeine to get going or to concentrate better. Others are content with their addictions as an escape from a life that has little to offer. Our analysis excludes these and any other areas of addiction that do not involve inner conflict and a sense of being out of control. For brevity's sake, we will henceforth limit our use of the word addiction to those habitual, self-destructive activities that generate inner conflict.

Our interest is to present a framework and analysis that shows why the inner battle is not essentially people's private struggle with their own so-called weaknesses, but rather involves the internalization of values that cannot be lived up to. We view this kind of addiction as a revolt against an inner authoritarian, addiction being just one way of trying (and failing) to escape it. Decoding this internal war has far-reaching implications for understanding inner conflict in general, and the social orders that engender it.

Limiting ourselves to the configuration of addiction that involves an inner battle about being addicted has the advantage of isolating the most elusive, controversial, and seemingly mysterious component—control. In focusing on the inner conflicts around control, including the ostensible loss of it, there are two related factors:

1. Doing repetitive behaviors that one feels either incapable of stopping or that take great effort to try to stop—and should one succeed, their possible return is always lurking in the background.

2. These repetitive behaviors are judged by the person involved to be (or in fact are) interfering in a non-trivial way with one's well-being—in short, they are self-destructive.

The two prevalent frameworks for addiction, the disease and the responsibility models, polarize around the core issue of control. Disease models see so-called addicts as being in the control of an illness, a bad gene—something that fundamentally puts them out of control. In contrast, responsibility models emphasize choice and will power, and challenge the idea that people are really ever out of control. Instead they see addicts as exercising varying degrees of control, using addiction as an accommodation to their lives.

Disease models are attractive because they recognize people's feelings of helplessness and minimize blame; but this is at the cost of elevating the acknowledgment of powerlessness to a virtue. In contrast, responsibility models enable people to feel they can change if they so choose, but fail to account for the deep feelings of being out of control and powerless which are at the core of most people's experience with addiction. We will show why both models not only miss the mark, but contribute to the problem because they both stem from the values that lead to addiction.

What does it mean to feel out of control? One thing it does not mean is being capriciously and chaotically blown by external factors. Addiction displays repetitive, largely predictable, very mechanical patterns. Such patterns indicate that the person is really not out of control, but rather in the control of something—but what? A substance? A habit? A genetic weakness? A biochemical shift in the nervous system? An early trauma? A predilection for short-term pleasure at whatever cost? A weak or perverse will? We do not deny any or all of the above could be factors in feeling out of control. There is, however, a deeper way to examine the basic question of who or what is really in control.

Ordinarily, within addiction there are essentially only three positions vis-à-vis control that one can occupy or shift around in:

1. Keeping control over the unwanted behavior. (People who define themselves as non-drinking alcoholics are an example of this.)

2. Totally giving in to it after a struggle, as exemplified by the bum on skid row.

3. Struggling or battling with it so that one flips between feeling in and out of control.

The struggle is the most usual state. And most who manage to keep some control believe they must be continually on guard lest they find themselves "out of control" again. So unless one has totally given up or totally conquered the unacceptable behavior, some inner conflict is present. Who are the protagonists in this drama and what is the battle about? Obviously both the battlefield and the battlers must live within the person. This means the psyche must be compartmentalized into different parts vying for control.

The Divided Psyche: Symptom of a Dysfunctional Morality

The idea that humans are or can be internally divided is of course not new. Many theorists who have looked at internal conflict have put forth the notion that a person has different parts or voices that are trying to be heard or given their place. If an inner battle for control exists, at least two distinguishable elements must be so engaged. The person is then, at least to some extent, divided. To Freud and his followers the conflict is between one's conscious and unconscious aspects; Jung added a conflict between the personal and the universal or archetypal; in Buddhism it is the conflict between the selfless and self-centered; and in Western religions it is between the forces of good and evil within. This list is far from complete.

Should one give the idea of an inner split credence, the next question is what is the nature of this division; and what ramifications does the split have on how and why people do what they do? Our view is that the oscillations between being in and out of control within addiction are largely a particular expression of a deeply divided psyche.

No matter how a given theory describes the divisions within the psyche, it is rare that the divisions are allotted equal value. Buddhism values the selfless over the self-centered; Judeo-Christianity good over evil (it's hard not to if reality is framed and divided in this fashion); and Freud believed it was necessary for the conscious to keep the essentially anti-social, unconscious forces of the id in check. (He thought repression necessary because as a Victorian he accepted the dualistic morality of the religions he disdained, not imagining that his tripartite model of the psyche could be a consequence of that morality rather than of human nature.) Jung is sometimes an exception to placing greater value on one side, which is where much of his innovation, current relevance, and popularity lie.

Since not all cultures produce divided psyches as the norm, an inner division cannot be an intrinsic part of human nature. Rather we see this split as developing in tandem with the renunciate moral orders that polarized existence by creating dualistic, hard categories between spiritual and mundane, soul and body, spirit and matter, etc. The job of life then becomes maximizing the "good" or moral side of the split through effort. For example, for a Buddhist one's work is to become a better person by becoming more selfless and less self-centered.[2]

---

[2]"The Power of Abstraction: The Sacred Word and the Evolution of Morality" examines the way hierarchical social orders based on accumulation both create and reinforce these polarities, which in turn define what is moral and immoral.

In all social hierarchies based on production and accumulation, doing one's duty is valued over doing something else, or doing nothing; consequently work is valued over play. They all make divisions between industrious and lazy, valuing the former. Industrious means producing, showing results. Laziness, which has a negative connotation, is defined as spending time in ways that do not yield anything to show for it. In these moral systems leisure has no inherent value other than as a temporary reward for hard work, its function being mainly recuperative. This is not real leisure. If having leisure is as important to a person's well-being as accomplishment or productivity, it is no wonder that those so deprived get involved in self-destructive activities that offer a temporary way out of a life where producing is not a joy, but merely a means for often meager survival. The sad truth is that in a society that does not value leisure, people largely have neither leisure nor meaningful work.

Addiction has been (and often still is) considered a moral failing bringing immoral acts. We, too, look at much of addiction as essentially a moral disorder—but one that results from a faulty morality, rather than faulty people. In our view the disorder comes from the person having internalized values that not only cannot be lived up to, but that involve renouncing and suppressing vital parts of what it is to be human. The part of oneself that takes on these values becomes the inner authoritarian that not only attempts to mold one's behavior to fit the values, but judges any deviance as bad or lacking. The values contain standards for accomplishment and an ideal of what it is to be a good or worthy human being. This aspect of oneself that tries to actualize the values is perceived as the valued, worthwhile, respected—in short, the "good" part. Familial and societal mechanisms of reward and punishment ordinarily support and reinforce this ostensibly good part remaining in control.

We view the fundamental division within the psyche as a reflection and internalization of traditional worldviews that all divide activities into hard categories of right and wrong. We are not questioning the necessity of concepts of right and wrong being interwoven in any social order. Rather, we are questioning the current and future viability of the worldviews that make good and evil absolutes from which static rules and principles of right and wrong are derived. Complex, changing societies need a non-static approach to morality where right and wrong are tied into processes that move society in an appropriate direction, for example: survival, social justice, and self-trust.

It is of course easier for a society to control its members through rigid, unchanging categories of right and wrong if people buy into them. A task of traditional religion is to ensure that people do. Underlying the moral divisions between right and wrong, pure and impure, good and evil, or (as in some Eastern religions) reality and illusion is the basic separation between the selfish and selfless. We have in many different places in this book described how and why this division between the self-centered and selfless, the egoistic and altruistic creates what we call a "renunciate morality."[3] Here selflessness with its corollary self-sacrifice is a core concept, for it is through ideals of sacrificing selfish desires to God's will (monotheism), the good of the group (communism), or karmic law (Hinduism) that morality is defined. Buddhism goes further and sees selflessness in and of itself as the key to morality and right action. This morality is essentially authoritarian as it pegs "the good" to the sacrifice of self-interest for some "higher interest," which it in turn conveniently defines.

Elsewhere we have also shown how the very concepts of self-centered and selfless are embedded in each other, and that they can only be meaningfully seen as such.[4] In our framework being

---

[3]"Religion, Cults, and the Spiritual Vacuum"; "Dualism and Renunciation" in "Oneness, Enlightenment, and the Mystical Experience"; and the last three sections in "The Power of Abstraction" discuss the nature and problems of moral systems that promulgate renunciation.

[4]"The Power of Abstraction" shows that the way concepts such as selfless and self-centered are placed in opposition is the result of a polarized moral order. "What is Selfless Service Serving?" in *Control* discusses the self-

self-centered is simply an aspect of being human, as is the capacity to truly care for others. Not only does each have its value and function, they are intertwined rather than totally separate or even separable. Any morality that separates the two, giving much more value to one (the selfless), cannot but deeply divide the psyche of those who accept this frame. What ensues is an inner struggle aimed at keeping the devalued aspect of oneself in check. Accepting selflessness as the highest value is where the insidious authoritarianism of the old order unwittingly seeps into many modern paradigms that attempt to be new.[5]

Even Jung, whose worldview involved acknowledging and balancing basic polarities relegated the so-called dark side of humanity to an archetypal concept he called "the shadow." Shadows darken whatever they touch, but they in themselves are insubstantial, with no autonomous existence. That Jung chose such a strangely disembodied image to represent the negative pole of humanity is an indication that he, too, was uncomfortable with it. Whenever there is a shadow, something else is always casting it. Actually it is self-centeredness, particularly unacknowledged or unconscious self-centeredness, that casts whatever shadows there are in the world. There are those who hope that by embracing the shadow or approaching it with compassion, it will magically disappear. Self-centeredness, however, is very real and does not vanish when embraced. This is why all moral and social systems attempt to curb or channel it into areas of acceptability.

No matter what the game, rules create a system of interaction and expectation, and also define cheating. Cheating is break-

---

centered component in enacting ideals of selflessness and gives an in-depth explanation of why any solution that makes selflessness a prescription for living not only does not work, but contains the seeds of corruption and further reactiveness.

[5]"Love and Control: The Conditions Underlying Unconditional Love" shows how the ideal of selflessness is destructive to relationships.

ing the rules (usually in a hidden fashion) in order to gain advantage for, of course, oneself. Rules for playing the game of life are called ethics; if self-centeredness did not exist such rules would not be needed. We are not making self-centeredness the basic core of all motivation. To do so would just be more either/or conceptualizing, not essentially different from elevating selflessness, which has been done for thousands of years. However, self-centeredness must be acknowledged as a real part of being human that is ineradicable, necessary, and even valuable. Denying this, or trying to overcome it, is self-destructive and dysfunctional, and does not resolve the very real problems that self-centeredness gives rise to.

The hypocrisies, lies, and justifications for the use and abuse of power, which have been a prominent part of the history of all civilizations, often come from a pretense that denies self-interest. Hitler justified what he did through an ideology that placed supreme value on the Aryan race rather than on the furthering of his own ambitions. That he cared little for Aryans, or anyone else for that matter, is obvious, as he destroyed anyone who stood in his way. He would not have been able to muster support had he said that all he was really interested in was power at any cost.

What one keeps hidden, often from oneself, is the particular flavor and extent of one's own self-centeredness. This is one of the deepest roots of unconscious behavior, largely because people are conditioned to feel guilty and ashamed of this part of who they are. Also, deep down not feeling good enough is a major factor behind the inner experience of feeling driven. This in turn brings the need to justify one's existence through accomplishment and constantly striving to be "better." Humans are the only animal driven in this fashion. Accomplishment and social approval do elevate feelings of self-worth. Yet since the taint of self-centeredness can never be truly eradicated, the striving is endless. This deeply ingrained need to justify one's existence is at the root of Puritanism. The motivational aspect behind Puritanism involves always trying to get better (purer)—a never-ending task without respite, given that purity is defined in a way that denies the essential worth of being human in and of itself. The major religions promote this by valuing purity, particularly purity of intent—meaning intention without self-interest. Low self-esteem, which is currently being blamed for a plethora of social ills, including addiction, is inevitable when one is taught to devalue a basic part of oneself.

We emphasize the self-centered/selfless dichotomy as a basic source of internal conflict because this is really how the battle manifests itself in so many people. All societies have implicit and explicit rules for interaction that inhibit, limit, and channel expressions of self-centeredness—this is what the socializing process is about. But the old moral orders did this by using authoritarian means that controlled people through implanting guilt and fear about this aspect of being human. Now people and society are more out of control because the old constraints are no longer working. We are proposing that any inner battle that is habitual is an indication of a divided psyche; and further, that by its nature this division has a moral or normative aspect. What is called addiction is but one expression of this.

Taming the Beast: The Inner Battle for Control

In describing the dynamics of the struggle for control within a divided person, a danger lies in conceiving the parts too literally as separate entities battling for ascendancy. (Reification is a danger of all models.) This is not our view. We look at the two sides as compartmentalized aspects of the person that are tied into and dependent on each other. That is, the way each side expresses itself when in seeming control is in reaction to knowing and often fearing the other side.

Even folk wisdom recognizes that the human mind creates compartments, and that each, when activated, mysteriously seems to take on a life of its own. ("Don't let the right hand know what the left is doing.") Why the mind creates boundaries within itself must involve something in one compartment being unacceptable to another. Values are what determine unacceptability. Each compartment contains a configuration of thoughts, memories, and emotions that need to compete for expression because they operate under a different, conflicting set of values.

Calling the struggle for control essentially normative means that values lie at the heart of it. Values are taken on, most usually socially approved ones, that define what a good person is. For simplicity, we call the valued or ideal part of oneself that internalizes and tries to exemplify these values the "goodself." In order to be the kind of person the goodself constructs as an ideal, control must be maintained over that which interferes. Of course, if living up to one's ideals were in fact all a person were about, there would be no need to employ control. One would simply display the wanted virtues without conflict, hesitation, or effort. What interferes are the parts of being human that do not fit the values. The very need to exercise control indicates that something else is going on that must be contained—something that would otherwise come out and not display the wanted virtues. We call this "something else" the "badself" because what comes out when it is not being inhibited by the goodself is very different, often the opposite, of the consciously proclaimed ideals.

We want to make explicitly clear at the outset that we call this devalued part the badself not because it is actually bad, but rather because the goodself and typically society judge it to be so. This caveat also pertains to the goodself. We are aware of the drawbacks of the nomenclature goodself/badself due to their connotations, which seem to imply they are actually good and bad. This we emphatically do not wish to convey. Although neither is essentially good nor bad in our eyes, we have found no better words to represent the psychological distortions that result from the old moral order's dualistic, authoritarian split into good and evil. Neologisms are justifiable insofar as they offer something new. So we are bending language by constructing one word out of two (goodself instead of good self), intending this contrivance to be a reminder that the goodself does not contain all that is valuable, and the badself is not devoid of worth. The nature of this inner split will become more clear as the chapter moves along.

Any model that purports to describe or explain aspects of internal life risks appearing overly simplistic or reductionistic. Yet, dividing the psyche into the goodself and badself is no more (or less) simplistic than the dualistic moral order that divides the cosmos into good and evil. If part of what is socially designated as bad is an inescapable aspect of being human, this context sets the stage for dividing people's psyches. It is from this split that an internal struggle for control ensues. The two sides are formed and perpetuated in reaction to each other, that is, by their ongoing battle. What results is that the goodself has aspects one would be far better off without; while the badself contains elements that need to be legitimized and expressed. Our view is that health and well-being involve truly being whole, which means not internally warring.

In general the goodself takes on some or all of the following constellation of values: A good person does one's duty; is responsible, reliable, truthful, temperate, industrious, and productive; works to improve oneself and maximize potential; can put aside immediate pleasures for more important future results; does not use or hurt others merely for one's own enhancement or enjoyment; obeys the rules that make society work; takes other people's needs and wants into account. Often the highest good is considered putting others or something other than oneself first. The job of the goodself is to remain in control to ensure these values are lived up to.

In contrast, the badself consists of the parts of oneself that are devalued, and often suppressed or repressed because of not fitting into the values internalized by the goodself. Because it is usually the underdog, this unwanted part of oneself lies or dissembles to get its way. It cares little about future consequences or their effects on others; it uses and manipulates people; it is hedonistic and often reckless in the way it gets and sustains its pleasures; it is more interested in fun than accomplishment; it pushes against boundaries, restrictions, taboos; it flirts with danger; and when crossed it displays so-called negative emotions and behaviors such as anger, pettiness, and vengeance.

Within this framework each side needs the other as a foil, and thus each has mechanisms (usually not conscious) for keeping the game going. So the two compartments or "selves" do not coincide with categories of conscious and unconscious, as each contains both. But the side more valued by society and the person would, for this reason alone, tend to be more conscious. Most people prefer to identify with (and show others) their goodself, especially given that society and others who have similar values praise and reward it. Consequently, the goodself has much support in maintaining control. Since the devalued part does not have moral legitimacy to stand up to the valued part, the way it fights for expression is through subversion, deception, undermining (often unconscious), and externalization—"The devil [or my addiction] made me do it."

We view the feeling of being out of control that occurs in addiction as a secular version of religious possession. Laying the cause of unwanted behavior on an invading external evil spirit is similar to blaming the drug itself. In contrast, we view compartmentalization and the ensuing struggle as a better explanation of both addiction and so-called possession. Feeling out of control really means the goodself is not in control, but instead an unacceptable part of oneself is.[6]

The remainder of this chapter will describe the workings of the battle for control in general and within addictions. We end by giving some indications about how a divided self can become whole, while pointing out the difficulties in doing this within social orders whose power is derived from having people remain divided. For it is this division that makes people especially subject to authoritarian control.

---

[6]See "Satanism and the Worship of the Forbidden: Why It Feels Good to Be Bad" for more on possession.

Values can be internalized, expressed, and reacted against in a variety of ways. That we are critical of the process by which the goodself internalizes and self-imposes values does not mean we are essentially challenging the worth of the values themselves. Although there is great variance in the way values are ordered internally, they are often organized in a hierarchy of importance. For some, duty may be a top priority. But this could be duty to country, God, one's children, the planet's ecology, or one's own spiritual development. For others duty might not be a major concern. It could instead be productivity, helping others, truthfulness, or integrity, etc.

Within the goodself/badself division, it is difficult not to place one's allegiance with the goodself. But the goodself is not as benign as its espoused values make it seem. Authoritarianism is usually masked by lofty ideals that appear to be life-affirming on the surface and are thus hard to fault. And here too, the seemingly impeccable values mask the process by which the goodself creates a driven, cut-off human being. To the extent that its ideals become criteria for living, the goodself becomes the inner authoritarian whose task is to keep the forbidden, "bad" parts under its control. This not only occurs within a person, for often in relationships one person's goodself can try to control another's badself, setting off a reactive battle for control between people.

The goodself embodies both the dominant and submissive aspects of the authoritarian personality. Since it uses external authorities to bolster its power over the badself and other people, it is conditioned to submit to authorities. The goodself then is dictatorial, judgmental, structured, often a puritanical harsh taskmaster; and above all it is fearful—fearful that without always maintaining control, one's life would unravel. If the goodself shows some benevolence toward human frailty, especially its own, it can at times (if not too threatened) allow and forgive little lapses of virtue—for after all, "One is only human." This safety valve works as long as things don't get out of hand. Addiction is one way things do get out of hand.

The goodself is involved in "taming the beast," meaning keeping the carnal, the animal, within acceptable bounds. The fear is that without constraints, the animal (or id, dark side, one's sinful nature, unabashed and uncaring self-centeredness) would rage forth, leaving destruction, including self-destruction, in its wake. This kind of inner division usually relegates much of self-centeredness and carnality to the badself, thereby distorting and exacerbating them. It also suppresses spontaneity, creativity, and enjoyment for their own sake because these expressions often undermine the goodself's control mechanisms. It is this division between the animal and the rational, the spiritual and material, and ultimately between the selfless and self-centered that does not allow the carnal and self-centered to be integrated and valued as part of a whole being. Ironically, the division itself with its suppressions ensures that if what is inhibited ever does break loose, it tends to go wild. This in turn confirms the worst fears of the goodself, verifying its need to keep in control. It is around this dynamic that we will describe our views of addiction.

Two different yet interrelated questions are relevant here: First, why is it that one wants or needs to express traits judged undesirable at all; and secondly, how does one go about doing so? The latter deals with how the badself gets the goodself to relinquish control.

Just as those with political power have the advantage of official ideology and sanctions over usurpers, so too do the goodself's judgments carry more weight. These judgments about what it is to be a good human being are programmed from childhood and stand underneath one of the most powerful control mechanisms of the goodself—guilt. Most parents rely heavily on guilt to control children's behavior by making them feel they are bad for being self-centered and disobedient.[7] This plays a primary role in creating a divided personality, as it makes people feel bad about basic aspects of themselves. A non-fragmented person could treat guilt simply as information that a discrepancy exists

---

[7]"The Ambiguity of Parental Authority" in *Control* goes into this.

between one's values and behavior, both needing to be reexamined to determine which, if either, is appropriate. In contrast, a divided person's goodself uses guilt as a driving mechanism to remain in control.

The goodself has all the weight of tradition, accepted morality, parental conditioning, and social structures on its side. Accumulation cultures all place high value on the means of accumulating, namely work. Having a divided self may or may not be essential in making a "work ethic" work, but it is essential in producing people who are driven to justify their existence. Humans are the only animal so driven, and here, too, guilt plays its part. Guilt about being bad often results in needing to prove to ourselves and others that we are worthwhile through achievement. Work and accomplishment, and the rewards and praise they bring, are mechanisms that can keep the goodself in control.

This endless need to get better creates a mysterious core of tension that is the motor driving many. Although living with this tension comes to seem normal, what results is an inner torture chamber from which another part of oneself is desperately trying to escape. So calling addictions "escapism" has a strange truth and irony. What is requisite for all of this to operate is a core of deep self-mistrust and even fear of oneself. Authoritarian moralities that denigrate the carnal and the self-centered implant the mind control that is necessary for such self-control. All mind control operates under the guise of self-control.

We are not denigrating either self-control or accomplishment. There is deep satisfaction in a job well done, in enlarging the scope of one's capabilities, or in helping others to do the same. Accomplishment and self-control are intrinsically tied to each other and are essential human needs and expressions—as are leisure and spontaneity. Rather, we are showing the mechanisms operative in the struggle for control in divided people who fear loosening control because they fear themselves.

In fearing oneself, what is actually feared is one's badself, and that without being continually pushed by the goodself one would end up a slothful person of no worth. We look at the inner battle for control as involving an inner authoritarian, armed with moral righteousness, caging needed human expression that does not have an adequate voice—i.e., a historically well-articulated alternate set of values capable of validating needed expressions of carnality and self-centeredness. (Carnality, our animal nature, which involves satisfying basic needs, has an intrinsically self-centered component.) Thus the badself's route to power is subversion, seduction, and casuistry to sabotage the goodself's rules. People so divided both cage themselves and reactively try to escape their cage. Here people operate under and rebel against implanted "shoulds," which guarantees a life of conflict.

Since society defines maturity as assuming roles and obeying rules, the badself often looks like a rebellious child next to the goodself's adult veneer. Although there is a similarity between the way the badself subverts and a clever child wheedles around adult authority, the goodself is no more truly adult than the badself it tries to contain. The badself's attempt to compensate for lacks of expression through extremes is just part of the game. It, too, is a symptom of a polarized authoritarian morality that has bought the framework which makes the goodself "good," and so it gets its pleasures the only way it can—through being "bad."[8]

The badself exerts a powerful allure—that of spontaneity, shameless self-indulgence, cutting loose, throwing caution to the winds, and other taboo enticements, including forbidden expressions of sexuality. Breaking out of the goodself's boundaries can release a charismatic energy that is seductive to others. Society's fondness and indulgence for fictional heroes who outwit authorities and break rules is legend, as is the romantic appeal of the frontier—that lawless place beyond convention. In contrast, portrayals of pure virtue, where the goodself reigns supreme, are of little interest. The mythic figure, the outlaw hero, vicariously offers an outlet for a repressed culture by igniting a safe collusion with people's badselves. Thus society puts forth a dou-

---

[8] See "Satanism and the Worship of the Forbidden."

ble message: "Rebellion is bad and dangerous," on one side; and "Rebellion is not only exciting and exhilarating, it is freedom," on the other. Double messages from parents have been shown to cause schizophrenia in children. The double messages a society puts out likewise must fragment its members, but here the resulting pathology is disguised by being the social norm.[9]

Groups easily form around eliciting and reinforcing either the good or badself; these alliances serve as a mechanism to bolster the control of that side. Whom people associate with is often based on needing allies to support one side or the other.[10] Gangs of young males urging each other on to rebellious deeds is an example of a collusion between badselves, while 12-Step programs function as a support for the goodself. In such support groups the goodself's inability to control the addiction on its own is what connects the members. Previous to joining, it was often also the addiction (getting high together) that connected them to others. In both the repetitive drunk and the strict teetotaler, the relation to alcohol is a foundation of personality and the central focus of life.

The badself has no monopoly on destruction, including self-destruction. Groups that exacerbate the inner split and justify violence also form when people surrender to a leader or an ideology. Here ideals of purity (and purifying) are the basis for rampaging violence via racist lynch mobs, "law and order" vigilantes, or armies under the lofty banner of righteousness or fulfilling God's will. They all use "doing good" as the grounds for callous brutality. Any culture or person whose identity is predicated on superiority, moral or otherwise, is particularly susceptible to this. Living up to images of superiority requires a severe

---

[9]"Why Politicians Lie" in *Control* describes why a dualistic morality creates a schizophrenic society prone to corruption, deceit, and hypocrisy.

[10]It could be worthwhile to use the good/badself framework to analyze the dynamics of control, reactiveness, and collusions within couples, families, groups and relationships in general. (A person's goodself or badself can try to control, seduce, and punish the good or badself of others, etc.)

inner authoritarian, which in turn vindicates external severity and ruthlessness as a means to some purified end.

Socially sanctioned violence, be it war or capital punishment, is capable of destroying anything as long as it can be justified with shared moral principles. We strongly suspect that the deeper the split is within a person or culture, the greater the potential for destruction. The highest and therefore most unlivable ideals cause the greatest split. This framework explains how a whole culture (Nazi Germany) could commit monstrous atrocities it later deplores.

In the struggle for control between the two selves, what is really in control is the polarized unconscious system itself. That is, neither side is conscious of participating in a system where each side colludes with the other. The goodself needs something "bad" to control, and the badself needs something to react against. In order for the goodself to justify its power, the badself has to be excessive. Each side needs the other to exist at all, quite literally, because each can only live in opposition to the other. So however torturous, both selves need to perpetuate the split. Ultimately, the inner battle for control depends on the dynamics between the two selves remaining unconscious. The more extreme and inflexible the inner compartments, the more people oscillate between them in a seemingly inexplicable fashion.

In our view, much of what is called psychopathology also displays the ways people accommodate this unconscious struggle within themselves. To hint briefly at this line of thought: Neuroses are ways of expressing self-centeredness and being self-absorbed that would otherwise be unacceptable—psychoses even more so. Whatever else psychotics are doing, they are creating a walled universe with themselves in its center that leaves no room for others. Psychotic "dis-integration" comes from an inability to integrate parts of oneself judged bad or wrong. Many psychotics are very sensitive and painfully aware of the hypocrisy masking so much of social interaction where people pretend to be far more virtuous than they are. They are unable to cope with the so-called negative aspects of being human, such as aggression, not only in others, but in themselves. Their solution is to leave the field of normal human interaction.

The sociopath or psychopath who has that mysterious ailment of being without conscience has adopted as a survival strategy the negation of the goodself, which results in loss of empathy and care. This adaptation is more likely the result of an emotionally impoverished childhood than of conscious choice. If intelligent, a psychopath maintains the guise of conventional morality and is never discovered. Elevating self-centeredness (the badself) as the only reality, the sociopath's access to human connection becomes power and domination. Although bright psychopaths are usually able to construct safe ways of getting their power needs met, some resort to violent outlets which can become compulsions, serial murder being an extreme example. The most heinous crimes are often committed by those who are noteworthy for being unnoteworthy. Serial killers, like Nazi leaders, are renowned for their outward ordinariness.

Addiction as Revolt against the Inner Authoritarian

The battle for control in addiction involves somewhat predictable patterns that shift control from one self to the other. Here a substance (alcohol) or activity (gambling)) becomes the focal point of the battle. Either can become a trigger mechanism that shifts control to the badself, allowing the expression of what has been suppressed. A "trigger mechanism" is any experience that offers some immediate release. It is feared or forbidden by the goodself because it can act as a doorway to undermining its control. A trigger mechanism (taking a drink or placing a bet) does not always escalate to where the goodself loses control, but an addict is never sure when it will.

The trigger mechanism is usually made the culprit ("demon rum"). Now a modern twist has faulty genes empowering the substance to explain why only certain people are susceptible. It is possible that particular genetic configurations affect susceptibility and predilections differently. For example, those with slower metabolisms could gravitate toward stimulants, while those with faster ones toward depressants. Yet even granting that genetics may be a factor, making genes the major cause does not explain why loss of control only occurs sometimes, nor why some who are susceptible cannot exercise moderation. One drink does not make anyone drunk or out of control. In contrast, locating the crux of the problem in a divided psyche that uses a trigger mechanism to sabotage its inner authoritarian does explain both the sporadic loss of control and the power of the first drink. Here whether loss of control (actually, a shift of control to the badself) occurs or not is a function of the context, which explains why those with more to lose often manage to maintain control when they need to.

When addictions shift control to the badself, this provides both an opportunity and an excuse to let out a lot of things that are normally held in. For instance, a mother killed two of her children while on cocaine. Afterward she claimed she loved them, displaying bewilderment ("I hadn't planned on it") and seemingly genuine distress as to why she killed them. This was taken as convincing evidence (by *Time* magazine at least—June 10, 1991) that the drug made her do it. Yet many people have taken large amounts of cocaine without killing anyone. Can one doubt that this woman must have had extreme conflict between loving her children and resenting the sacrifices that taking care of them imposed on her? To us, that she was truly confused as to why she did it corroborates that she has a deeply divided and compartmentalized psyche. When back in her goodself, she was unconscious of the depth of her ambivalence about motherhood. This is an extreme example of how cultural idealizations of maternal self-sacrifice can divide a mother to where her goodself cannot acknowledge how much resentment is actually there.[11]

---

[11]"Self-Sacrifice, Power, and Passion" in "Love and Control: The Conditions Underlying Unconditional Love" discusses the relation between self-

As it is a part of a larger inner dynamic, what triggers the shift in control can be most anything that brings immediate gratification: consciousness-altering drugs, food, shopping, gambling, stealing, anything taboo, etc. Trigger mechanisms ignite memories of previous states of pleasure and release. The very act of, say, placing a bet shifts one out of wherever one is into anticipating something better. Even the disappointment of losing can be immediately altered by placing another bet. Whether winning or losing, compulsive gamblers have gambling as the focus of their lives because they use it for release—that is, to get away from their goodself.

The struggle for control is composed of cycles in which each side gains the upper hand temporarily. The inner dialogue of the addict reflects this battle. The goodself lays down the rules and reasons (all good) for maintaining control. Hungering to escape the confined, idealized, and regimented life the goodself tries to lead, the badself's voice is more subdued in the background—a siren song whispering words of this ilk: "I need to relax. One drink won't hurt—this time I'll stay in control; I've been good and need a break; I'm losing my friends because I'm no fun anymore; I feel just as bad when I don't drink—so what's the difference?"

Since the life as constructed by the goodself has a driven quality (toward success, improvement, or merely keeping forbidden impulses suppressed), any unwanted occurrence can overload an already stressed system. An argument with a loved one, feeling abused or unappreciated by one's boss or mate, losing money in the stock market, a car accident—such difficulties are sure to come, as they are a part of life. This brings the hardest thought to resist: "This is too much—I can't take any more." One knows exactly what will ease the tension. The first drink does bring a real letting go. This is not primarily owing to the drug's effects, but

---

sacrifice and power in the traditional mother role, and how this affects women so involved.

more because taking it ends the immediate conflict about whether to take it, bringing a momentary release from the over-all struggle. Where the nerves were screaming, tension begins to melt away, leading to the justification, "God, I really needed that; the things I have to deal with."

For simplicity, we will focus on alcohol addiction as a prototype for a number of reasons: it is a classical addiction as it can have physiological dependency and withdrawal; it is a major social problem; the drug is socially acceptable and available in much of the world, and thus extremely accessible. Also, most who use it do not become addicted. Moreover, alcoholism as a disease was a key concept in the development of 12-Step programs, the most widespread addiction treatment.

Those labeled addicts often go over the edge to where drinking makes them dysfunctional. From our point of view, this is because the hidden purpose of addiction is precisely that—to make the goodself dysfunctional. One drink loosens the controls enough to lead to another, but not enough to do away with the goodself's behavioral constraints. So the addict drinks until that occurs. As tolerance to the drug increases over time, more is needed to incapacitate the goodself, which brings about social and relational problems as well as physical damage. This in turn reinforces the goodself's values and need to stay in control. The goodself must become even more rigid lest the unwanted parts come out; while the badself, through devious means and sabotage, attempts to undermine its control enough to allow the trigger mechanism entry. Thus, in a psyche so divided, no matter how much power the goodself seems to have at any moment, the badself is always lurking underneath, waiting for the right moment to take control by seemingly going out of control.

Once the badself is on a roll it resists restraint, knowing it will be caged again. Eventually, as a binge plays itself out, the extremes of self-abuse and unacceptable behavior (becoming truly "wasted") act like another trigger mechanism that lets the "righteous self" regain control. Control usually shifts back to the goodself when the badself's cutting loose reaches a point of excess that can no longer be handled or integrated. Excess eventually occurs since the badself is reactive by nature, mechanically rebelling against the goodself's constraints and judgments, including those that do have real survival value. Then come the judgments, self-recriminations, and vows which the goodself uses to bolster the constraints necessary to keep the badself submerged.

The victory is Pyrrhic, however, for all its carefully constructed defenses can unravel in an unexpected instant. The goodself knows deep down it really isn't in control, because it can never be sure that in a moment of "weakness" or temptation its elaborate edifice of controls will not again crumble. So it must always be on guard. This is why some popular frameworks of addiction are emphatic that addicts can never really be cured. In actuality this is only true as long as the person remains internally compartmentalized. Unfortunately, the very belief "Once an addict, always an addict" is a self-fulfilling prophecy because it ensures self-mistrust, which keeps a divided self divided.

The longer one is involved in the inner battle, the more self-trust deteriorates. Perpetually making and breaking resolutions gradually erodes the goodself's credibility with itself as it secretly loses faith in its capacity to maintain control. What results are people who do not trust themselves at the deepest level. Part of their tragedy is they have no good reason to. Even those who have kept control over their lives for an extended period of time still have to take it "one day at a time."

Severe dysfunctional addiction is only one of the more obvious manifestations of the power struggle in people torn between their good and badselves. Because the divided self is the norm, much of so-called normal life contains varying degrees of this inner conflict. Many suffer from and often hide a raging inner battle which brings not only self-disparagement, but severely blocks energy. Food addiction (what many would call a compulsion) is a good example. Eating (like sex) is an essential human activity with immediate gratification that can get caught up in a struggle for control. Though socially safer than many other so-called addictions, struggling with food still involves some kind of inner revolt against the rules and structures of an inner authoritarian. Here too, the feeling of not being able to control oneself can only mean that another rebellious part of oneself is in control.

The easiest way to try to control a habit is to avoid the trigger mechanism altogether through unambiguous rules of total abstinence. This makes it harder for the badself to seduce, tempt, and rationalize. Compulsive eating is complicated by the fact that total abstinence is not a possible solution. With overeating, as in any addiction, using will power is not reliable, because self-control in a divided person is really "goodself-control," which has inbuilt reactiveness. Thus whenever eating, a divided person faces the possibility of "losing" control, since any bite can become a trigger that shifts control. Even more, given that food is everywhere and abstinence not an option, the badself's propensity for rationalization and sabotage can manifest whenever food comes to mind. Ironically, since food is often used as a reward or to celebrate, many people are conditioned to overindulge as a payoff for being good.

Of course, different substances operate differently. Cultural values determine which addictions or compulsions are socially acceptable. When productivity and expansion are primary values, work—and its mirror image, consumption (the reward for work)—as well as money and power, easily become addictive. Not surprisingly, drugs that enhance work or bring release in socially safe ways are favored. For example, caffeine and nicotine are often used to maintain control and focus. Both are socially acceptable, as they can aid productivity and fit into normal activities. With neither drug does excess lead to the release of suppressed aspects of oneself nor anti-social behavior.

Upon becoming truly cognizant of nicotine's detrimental effects, even though it is highly addictive physically, some people stop smoking and go through withdrawal with a minimum of fuss, while others torturously try to eliminate it and fail. Why is this so? As with other addictions, in smokers the battle for control is between the "good" part of oneself that knows what's best, and the rebellious part that justifies momentary pleasure with a devil-may-care attitude toward self-destruction. Those who stop manage to shift priorities upon seeing that the habit is not worth the consequences, and that clarity defuses the struggle. Whereas those who say they wish they could stop but cannot or "are not quite ready" really don't want to but think they should. Here just thinking about stopping is enough to trigger desire. The seeming inability to resist is used as permission to continue. Perhaps having previously tried and failed, such people fear losing the battle again.

Nicotine is a strange drug which seems to be both a brain stimulant and a muscle relaxant that easily gets hooked into daily work habits. Many smokers become very anxious without nicotine because it dampens emotions, giving more control over unwanted ones. Smoking serves as a momentary release and aid to a nervous system over-burdened by maintaining control in other areas. What makes nicotine so difficult to "kick" is that it supports the goodself's agendas while giving the badself an emotionally safe, routine venue for rebellion.

On the other end of the spectrum are compulsions that are not only anti-social, but hurtful to others. In violent compulsions such as repetitive rape and serial murder, a buildup of inner pressure leads to the fix (i.e., release) that cools the person out. In those who are driven in this fashion, the addiction is to a guaranteed form of power that not coincidentally is a release of hatred or rage. "Getting off" on others' extreme pain, fear, or even death can only come with shutting off all empathy. In our framework this is not because one is a bad seed or congenitally deficient, but because one has learned to feel good mainly through being bad. These people become human time-bombs because their badself is their only access to power and release.[12] Then too, there is the recurrent mystery heard about far more

---

[12]See "Satanism and the Worship of the Forbidden." "Abortion: The Old Morality is Killing Us" in Control discusses the link between unwanted, uncared for children and such violence.

often than is comfortable: the seeming incongruity of a supposedly ordinary, "nice," upstanding person going berserk on a killing rampage usually ending in suicide. For us going berserk is another sign of a rigidly compartmentalized psyche seeking release.

Repeated wife-beating can be looked upon as an addiction. Batterers talk about being "out of control." Like other addicts, they are also notoriously two-sided, one side being sweet and loving, even charming, the other violent and vicious. The woman often gets stuck in confusion and ambivalence, wondering which is the real person. The answer, of course, is that both sides are equally real. Habitual battering involves a syndrome where violence releases built-up tension.[13]

Lest it appear we are placing self-destructiveness solely in the badself, we emphatically are not. On the contrary, self-destructiveness comes from having a self so severely divided that each side is trying to destroy the other. Within this framework, no healthy solution can emerge. Being a bum on skid row is one way of seeming to end the battle by surrendering fully to the addiction.[14] A victorious badself is obviously self-destructive and also leads a very constricted life. Here the fear is that any attempt at sobriety will bring back the more unbearable battlefield of conflict. A victorious goodself is also self-destructive, but less obviously so. What has been destroyed are self-trust and vital aspects of self-expression. Also, the rigidity that comes from suppressing elements of one's nature over time often takes its

---

[13]"Love and Control" shows why it is no coincidence that most personal violence occurs within the family, where unlivable ideals and the taboo against boundaries exacerbate the goodself/badself split. Its section "Forgiving and Letting Go" discusses why the goodself ideal of forgiveness as a virtue rewards abusive patterns. This is especially easy to do when the abuser's goodself becomes remorseful. The section on "Love Addiction" describes how imbalances of power can mechanically arouse passion, sometimes feeding abusive patterns.

[14]This has a structural similarity to satanism, which purports to end the battle through aggressively affirming the "bad." See "Satanism."

toll on the body through stress-related ailments. Tension is always present because the goodself can never truly relax. Which of the warring selves is the real person? The answer is both and neither—both because each is a real expression of who the person actually is; and neither because there is no way to know what an integrated person free of the struggle would look like. Truly ending this inner battle through integration is far more difficult than giving one or the other side ascendancy.

Most ways of dealing with addiction do not get at the root of the split endemic to cultures that dualistically categorize good and evil. Instead they attempt to strengthen the controls of the goodself to where the badself is sufficiently contained. Although this can work in making people more socially acceptable, even to themselves, it does not free them from the inner battle. Societies whose values create and reinforce this personality split not only make integration difficult, but spawn an underbelly of corruption as the devalued side creates clandestine avenues to express itself. Corruption is hidden self-centered activity that is contrary to the values a society professes.

The Failings of Disease and Responsibility Models

If substance addiction is thought of as a disease, it is certainly not one in the ordinary sense, as there are no invading microorganisms to dispel, nor any way of physically detecting it when the substance is not present. Moreover, addictive substances do not affect everyone uniformly; nor do they even have a uniform effect on the same person all the time. Non-substance "addictions" (eating, shopping, stealing, gambling, etc.) are even more difficult to place in a disease framework. On the other hand, locating the problem of substance abuse totally in the psychological realm stretches the meaning of the word disease too much. Here, there would be no more reason to call addiction a disease than to call fear of heights (or any neurosis) a disease.

So to postulate that those who do get addicted are suffering from a disease can only mean something is wrong with, or lacking in, their physical makeup.

What meaning addiction as a disease could have is that because of genetic predilections, chemical imbalances, or other physiological factors, one is unable to handle a given substance without loss of control. Here addiction is viewed as being similar to an allergy, with the symptom being that the first drink triggers an uncontrollable need for the second. (If this were true then total abstinence would be the only solution.) This doesn't explain why people often move from one addiction to another, or have non-substance addictions. The other problem with this theory (besides the fact that much research claims to disprove it) is that typically once people identify an allergy, they simply avoid what causes it. Backers of the allergy theory could contend that most ordinary allergies initially feel bad, while addictive allergies initially feel so good they are irresistible. But this places addictions in a different category; and it still fails to explain why some people continue after knowing the problem, while others desist.

More tellingly, it also fails to explain why those who believe they are allergic to alcohol take the first drink at all. This means loss of control can precede the first drink, making it hard not to take it. Unless a residue remains from previous drinking, the temptation and subsequent loss of control cannot be a function of the physical effects of the alcohol itself. A hangover is a residue, but other than that, there's no way to predict when and why the first drink is taken when the person is sober. The real problem, however, is that people notoriously start again after drying out. Thus the urge to take the first drink must come from some place other than physical need.

The great appeal of the disease model to people struggling with addiction is that it gives them a reason for their plight other than a flaw in their character. The addict is no longer seen as depraved, weak, or just plain no good, but rather sick. Just as those with pneumonia are not expected to go it alone and cure themselves, neither should this be expected of those suffering from addiction, especially if it is an illness. The problem is that pneumonia can be cured medically, while addiction cannot. The physiological effects of addictions can be eliminated by simply shutting off access to the substance for a sufficient length of time. But this does not necessarily ameliorate the propensity to become addicted, which is what a real cure would be. Removing people from internal and external blame does have value, as does encouraging people to seek help. But the disease framework of addiction is flawed not only because addiction neither looks nor acts like any other kind of illness, but also because the model itself becomes an important chip in the power game of "Who is in control?"

The widespread popularity of the disease model becomes understandable when one sees the available alternatives in the current moral climate. In our society wrong actions (being "bad") are to be punished, while the sick deserve compassion and the allocation of resources for cures. In order to be cured, there has to be an illness. Since our society's major solution to crime and other unacceptable deviance is punishment, not rehabilitation, one escape valve that allows for merciful treatment is the concept of diminished capacity. If a disease makes people lose control, their capacities are certainly diminished.

Given only these two alternatives—bad or sick—addicts, those who care about them, the health-care industry, and society in general would understandably much rather look at addiction as an illness. This frame at least offers the possibility of a humane approach to the problem. In terms of the divided self, judging someone "bad" leads to punishing the badself, while the designation "sick" permits helping the goodself. It is not surprising, then, that all the contradictions within the disease model, as well as the body of scientific research that is contrary to it, are largely ignored. This is in part because people fear that if addicts were not considered sick, society's solutions would be harsh and punitive. Also, the rubric of illness is the official ticket to ameliorative (instead of punitive) funding, grants, and insurance benefits which fuel the multi-billion-dollar rehabilitation business.

Older views saw excessive anti-social behavior as either bad or possessed by something bad. They tried to control it through censure, punishment, or some form of exorcism (often another guise of punishment—"beating out the devil"). And although drunkenness (or insanity) could excuse moderate indiscretions, when control was applied it was largely punitive. In short, the errant individual was taken to task and made responsible.

Certain contemporary theories also hold that, bottom line, the individual must be held responsible. We thus call them "responsibility" models, the more sophisticated of which are also concerned with society's responsibility, as well as prevention and rehabilitation. Their approach is to empower people so they can conquer their addictions, rather than making them feel powerless before a disease, which necessitates going to some outside agency for a "cure." These models hold that individuals should ultimately take the credit or blame for what they do, although they also acknowledge that society has a hand in shaping people. This justifies wanting society to engage in prevention and rehabilitation, but in a way that still makes the individual responsible. Although these models are couched in scientific and humanitarian language, there is nevertheless trenchant resistance to them. This is partially out of fear they could lead back to the old harsh handling of people that previously occurred before disease models reframed addicts from "bad" to "sick." The line between responsibility and blame, as well as rehabilitation and punishment, is thin indeed.

We will only be concerned with modern responsibility theories that directly challenge viewing addiction as an illness, and which postulate that choice and will power (taking responsibility) are the way to recovery. Whereas loss of control is at the core of disease models, denying the addict is really out of control is at the core of responsibility models.

Responsibility frameworks break down in two places. Few would argue that a person is totally immune from social contexts. Evidence shows that some contexts produce more addiction than others. So how and where does one affix responsibility (mostly a euphemism for blame)—on the person or on society? This leads to a confusing double message: "People must be held responsible, but society is also to blame."

The most telling place where these models go awry is in the presumption that addicts are capable of being in control when they want or need to be. There is an unwarranted assumption that if addiction is not a disease, then control isn't really destroyed. Some theorists "prove" this by showing that seeming loss of control is inconsistent. Here many studies and experiments (in institutional settings) are cited, showing that so-called addicts can control, regulate, and adjust their intake and behavior to accommodate changing circumstances—including what they can get away with. In all this the unfounded presupposition is that loss of control has to be consistent for it to be real. This underlies the faulty conclusion that showing addicts can exercise control in highly controlled situations proves they are capable of doing it whenever they so choose. This *non sequitur* not only leaves no room for unconscious factors and contextual influences, but contradicts the very real and deep feeling of being out of control which those addicted have experienced. Responsibility models also leave unexplained where this curious drive to self-destruction through excess comes from.

These models are correct in asserting that addicts are not as out of control as they often appear. But they fall down in assuming that therefore the addict is really in control, and thus all that's needed are ways to increase options and will power so the **right** decisions can be made. Their premise is that addicts can control their lives—so let's help them do it better. The solution here is that addicts must be made to take responsibility for their actions and be helped (not coddled) into making the right choices. Of course, these "right choices" are the ones aligned with society's values. What this actually means is helping the socially sanctioned self, the goodself, keep control. This does not address the problem that many of these very values divide people's psyche to where addiction becomes a compulsive mechanism of release.

Some who favor responsibility models fear that defining addicts as sick or handicapped could protect them by law from facing the consequences of their actions. A corollary fear is that protecting them as sick could potentially punish those not under this umbrella. For instance, this could force employers to keep those who claim to be recovering addicts over more responsible candidates. This in effect would reward people for being addicts. Another major worry of some responsibility proponents is that the disease model undermines moral responsibility, and thus the very fabric of society. The fear is that denying responsibility and choice exacerbates the moral breakdown currently underway. Our view is different: We see the overall moral breakdown that is occurring worldwide not as an indication of the present lack of moral fiber in people, but rather as due to the crumbling of age-old authoritarian moralities that many people can no longer live by.

Responsibility models can only offer reprogramming that attempts to strengthen the will, training people to "be responsible"—meaning choose socially sanctioned behavior. It is not surprising that often the methodology utilized for change involves behavior modification techniques based on conditioning procedures of reward and punishment. Rewards and social reinforcements can strengthen the goodself; punishment, especially if severe enough, can contain the badself. However, these short-term solutions not only leave the root of the problem untouched, but they, like the disease model, exacerbate the inner split by only strengthening the goodself.

Those who promulgate responsibility as the key to dealing with addictions do see clearly that disease models foster a victim mentality. They hold that taking responsibility is necessary to empower the addict to change, while feeling the helpless victim of a dubious disease panders to irresponsibility—offering merely an excuse, not an explanation or solution. Yet having a split, warring psyche where each side victimizes the other does bring about a loss of power and control that makes people feel like victims. The disease model does bolster the victim stance by building an ideology claiming that mainly biological forces control what's going on. Seeing addiction as biologically based essentially means being a victim of one's own body. Legitimizing the victim mentality exacerbates the inner battle by reinforcing the badself's capacity for sabotage ("I can't help myself") and the goodself's need for constant vigilance, which further breaks down self-trust. We are all victims of circumstance in one way or another, but to feel like a victim of oneself (genes, etc.) makes self-trust impossible.

What responsibility models do not do well is explain the very real feeling people have of being out of control. Although it is true that people will readily latch onto a good excuse, the more important reason why so many people resonate with the idea that addiction is a disease is that they have truly felt out of control. To date, the disease model has been the only theory to propose a cause for this people can somewhat understand. Responsibility frameworks really cannot even acknowledge, let alone handle, a truly out-of-control factor. For if you're not in control, how can you be held responsible? Actually, beneath their adversarial stance, the two models share a common moral frame that generates a psyche at war with itself. They are opposite reflections of the same polarized moral order that can only view problematic behavior as either sick or wrong. They mainly differ in their strategies for strengthening the goodself.

In contrast, the model of a divided psyche does not promulgate a victim mentality; yet neither does it negate the inner experience of those who at times do feel driven and helpless. It also allows for inconsistency around control. From our perspective, what are called addictive types or personalities (those prone to addiction) utilize the battle for control to express their deep internal division, which permits occasional escape from their inner authoritarian. The battle itself becomes the focal point of life. This is why they can have several addictions or move from one to another. Our framework views self-destructiveness as inherent in the divided self as each side tries to dominate the other. In addiction the badself is usually the underdog using whatever means it can to destroy the controls of the goodself.

Proponents of disease and responsibility frameworks for dealing with addiction both show evidence that their approaches can at times help people gain control over their lives. Their criteria for success understandably is a lessening of the use and abuse of substances over time. We do not question the value of systems of relief that offer individual or even short-term help. But we do not think that either theory can stem the rising tide of out-of-control behavior because neither really addresses the basic issues involved in the very nature of control.

Twelve Steps to Where?

The disease model shifts the framework of addiction from "bad" to "sick" by viewing addicts as victims who are out of control. But it does so by fostering the idea that the individual is powerless in the face of the addiction. Its strategies for help involve reinforcing the control of the goodself, ensuring the person remains divided. One way the goodself maintains control is through being a member of a group that rewards its values. With the erosion of traditional structures that have functioned as a support for the goodself (church, community, family), 12-Step groups have come to fill that vacuum. Ironically, the label "self-help" has been affixed to these very groups that foster the belief that people are helpless on their own.

It is no accident that approaches that work by supporting and strengthening the inner authoritarian through group pressure favor the disease model. The prevalent 12-Step groups work only if there is total capitulation to their precepts—the 12 Steps. The disease model furthers this along by locking in the belief in one's helplessness that is necessary for such submission. The 12 Steps are authoritarian insofar as they are unchallengeable rules to live by. The demands can be summarized as: admission of ultimate powerlessness; total surrender to a higher power (God); working to eliminate character defects with the help of this higher power; doing a *mea culpa* and making amends; helping others through spreading this message (the Word).

Although eventually Alcoholics Anonymous embraced the physiological disease model, originally it looked at drunkenness as a character defect and thus focused on traditional moral betterment. So, it is not surprising that the values underlying the 12 Steps come straight from religion's moral division between good and evil. Whatever "higher power" one surrenders to, however personal, eclectic, or seemingly modern, the morality that is assumed to flow from it is traditional, devaluing both carnality (the animal) and self-centeredness. Power is the key word in "higher power," as the goodself gains strength by drawing on the idea of an omniscient power that defines virtue. The way the higher power is envisioned doesn't matter because it is still the source, support, and moral foundation of the goodself. Like most authoritarians, the goodself seeks power under the presumption that "It knows best."

Since A.A. is the original 12-Step organization and model for numerous others, we focus mainly on it. Although overtly leaderless (actually, old-time members assume leadership roles), A.A. shares many features of authoritarian cults: an unchallengeable written authority ("The Word"); commandments or rules to live by; a conversion experience achieved through inducing surrender to a super-human power; and dependency on the group, which often undermines relationships with those who do not accept the sanctity of the 12 Steps. Disagreement with any of the Steps is labeled denial or resistance. Like other authoritarian groups that manipulate fear and desire, fear of leaving is instilled by the often repeated warning "You can't make it without us."

As is true of every authoritarian structure, surrender is the key to making it work. Part One of this book details how the act of surrender itself has potent psychological repercussions. Giving control to something envisioned as more powerful and worthy than oneself not only temporarily eliminates conflict, but often enables one to feel renewed and even reborn. Feeling "reborn" is characteristic of all religious conversion experiences which, when combined with repentance and amends, gives an aura of wiping the moral slate clean. In A.A. what one is actually surrendering to are the 12 Steps and the unchallengeable assertion that if one "works the Steps" properly and long enough, they will perform the miracle of sobriety. But this miracle still requires continual group support because the 12 Steps do not eliminate one's inner split, but rather act to strengthen one side by suppressing the other. The goodself cannot contain the badself all on its own, no matter how lofty an ideology it assumes (or surrenders to). This is why it is important for such programs to have people acknowledge powerlessness for life, and thus be in continual need not only of the 12-Step ideology, but of group support.

The A.A. model not only programs people not to trust themselves, self-mistrust is essential for it to work. Its litany is "The 12 Steps work—don't question them." When someone does drop out, sure enough the addiction (the badself) resurfaces—as warned. On returning to A.A., the "We told you so" smug reproof further locks in the belief of being powerless. The group acts like a chorus of goodselves whose refrain is "You'll always lose control on your own." A.A. interprets its ability to predict relapses as a verification of its ideology (rather than of its ineffectiveness), using this to tighten authoritarian control over its members. But the model of a divided self explains far better why even after years of sobriety the siren-song of excess lurks beneath the surface, leaving no choice but to "take it [sobriety] one day at a time."

Any compulsion or addiction must contain a deep fear of a past state that in some fashion the addiction ameliorates. What is often feared is the dry, regimented life of being bottled up by the goodself with no outlets. Thus the life the badself creates has to become really bad, often life-threatening, before sobriety, which here means a return to the constraints of the goodself, has any real appeal. This is why A.A. continually emphasizes addicts need to hit bottom to change.

A.A. can serve as a stepping stone to major life changes. Some have successfully used it to gain stability long enough to shift priorities and find other sources of fulfillment. The strongest argument for such programs is that they work, or rather, work better on a mass scale, and cost less, than anything else available. Although there are some, particularly proponents of responsibility models, who seriously challenge the long-term efficacy of A.A. and its success rate. How well A.A. actually works is not our focus. Authoritarian structures of all sorts do indeed work to the degree that those in them obey their precepts. Like most authoritarian belief systems, the 12 Steps provide a powerful, mechanical strategy with fairly predictable results for those who conform.

A key question is how is "work" defined? We do not doubt that abstinence through A.A. could be far better for some than their previous desperate, dysfunctional lives. These programs can enable divided people to function in a social order whose values promulgate their inner division. Yet leading a manageable life only through believing one is unalterably sick is a very limited view of recovery. If stability is dependent on continually acknowledging one's basic powerlessness, it is seriously flawed. What remains is the underlying fear that one is untrustworthy at the deepest level.

"Cures" that do not bring an integration are disabling in their own way. People who fear being taken over at any instant by an element within themselves are crippled, though often less overtly so than before the goodself (with outside help) gained the upper hand. Any framework that does not take the division within people into account can never truly implement a cure, if by cure one means an integrated being who has self-trust, and thus is not susceptible to authoritarian manipulation. To live in fear of oneself is to be psychologically crippled.

A way of taking issue with our perspective takes this form: "Being critical without offering something better is questionable at best and arrogant at worst." We are in no way saying that people and the world (as it is now) would be better off without such programs. People do what they must to function and survive. This chapter does not offer a simple cure nor a specific therapy for addiction. Rather, it places the kind of addiction that involves conflict over control within the basic framework of authoritarianism. Our purpose is not only to show why such addictions belong there, but to offer a different frame for viewing it that does not foster adaptation to a dysfunctional social context that is itself increasingly out of control. Any "help" that contains unwanted behaviors through generating self-mistrust is just the old authoritarian machinery in disguise. And although this may bring some relief, it does so at the high cost of further crippling self-trust.

If addiction is an illness, the disease is authoritarianism. As in so many other areas, the cure society offers for the ills it creates and exacerbates through coercion is more coercion. Not only are 12-Step programs authoritarian, people (teens, employees, drunk drivers, wife-beaters) are being coerced to enter them as an alternative to more severe punishment. The 12 Steps work to the extent they do because they mirror the division within the social and moral order, helping divided people fit into a society that helped divide them. Authoritarian structures have been in operation for millennia because they "work"—i.e., they are good at accomplishing certain ends. But, by defining the rules, limits, and framework of change in advance, they are incompatible with a truly evolutionary model.

It is not surprising that a society with a polarized morality and a deep fundamentalist strain frames addiction as either bad or sick—"sick" becomes an ambiguous category that is at least not bad. The somber truth is that addicts are neither ill nor evil, but caught up in a social context, as we all are, that makes sanity and wholeness difficult to achieve. Whenever the root of the problem is the context, which exists not only in social structures but also in people's minds, there is a different way to implement change other than through therapies, cures, and behavioral controls. Trying to shift a deeply ingrained, even though outmoded, social and moral context can seem hopeless. But once it begins to lose its power to define and thus control, personal and eventually social change begin to accelerate. The remainder of this chapter speaks to this, with broader concerns than just addiction.

Developing Wholeness and Self-Trust

Feeling powerless and needing to surrender to an authority, be it a person or an ideology, is a deep part of our heritage. The struggle for control between the goodself (the compartment that has adopted values that cannot be lived up to) and the badself (the part judged to be base) has ramifications far beyond the individual level. Historically, in cultures that have taken on this division, controlling people through an ideology that fosters an inner split makes control much easier on a large scale. Once this division takes hold and the battle for inner control ensues, the sure outcome is loss of self-trust. Once self-trust is lost, looking to an external authority is inevitable.

Traditional religions that set up the division between the spiritual and the carnal, the selfless and the self-centered, propped up the goodself through threat and promise. With their moral authority they justified hierarchical authority, which made control at all levels of society possible. This reached deep into the basic unit of control where this division and the self-mistrust that comes from it are first implanted—the family. The traditional family conditions obedience to authority by undermining self-trust.[15] It is ironic that the so-called self-help programs with their 12 Steps create an extended family that does the same thing—undermine self-trust.

The spread of addiction is just one sign that the traditional moral props that have kept the devalued parts of being human

---

[15] "Love and Control" shows why the family, which promulgates the highest ideals around openness, support, loyalty, and unconditional acceptance, not only fosters the good/badself split, but is also where the badself most usually and violently displays itself. "The Ambiguity of Parental Authority" in *Control* describes at length the ways self-mistrust is conditioned by parents.

contained are not working. From our perspective it is authoritarianism, not limited abilities, that is preventing our species from finding solutions to controlling its self-destructive habits and appetites. Similarly, it is the inner authoritarian preventing people from finding new solutions to their own self-destructive proclivities. In order not to be subject to authoritarian control, whether internal or external, one must have a basic self-trust, which can only come if one is not at war with oneself. It is truly unknown what people's potential would be if they were not at war with themselves, as well as with others. The two types of conflict, internal and external, are not unrelated, as authoritarian hierarchy fosters both.[16]

Human beings are capable of and also need a wide spectrum of expression which has been divided by the old moral orders into what is considered the good (with selflessness as the paragon of goodness) and the bad (the selfish). Once this split is internalized, the goodself becomes the inner authoritarian trying to keep the devalued aspects submerged. Impossible ideals eventually give rise to extreme reactions. The occurrence of a rampant id on the loose (primitive self-centeredness) or a shallow society of me-firsters is far more likely in a world whose dualistic moral base divides people internally. The world we are living in is a testament to this. Actually real altruism—real selfless action not based on trying to live up to ideals and images, but which comes from empathy and care—is far more likely in a whole person.

Wholeness is not a chimerical nor fanciful concept. Those who have associated with tribal people sometimes marvel at their seeming wholeness compared to us more "civilized" folk. They in turn marvel at how we can complicate what for them are the simplest things. Their mysterious wholeness basically derives from animistic worldviews that do not dualistically separate the spiritual from nature, thus internally dividing them.[17] Although much can be learned from examining what makes

---

[16]See "Authority, Hierarchy, and Power."
[17]The chapters on animism in *Control* discuss this.

such people feel whole in themselves, connected with others, and in harmony with nature, their ways cannot be imposed on a modern technological culture. This is because their solution for curbing self-centeredness involves minimizing individuation and thus innovation. When such cultures face the need to change they usually disintegrate, as they don't have the internal mechanisms to do so. Yet that such people exist at all shows that being divided is culturally imposed rather than human nature.

There is a use of the word "wholeness" currently in vogue that really comes from the old polarized moral order. Here the ideal of wholeness is really selflessness in disguise, for a whole person is presented as giving, unconditionally loving, "a light unto oneself"—meaning not needing others, and the like. Within this view the so-called "negative" emotions (i.e., anger, possessiveness, and the need for self-enhancement) have either been conquered or are sufficiently small so as to no longer be a problem. Here, in trying to become whole, what people are inadvertently doing is trying to become better by curbing the badself. Not surprisingly, the way to achieve such wholeness is often thought to be through following teachers, including gurus, who present themselves as being whole. All this is just the old authoritarian morality with its renunciate values that perpetuate inner conflict. Bringing division while masquerading under the concept of wholeness is just another example of how authoritarian power hides behind goodself ideals.

Survival problems are global, involving the whole world. From our perspective it will take people who are whole to create the structures that can keep the world afloat. A conundrum for the times is how to become whole in social orders that create and reward divided people. This dilemma is one reason the framework we are offering does not lend itself to a facile therapy that can help people fit into the existent power structures. For the real problems are not merely personal, but structural.

Ultimately a morality is needed that can develop whole people through integrating and valuing both sides of the divided self. What this would necessarily mean is synthesizing the spiritual and animal (carnal), the selfless and self-centered, the altruistic and egoistic, so they can live comfortably with each other. This involves integrating the life-affirming aspects that are usually expressed by the badself: the spontaneous, the immediate, the pleasure-oriented, the so-called lazy (really that part of oneself that can luxuriate in timeless leisure). It does not mean discarding the equally valuable traits of the goodself: the productive, the capacity to defer immediate pleasures for future results, the responsible (the capacity to respond that takes account of implications), and the truly altruistic.

What to do? How does a divided person move toward wholeness? If authoritarianism is at the root of the division, then being told what to do cannot be the answer to building self-trust. Once trust is lost between people it is difficult to rebuild; the same holds true when self-trust is lost. So how does one build self-trust if it's not there? This personal dilemma is similar to a parallel quandary on the social level: How can people restructure social systems, a world leading to self-destruction, while having to operate within those very systems? Restructuring, whether psychological or social, is a bit like picking oneself up by one's own bootstraps.

The key to building self-trust in a changing world is the ability to utilize one's own experience, including mistakes, to change. This can be done even if one does not initially trust oneself. Self-trust is gained only by experiencing positive change through utilizing one's feedback, which begins to break the loop where mistrust breeds mistrust. Being in the throes of an internal war is one huge piece of feedback, not only that one's life isn't working, but also that one has a divided psyche whose parts thrive on the conflicts and drama engendered. Moreover, being fragmented makes it nigh impossible to tell the difference between what one really wants and "shoulds," which are often mistaken for true desires. Conflict, resistance, procrastination, and guilt can be indications of a divided self that acts differently than it thinks it ought.

We have no easy fixes to offer, yet one must start somewhere. Addiction has its own self-perpetuating momentum. Part of what makes addiction a closed system is the framework in which it is viewed by the person and by society at large. Changing the basic framework can not only open the system, but begins to change a person's capacity to read and integrate feedback. Fortunately, once restructuring is set in motion, if it brings a more appropriate way of dealing with life, it too has a momentum of its own. Societal structures, interpersonal activities, and even what one often considers the foundation of one's own personality are interwoven. The way they are constructed and viewed is largely a function of the human mind, which needs frameworks both to integrate experience and to have a culture that can be passed on to the next generation. Thus a shift in mental structures literally changes the way one perceives both oneself and the world at large. Such shifts are always a prerequisite of lasting change.

It is our hope that the perspectives offered in this book can be a tool for broadening awareness of the insidious and destructive nature of authoritarian control—whether external or internal. Seeing the nature of the division in oneself, including how both sides need each other to exist, begins to defuse the power of each. The inner battle depends on the dynamics between the two selves remaining unconscious, and so the more conscious one is of the split and its ramifications, the easier it is not to be mechanically driven by it. Once one begins to see the way the system works, the parts begin to lose their mysterious hold. The problem is that much of personality is built upon this division so that when both sides lose power, it can feel empty, and perhaps even a bit like dying. Yet it is only through a capacity to die to aspects of oneself that are not viable that any transformation ensues.

Becoming interested in seeing the nature of the game brings a crucial shift in awareness that allows one to discover for oneself the workings of one's own inner battle. Replacing the reactiveness of each side with curiosity and a respect that acknowledges the importance of each can be the beginning of a more healthy inner dialogue. Both the good and badself have powerful, compartmentalized, subjective filters that justify not only their existence, but their right to maintain rigid control. Becoming interested in the nature of the two selves and their collusions brings an emotional detachment from the drama that can allow the two sides to integrate. From this more objective vantage point the two selves can be viewed as a mechanical, static system in which neither side values nor trusts the other's point of view. This more inclusive perspective can allow one to transcend the power struggle as wholeness gradually develops, and with it a more fulfilling life.

Substance abuse is also an area where the problems lie not in substances, but in having people who are not whole. Now and throughout history, people have been using substances to alter consciousness in just about every culture known. There are scientists who maintain that not only do humans have a drive to alter consciousness, but so do many other animals as well. This is backed by both ethological and laboratory studies. Whether this is true or not, the idea that ideology and repression will stop most people from using or abusing substances is whistling in the wind.

Without an inner split, substances would not be needed to release the caged beast. Just as wholeness involves developing one's own relation with control and spontaneity, a whole person can also develop a healthy relation to substances. Once the realization that one is not fundamentally self-destructive begins to grow, self-trust and self-control also grow. This occurs not through effort, but rather as one stops doing what interferes with living. Since in this arena there can be no formulas, this would look different in different people. Some might decide that using certain substances at certain times enhances their lives and would use them as long as this were so. Others might find substances irrelevant to their lives and simply not use them. Still others might decide that substances are a hindrance to strengthening their whole self and would stop as long as they felt this way, without having to make absolute promises to themselves about an unknown future. Resolutions often stem from fear of oneself. By creating a cage the badself reacts against, such promises become inverted self-fulfilling prophecies in that they bring about the opposite of what is hoped for. This, of course, also erodes self-trust.

The emerging whole self does not judge the badself nor make resolutions like the goodself. Rather, it utilizes the information from each to construct something different and viable. This process is necessarily self-referential and thus involves paying attention to feedback of all kinds on a daily basis: What brings and deflates energy? Are one's "shoulds" and "oughts" (along with their rewards) what one really wants or were they mechanically programmed? Is the overall context of one's life enhancing or unfulfilling? Pain is information that reveals the limits of pleasure (i.e., when pleasure crosses over into self-destruction). Really, neither substances nor ostensible susceptibility to them is the problem. Once the good and badselves are disempowered through awareness and a way of living that makes them irrelevant, substances no longer trigger repressed energy that makes one "lose control."

In each moment life contains both the accumulations of the past and the seeds of the future. Creating something new out of the old is what makes the future different. Authoritarian moralities do not value or support anything that threatens their hold on people's minds. This is why creativity is often taken over by the badself. It is not unusual to see it associated with self-destructiveness. Some, being out of step with the social order, can only loosen the constraints of their inner authoritarian through drugs or "anti-social" behavior.

Addiction is just one expression of a world that is morally dysfunctional. The old moral orders used to work neatly within accumulation societies that utilized authoritarian hierarchies of power to maintain order. Moralities that adulate sacrifice dictate the sacrifice of the individual to whatever higher cause the power-holders construct as higher. Having people who are inwardly divided without self-trust, who are given some security and a modicum of authority over others based on accepting their position in the hierarchy, makes authoritarian power work. (Even the lowest-ranked males were given authoritarian power in the family.)

Feelings of powerlessness that go far beyond addiction are rife. This is because the old authoritarian mechanisms for bestowing power are crumbling—crumbling because they are not viable in a world demanding more awareness and consciousness from all of humanity in order to survive. In this time of social and moral upheaval, whole not divided people are needed to help construct survival-oriented strategies and structures. We are not suggesting there is a simplistic, universal explanation for all the world's ills. However, any moral system that denies or devalues basic human dispositions must divide people's inner being. This results in an ongoing battle for control with a wide array of dysfunctional and destructive consequences. Given that authoritarianism is deeply embedded in the morality and socialization process of much of the world, it is not outlandish to postulate it is a core element within planetary problems.

The old mechanisms of social control are predicated on group cohesion, rewards for obedience, and fear. What has been feared is not only punishment in secular spheres, but also that an omniscient intelligence is tallying up the moral score that will decide one's fate (in this life or the next). Social control depended upon a propped-up goodself. Now the props are failing, the social order is breaking down, and badselves are breaking out all over. Rampant addiction is a particularly graphic symptom of a society gone awry. Any solution that does not address this is merely a Band-Aid that misses the mark. Instead of trying harder to fortify the goodself, which will not work, a process-oriented morality is necessary that can help bring about whole people.

This is why we call addiction a moral disorder. The challenge the world faces is not only restructuring the authoritarian sociopolitical mechanisms of power and control, but also restructuring the authoritarian climate of values to foster human beings who can wholly express the full range of being human. Global survival can occur only by unleashing humanity's potential for intelligence and creativity. Thus, not fostering whole people is now the real threat. We maintain wholeness can occur only through truly caring about something other than oneself, without denying one's interest in personal enhancement. On a larger social scale this would necessitate a more livable moral framework that gives equal validity and value to both the selfless and the self-centered.

Our perspective of wholeness could be criticized as another panacea that is not within the range of most people, who have to struggle with the harsh constrictions of their lives and the reality of who they are. Consequently, its relevance could be questioned. It is true that becoming whole involves the kind of deep changes that are difficult. Nevertheless, to bring about a workable world more people must become whole, through whatever process or miracle. Divided people cannot truly trust themselves and so must look to authorities for their sense of worth, as well as to solve the endless conflicts being divided brings. Unless a social movement toward wholeness occurs, which means new values, the answer to the question "Who is in control?" will be sadly repetitious: it will be those people and structures whose vested interests and power depend upon having divided, fearful people. Here who is in control is ultimately whoever or whatever controls the mind by dividing it. This is the deepest meaning of mind control.

Love and Control

The Conditions Underlying
Unconditional Love

The experience of love is so primary and vital that examining it could risk missing its essence. We take this risk because, like it or not, experiences of love are conceptualized, and the ways this is done impact the ongoing nature of the experience. If ideals of what love is, or should be, come from authoritarian ideologies, love becomes another human emotion that is often unknowingly bent to the service of authoritarian control. Moreover, if ideals about love are unlivable, this both distorts emotions and makes covert control in the name of love inevitable. In order to clarify why we think it important to examine love and control together, we first map out the basic issues and concerns before going into specific areas and more practical examples.

Many people want to keep love and control separate, perhaps because they have experienced being controlled in the name of love. Parents give and withhold affection as reward and punishment, as do adults with each other. Traditional religions have God give love for obedience, and make obedience the proof of loving God. Love for king or country is displayed by a willingness to die or kill for them. Mothers who use self-sacrificing love to generate guilt as a way of controlling their children are legend in psychological literature. Examples abound of utilizing the power of love to control. What these examples have in common are conditions; that is, receiving love is dependent upon meeting externally imposed conditions.

Is there a kind of love that does not set conditions or boundaries, that does not wax and wane with the vicissitudes of time? The concept of such a love and its existence are very important to many people, both to be able to give and receive it. Unconditional love is presented as the pinnacle of love. The concept permeates our culture and fantasies and is described in many ways: eternal love, absolute love, undying love, true love, selfless love, pure love that asks for no return, love that knows no bounds and does not measure, love as total acceptance, and love so boundless it can encompass everyone, perhaps even everything, without preference.

Are there then two kinds of love—conditional and unconditional, impure and pure, temporal and eternal, carnal and spiritual? Or is the former an inferior and incomplete expression of the latter? Or is conditional love not really love at all, but rather a hidden expression of self-centered desires? Or as some cynics have said, is all love merely a romantic invention? From our perspective, the above questions come from a specific framework about love—a framework that artificially divides the selfless from the self-centered. Our main concern is to show this division is at the root of the confusions about love.

At this point we ask the indulgence of the reader who may become impatient with such analysis, for popular wisdom has love as essentially undefinable. Even more, some say any attempt to define it sullies it, destroying its magic. We do not take issue with the inability of words to capture the essence of love. Words cannot ultimately encapsulate much of life, let alone its deepest emotions and experiences. Even something as prosaic as experiencing the color red cannot really be captured by words. Yet one can say that red is more similar to orange than it is to green; and love is more similar to affection than it is to disinterest. The point of this chapter is not to play word games, but to show that what is called love is indeed conceptualized, that the ways this is done inevitably impact the experience of it, and that traditional conceptualizations are limiting its natural expressions. More-over, the way love is conceived of is part of the structure of hidden control within a social order.

What Is Unconditional Love?

We do not doubt the magical quality of love, nor its central importance. A life without love is barren. Yet people are having difficulties with intimacy and love—from the prevalence of unhappy and violent families, divorce, and loneliness, to new types of problems such as reluctance to get involved, "women who love too much," and "love addiction."

We focus on the ideal of unconditional love because it is a concept deeply interwoven in the fabric of both social and personal control. We wish to show that the vital human experience of love has been conceptualized by a polarized moral order that structures, distorts, and even sabotages natural expressions of love, care, and bonding. The concept of unconditional love does not stand alone but is part of a broader constellation of values that separates the pure from the impure, the selfless from the self-centered, and the spiritual from the worldly. These are the two poles around which traditional morality revolves. What we wish to show is how this polarization unrealistically pits self-enhancement against care for others, as if they were isolated from and antagonistic to each other.

The very ideal of unconditional love contains seeming paradoxes. On one level it is presented as love beyond measure or measurement; yet on another level, it sets a standard for love against which other expressions of it are measured. So love that does not measure is made the measure of love. Also, to the extent that people need to experience love, that need is self-centered; yet the need for love can only be filled by breaking out of self-centered needs. Do I love you simply because you're you, or because doing so ignites emotions in me that are fulfilling? Love is only fulfilling when I break out of myself and connect with you. It comes by breaking through the boundaries of the very self that needs it. And that experience in turn feeds the self, so much so that one becomes attached to who or whatever brings it about. The paradox stated another way is that to satisfy me, I have to break out of me. These conundrums are artificial and unnecessary in that they come from the way thought creates a hard separation between self and other, and between the selfless and selfish. Unconditional love is a concept that derives from such polarizations.[1]

Generally, placing conditions on others stems from some self-centered concern. Each of the following refers back to oneself: "I'll keep loving you if you return my love; don't hurt me; do what I want; don't interfere with what I want to do; don't try to change me; make me only feel good"; etc. Unconditional love can only mean love that does not vary with how one is treated, or with anything else, for that matter. The ideal of unconditional love is that it gives unendingly without measure, while asking for nothing in return. It is, in short, selfless. Also, to feel one is the recipient of unconditional love, whether from a person (mother) or an image of perfection (Christ or a guru), means feeling totally accepted, no matter what.

When the ideals that surround love cannot be lived up to because they negate or demean vital aspects of being human, what results is more than merely disappointment. The internalization of unrealistic values inevitably creates serious personal and relational problems. Insofar as people try to embody unlivable values, they must either knowingly fall short or delude themselves. Also, eventually feeling let down or even betrayed is built into having such expectations of others. Another result of internalizing unlivable ideals is susceptibility to manipulation by

---

[1]"The Power of Abstraction: The Sacred Word and the Evolution of Morality" describes how dualism and either/or thinking have been used to build concepts for social and moral control. The nature of paradox and its use as a dominance ploy are discussed in "The Assault on Reason," "The One-Sidedness of Oneness" in "Oneness," and in the section on Buddhism in *Control*.

individuals who purport to exemplify these ideals.[2]

To say the concept of unconditional love is part of the foundational edifice of authoritarian beliefs at first appears to be an anomaly. For is it not the very antithesis of control? In order to clarify this it is necessary to examine these issues:

1. Why the concept resonates with people and has the great appeal that it does.

2. The worldview and implications embedded in the concept.

3. How the concept is part of a polarized moral order that dualistically separates the selfless from the self-centered, valuing the former and denigrating the latter; and how this split is utilized for authoritarian control.[3]

4. How the want either to give or receive unconditional love sets in motion unconscious forces that keep people from being whole.

People flourish when feeling connected to others. The question is if there is, as with other social animals, an inbuilt capacity to connect, why are many people experiencing great difficulty in doing so? In examining these issues, we will discuss many problematic aspects of today's relationships, such as power, control, boundaries, unconscious roles, measuring, holding on, and forgiving.

A good deal of the powerful appeal of the concept of unconditional love lies in it not merely being an abstract fabrication. It is grounded in people's experience in two ways: at times the experience of love does, in that moment, feel free of any constraints, boundaries, conditions, or expectations. And also, most people have had a period (early infancy at least) when they were the recipient of total acceptance, no matter what. Both experiences are very powerful, the memory of which brings a yearning

---

[2]See "Guru Ploys" for examples. "The Seductions of Surrender" shows why people confuse surrender with love.

[3]"Good and Evil" in "Satanism and the Worship of the Forbidden: Why It Feels Good to Be Bad" contains more on this split.

for their return. There is also a natural desire to feel special and be loved and accepted for what one is, which easily translates into a yearning for total acceptance all the time.

If it is possible to experience something akin to unconditional love, both as a giver and receiver, why call it a concept? With some trepidation, acknowledging the limitations of words, let's examine what's involved. The actual experiencing of love brings an energy, a level of excitation that breaks through personal boundaries as one connects with something outside oneself. In that moment, the concerns and import of one's internal dramas vanish. Along with this, an emotional bath permeates the whole nervous system in a way that feels more than good. It feels wonderful in the full meaning of the word, for it includes a sense of wonder. The capacity to connect and bond over time is part of being a social animal.

This experience is basic, primary—it is what it is, and while in its spell, questions of its nature do not arise. It is when its intensity fades that the mind compares love's presence to its absence. Then it can be described as timeless, eternal, selfless, conditionless—in short, all the characteristics that distinguish it from other experiences. The basic mistake is in taking an experience that feels timeless and saying one could and should be that way "all the time." This in effect puts love back in time, while projecting timeless qualities onto it. That is, the experience of love without conditions occurs in a timeless-feeling living moment, but the concept of unconditional love is drenched with future considerations wherein one expects to love or be loved timelessly all the time. This confusion lies at the heart of the concept of unconditional love.[4]

So what? One can easily wonder what difference any of this makes. This is not merely an intellectual exercise to show logical inconsistencies. Rather, insofar as unconditional love is consid-

---

[4]See "Oneness, Enlightenment, and the Mystical Experience" on the analogous confusion between mystical experiences that feel timeless and the ways they are conceptualized into an ideal state of being timeless all the time.

ered the pinnacle of love to which people aspire, what results is internalizing the historical split that defined the spiritual as self-less and denigrated fulfilling both carnal and self-enhancing worldly needs. In practice what this means is love, like spirituality, becomes tied to sacrifice, particularly self-sacrifice. The ramifications of this are gargantuan, for this pits people against their animal nature. It is another way of compartmentalizing the psyche into a pure part that at least tries to give without expectations, in the name of love, while labeling the part that wants some reciprocity impure. This fosters masochism and martyrdom, resulting in such diverse phenomena as women taking abuse and men sacrificing themselves for this or that ideal, no matter what the consequences.[5]

Conditional and unconditional are themselves abstract categories within a dualistic framework constructed by thought. When these two concepts are placed in opposition they display this conundrum: to want to give or receive unconditional love is to place a condition on love—namely, that it have no conditions. This is not just a play on words. Abstractions by their nature leave out the living context, and when dealing with emotions, this is particularly treacherous. If the abstraction omits or denigrates important aspects of the living situation, strange and often harmful consequences and distortions result. To adequately capture the confusion within the ideal of unconditional love and the conflicts this ideal causes, it is necessary to go into the relation between time and the timeless.

---

[5]"Religion, Cults, and the Spiritual Vacuum" and "The Power of Abstraction" show the link between religion, morality, and self-sacrifice. The latter describes the evolution of this split between the pure and impure, its link with authoritarianism, and how seemingly remote abstractions impact life. "Who Is in Control?" details how authoritarian ideologies internally divide people, creating a divided self locked in inner conflict.

Love, Time, and Timelessness

We will leave aside the metaphysics of time, which involves such issues as whether time is an objective property of the universe; whether it is tied into the subjective way the human mind experiences the universe (as Kant thought); or whether it makes any sense even to try to distinguish those two conceptions from each other. What is important is that people do experience both being in time and being timeless, and that these two modes feel different. Whenever one is totally absorbed in anything, or when thought stills, the feeling of the flow of time disappears, for one is simply involved in the present. Feeling love can be absorbing, thus timeless.

Experiencing oneself as part of the flow of time ("being in time") involves the mind being aware at some level of the past and future. Goals, agendas, desires, fears, expectations, and ambitions involve utilizing memory to project into the future, giving a sense of continuity, thus time. All these attempt to create conditions in the future. In fact, conditions can only be placed on the future, not the present. The present, similarly to love, just is what it is. Anything one might want another to do or not do has to be in the future, by definition. Thus the very act of placing conditions puts one in time. One can want something now; but although the wanting occurs in the present, it can only be realized or not in the future. This includes wanting a state one is in to continue.

Of course all moments, including projections into the past or future, occur only in the present. It takes awareness of the past and future to give a sense of continuity and thus time in a given moment. An experience is called timeless to distinguish it from instances when one more feels the flow of time. The word "timeless" only has meaning because it stands out as different in a context of experiencing time's flow. The inner psychological state of experiencing the flow of time and the experience of being timeless each need the other for contrast to be perceived at all. The concept of timelessness itself can only arise by comparing the memory of a timeless moment to other more time-bound ones. It takes a being who can remember, project, and think about the past and future to recognize a different state that feels out of time. This pair of seeming opposites, time and timelessness, are actually embedded in each other and thus have what we call a dialectical relationship.[6]

Ideals of unconditional love sacralize only the timeless by describing love as not fluctuating with time. Examples of such ideals are that true love asks for nothing in return; it doesn't try to change the other person; and even that it lasts forever. Interestingly, these concepts which appear to be beyond the encroachments of time all have a referent to time: "forever" refers to all of time; no change or fluctuation can only occur through time; asking for nothing or not trying to change the other implies continuity within a way of being over time. All these are reactions against time that involve time by projecting an endless continuity into the future.

Even though the experience of love can feel timeless, without conditions, what is often ignored is that the experience always occurs in a given context. The context is very much in time and contains conditions. People do not experience a timeless moment in a bubble, but come to it with a past and with hopes and expectations for the future. Wanting the feeling of love to continue, fearing its loss, or being disappointed by a lack of reciprocity all inoculate time into a timeless moment, thus changing it. Though love feels timeless, saying "I love you" usually means more or is taken to mean more than "I'm feeling these emotions now, and that's it." "I love you" suggests some continuity in time, and implies at least some ongoing context that allows the feelings of love to root and flower.

We wish to make it clear that although love in the moment feels unconditional, this only occurs in a setting that both has

---

[6]"Transforming the Symbol System" in "The Power of Abstraction" explains more fully what is meant by dialectical.

and needs conditions for its continuance. So timeless love is embedded in a context of time. Though the actual feelings do occur in the present, they filter into and are reflected in the temporal context of one's life in such a way that love is not merely a momentary occurrence. This is why saying "I love you" has future implications.

The magic of love is that it can occur unpredictably; and when it does, it opens up a path or valence for its special chemistry to reoccur. Once love comes, unless one is highly defended and fearful, it is most usual to want to stay open to it. Of course, if one has been badly hurt, feeling love again can be frightening enough to cause withdrawal. The real issue and difficulty in human relations is maintaining a context that allows love to keep regenerating. Since many contexts do just the opposite, it is common to try to cage and possess love with contracts out of fear, in the hope that this will make it stay. The problem is that for a context to allow regeneration it cannot be static, but itself must be changing, as are the people involved. What is changing through time are the conditions that keep the valence for love open.

Self-Sacrifice, Power, and Passion

When selflessness is made the essence of virtue, and being self-centered is considered if not out-and-out bad, certainly less than good, this causes great confusion around matters of the heart. Do I love you because you're you? Or do I love you because you ignite powerful feelings in me? Is it my deep feelings that count, or is it you? Is one "in love with love"—with one's own feelings of being in love—or with the other person? What am I to do if because of conflict, anger, disappointment, or just lack of newness these feelings erode and someone else appears who reignites them? Do I sacrifice these new feelings for your sake in the name of love, or do I follow wherever the intensity of passion leads? Resolving this difficult quandary is not helped by framing love as selfless giving, and passion as carnal and selfish. This turns loving into a duty because of promises, ideals, or an understandable

268

reluctance to hurt the other person. This further erodes love by not taking into account the context, which has changed to the extent that the old magic is dulled. Reigniting a waning love does not come from duty or self-sacrifice, but from changing the context that no longer provides the necessary ambiance.

Many of us when we were young fell in love with someone dazzling and out of reach, perhaps an older classmate or a movie star. And although the emotions were both excruciating and exquisite, the context could not sustain these feelings because it did not contain certain conditions necessary to do so. Mainly the flow of emotion was just too one-way. To say that this is not real love but merely an infatuation is to place an arbitrary judgment on deep feelings. Such feelings usually occur in a particular context, adolescence, that ideally one outgrows. If true love should truly ask for no return, then keeping such unrequited emotions going would be laudable and healthy, which it is not. This love could not sustain itself because it is totally unbalanced—as is the ideal that true love asks for no return.

Getting into a calculus of who's giving and who's getting seems an anathema to love. Yet equating love with only giving becomes a covert authoritarian prescription on how to be, and is an artificial construction of a morality that depends on a selfless/self-centered dichotomy. Love does not fit into this dichotomy, and to try to make it do so disables people from intelligently giving or receiving information. "You're being selfish"; "You don't love me anymore"; "You're trying to control me" are commonly used when ideals are not being met. These are all signs that something is missing or has eroded in the context that needs examination. Ideals of unconditional love not only do not help this but can further divide people from each other, and also divide them internally as they struggle with their selfish and selfless parts. When love is present there is no struggle, as giving and getting are not separable. When people separate them it is a sign of imbalance.

Internalizing the concept of unconditional love is damaging to the creation of a context in which love can thrive. It is yet another way of taking on an unlivable ideal that either makes people feel inadequate insofar as they are not living up to it, or unconscious insofar as they think they are. It also sets up an illusory ideal of purity whose verbiage is deeply interwoven within the framework of authoritarian control. Of course, through loving one may give unconditionally at any moment. This is not at issue, nor is it what the ideal is really about. Rather, the ideal of unconditional love entails being unconditional all the time. Such ideals not only create dysfunctional relationships but lead to unconscious expressions of power and control that are detrimental to love. Control itself is not necessarily damaging and may even be enhancing, if those involved are exercising it consciously and with care.

Love has an energy that breaks open the boundaries of the self, and in doing so is a connector that brings joy and meaning beyond self-enhancement. The experience of love can feel selfless, and when in love people often do put the other's concerns first. Because this does occur in love, it is easy to assume that one can recreate love or show it by putting the other first. This is how the ideal of self-sacrifice gets tied to love.

Images of this abound in religion, which sets the tone. In Christianity God shows love for his creation by sacrificing that which means most to him (his son) in order to save a tainted humanity (tainted with self-centeredness). The image of Christ on the cross equates love with suffering, and suffering with atonement. Christ, as the only pure (meaning not self-centered) temporal being, gives his life and love totally and unconditionally to save others. Monotheism itself, with rare exception (deism), makes selflessness and subservience the supreme virtues. If one is the creation of a willful God, then what other purpose can there be than serving his divine will? To counter God's dictates would not only be "bad," but foolish. Christ as the dutiful son of an authoritarian father is the perfect model of willing self-sacrifice and submission to "higher" purposes.

The Eastern concepts of enlightenment and cosmic unity likewise have intrinsic implications that idealize selflessness:

Here the image is of the perfect master or enlightened one who has merged with the godhead by going beyond the illusion of separateness to the extent of no longer identifying with oneself as a separate entity. Hence there is no ego, and all activities that spring from such a being are solely for the benefit of others. "Enlightened masters" are presented as loving all of humanity unconditionally, having incarnated (returned in human form to the wheel of rebirth) for the sole purpose of leading others toward higher states.[7]

It is one thing to put aside self-interest as a natural expression of care within a living context; it is quite another to be expected to do so as proof of love. This expectation can be from others or oneself. The concept of pure love automatically becomes institutionalized, as such expectations bring roles, duties, and rules that structure and control behavior. Christ's love is supposedly pure and unconditional; yet unless one obeys Christianity's rules one ends up in hell or purgatory, or in a more sophisticated version of divine retribution, one is denied God's presence. The guru claims to love unconditionally; but unless one surrenders to him totally (meaning obeys his rules) he loses interest. Parents are supposed to demonstrate love for their children by sacrificing for them; in return, children are supposed to obey. The wife's traditional role in the family has been to sacrifice her individuation for husband and children in the name of love.

We do not question the necessity of mothers, society, or the human species as a whole giving priority to the well-being of children, which includes loving them. All societies pay lip service to the importance of children but still expect parents, especially women, to do what is necessary. One reason our species is at risk is that children's well-being is left to isolated families in general, and mothers in particular, who are no longer equipped to do

---

[7]See "The Function of Enlightenment" in "Oneness." "What Is Selfless Service Serving?" in *Control* discusses the contradictions and ramifications of this value within Buddhism and other renunciate religions.

271

what is needed on their own. In this regard society is similar to an absentee parent. The old social and moral orders are built on women placing children and men first. No matter how modern one is, it is difficult not to have either deeply rooted expectations or reactions coming from these foundations and values.

The ways values are constructed in a society and internalized by its members are an integral part of both social and intimate control. Not only does society justify control through its values, it also uses them to allocate resources and determine priorities that then control the direction society goes. If a prime value is being the strongest military power, this trickles down very tangibly to control the lives of those under that prescription. Also, and not incidentally, values are what people use to control themselves.[8]

We are not questioning the value of values. There must be shared values, at some level at least, in order for people to cooperate at all. Rather, we are elucidating how valuing purity comes from a polarized moral order that uses a misleading concept of purity as a standard of measuring worth. The more absolute a standard, the easier it is to use as a measuring rod. This is why gold, whose purity can be measured relatively easily, became the standard for measuring material wealth. Investing the concepts of both love and virtue with purity sets an identical standard of selflessness for each that is used to establish worth along a linear, hierarchical scale of value—that is, the more selfless one is, the better.[9]

Pure and impure are concepts embedded in each other. Like so many other oppositions, they have meaning only in relation to each other. A moral order that values purity over impurity sets up a hierarchy of value whereby what is considered not totally pure is measured against a standard of purity. Thus in the designated impure sector, the purer the better. So if pure love sets no conditions, then the less conditions impure love sets, the better.

---

[8]See "Who Is in Control" on the inner conflict that is a reaction against self-control based on authoritarian values.

[9]"Renunciation as Accumulation" at the end of "Oneness" shows why ideals of purity, ironically, are a product of the accumulation mentality.

And also, if pure virtue is defined as selfless intentions, then the more selfless one's intentions are, the more virtuous one is. That is why the concept of unconditional love as beyond measure is actually a measuring device. If pure love is linked with sacrifice, then the purity of one's love can be measured by how much one sacrifices. Ideals of purity are necessarily only linked with individuals, which leads to an atomistic view of relationships. This notion cannot incorporate the idea that relationships are systems that affect the nature of individual control. Instead such ideals presuppose people could be (and should be) totally in control of how giving or sacrificing they are, as if the relationship had no effect on this. The logical extension of this framework would conclude the worse a relationship is, the more one can prove one's purity and love through sacrifice.

Nothing occurs purely as if in a vacuum, outside any context. Authoritarian hierarchies of power have been a pervading context ever since humanity moved into its early accumulation phase. Love, too, as a natural human expression only occurs within a context.[10] Perhaps one of the most uncomfortable areas to examine with honesty and clarity is the relationship between love and power. Would one surrender to and love God, a leader, or guru if they were not perceived as powerful?[11]

The ideal of unconditional love places love in a realm beyond power, which is thought to tarnish the purity of love. What this actually does is promote a double standard for morality. The concept of selfless love reinforces a double standard by compartmentalizing not only a social order, but the psyches of those within it. There are supposedly two spheres: that of love, which telescopes into spirituality, and that of power, which is so obvi-

---

[10]"The Seductions of Surrender" describes the mechanical ways passion occurs in authoritarian contexts of submission.

[11]"The Power of Abstraction" describes the way accumulation shifted the structures of power and morality. This development is covered in more depth in "The Roots of Authoritarianism," a section in *Control.* "Satanism and the Worship of the Forbidden" discusses the intrinsic link between worship and power.

ously corrupting. The arenas where selfless virtue can at least be attempted are mother-love, romantic love, spiritual questings, humanitarian causes. And then there are the areas of competition and power where "dirtying one's hands" is expected. Thus the priest, holy man, or mother is expected to be pure or more pure than the soldier, politician, businessman, or actress. A double standard of morality means that the rules of the game are different for each arena. The former are supposed to devote their lives to being a model for others through serving, while the latter devote their lives to achieving—which more often involves sacrificing scruples than self-interest. Historically, the split between the pure and impure also displayed itself along gender lines whereby women were expected to be sexually and morally more pure (meaning chaste and giving), and men were allowed far more leeway.

Wanting to keep these two spheres separate is an attempt to keep love incorruptible, thus pure. This cannot really be done, however, for love is not only expressed in contexts of power, but is itself, potentially at least, a manifestation of power. Popular maxims that refer to "the power of love" or claim "Love can move mountains" attest to this. Where love and power interface is where the difficulties arise. Attempting to purify love by eliminating power does not do so, but instead makes the way power is expressed less conscious and more covertly manipulative.

There can be great passion in surrendering to another. In authoritarian hierarchies surrender is structured in through submission. In hierarchical religions submission is to God or the guru; in traditional patriarchies it is to the ruler and to males. Dominance and submission create a context for emotional surrender. We call this "authoritarian surrender," as it involves submission without resistance through internalizing authoritarian values. Like surrender in other contexts, it opens boundaries that can allow feelings of love. As long as one is content to accept the submissive role, the good feelings can be sustained. One reason people do remain submissive in such a structure is that it is easy to become attached to the emotions generated by it. Here through surrender to roles, what feels like unconditional love is really a function of a context that is conditional on submission. Loving God is always a sure bet to generate passion because submission is built in.

Mother-love, the world's paragon of unconditional love, demonstrates the connection between love and power both on a personal and cultural level. The most usual context where unconditional love is experienced is between mother and child, particularly between mothers and young children. It can, of course, occur between fathers and children, too. However, it seems that men have an easier time maintaining their boundaries, especially with infants. Since women bear and nurture children with their bodies, it makes evolutionary sense for them to have some genetic hard-wiring that makes it more difficult to maintain boundaries with their children. One only has to observe the different effect a crying baby has on a man and woman. Whether or not such gender differences are genetic, the archetype of mother-love is that of acceptance and giving that starts with the breast and is sustained no matter what. The popular cliché "Only a mother could love him" expresses the expectations placed on the steadfastness of mother-love.

In many cultures where sex roles are sharply divided and male dominance a given, motherhood is held sacrosanct. These kinds of statements are inherent in such cultures: "My mother is a saint"—meaning she sacrifices an inordinate amount for others. And from a mother to son, "No one will love you as I do"—meaning no one will put him first the way she does. Placing mothers and motherhood on a pedestal can be so extreme that insults to either have been known to have mortal consequences. In such cultures not only is the primary emotional bond usually between mother and son rather than husband and wife, but a woman's power comes through her sons. The woman without sons is pitied.

Women, like men, are interested in protecting their survival, well-being, and position in a social order that impacts the quality of their lives. When women are denied direct access to power they have little alternative but to utilize men to gain security. Since their basic well-being is physically dependent on men, the traditional route of female power is to have men emotionally dependent on them. The ideal that a woman should be self-sacrificing controls her, and through it she controls (or tries to) those she sacrifices to. This is the stuff of guilt and resentment for all concerned. The unacknowledged, opaque intertwining of control and self-sacrifice has propelled people into endless hours of therapy and fills countless pages in novels and psychology books.

Rigid sex roles develop different spheres of power between the sexes, where each considers the other naive, even childish. As their development in the other's sphere is stunted, there is some truth to it. Women often say, "Men are really little boys," meaning their emotional development is arrested and they are self-absorbed. Men say, "Women are like children, they need protection," meaning they are weak and could not survive or even understand the harsh realities of the world. Traditionally both men and women had a vested interest in keeping separate, complementary realms of power, as it gave security and shape to their lives. This kept each sex childish in the other's realm by having them continue as adults to act out the roles of mother and father for each other. Traditionally women relied on men for economic support and physical protection; men relied on women for emotional support and physical maintenance.

When denied power in one sphere, attempting to get it in another that is culturally acceptable is inevitable. This is why women's power came from emotional and sexual manipulation. Although in modern societies sex roles are blurring, the traditional spheres of power are not as removed from modern life as it might seem. Many modern women complain that what men really want in a wife is a mother—someone who puts them first and builds her life around them. To the extent that a woman makes sacrificing herself for her children her prime identity (especially as they get older), she is teaching them that love is sacrifice. This usually translates differently to male and female children. Males come to expect being put first by a woman and associate that with being loved; females learn that's the way to get and keep a man and often equate others' need and dependency with being loved. Also, mothers come to expect their daughters to embody and display love for them through sacrifice, which is why the mother/daughter relationship usually comes with the most painful, convoluted baggage.

Many contemporary families have a usually unconscious collusion around power and authority that has the ideal of unconditional love woven through it. Now that the authoritarian father is out of fashion, the covertly authoritarian mother often fills the power vacuum. Mothers typically equate their willingness always to put their children first with the idea that they know what's best for them. This culturally supported belief can be used to control the entire family: "It's time to go home, dear— the children have to go to bed."

Many fathers happily collude with this because they cannot or do not want to compete with the amount of giving mother-love is customarily thought to involve. So they usually abdicate bottom-line responsibility for the day-to-day well-being of the child. This creates a vicious circle, for when men leave the field they do become more out of touch with their children, thus reinforcing the woman's conviction she does indeed "know best." How often does one see a father eagerly hand over a crying baby, saying a little sheepishly, "There's nothing like a mother." The woman's contented and sometimes condescending look comes not only from her belief that she alone can quiet the child, but also because this is her source of emotional fulfillment and power. Fathers could quiet a child, too, if they cared to figure out how.

When fathers do directly care for children, mothers typically think it should be done by their standards, which the men generally fall short of. Society promotes the value that good mothers always put their children first. Men concur, but rarely wish to meet such high standards of sacrifice themselves. They thus collude with mothers being child-centered, and seek avenues of power and amusement outside the family while the woman becomes the family's emotional bedrock. Mother-love, in becoming connected with service and sacrifice, often also becomes the basis of unconscious authoritarian control.

Many men initially make promises to share the responsibility equally without really knowing what's involved. Women often feel betrayed when the men fail to do so. They resent being more responsible for the children, especially if they have another job. Yet they are generally unconsciously attached to being their children's primary emotional center and authority on what's best for them, and to the overall power in the family this brings. They want more help, but on their terms, retaining the centrality of authority. Since this essentially makes the mother the father's boss around childrearing, he predictably resists involvement, which brings more resentment from the woman.

This not unusual scenario has deep ramifications in the nooks and crannies of control within a family, including damaging a couple's erotic life. An alternative to what we call "child-centeredness" (making the child's needs primary) is to realize the best and most secure thing for a child long term is for the parents to be fulfilled as individuals and happy with each other. This would involve a different context of responsibility and power aimed at balancing the needs of all concerned. It also involves making the couple's intimacy and sexual connection a priority.[12]

Control and Boundaries

Modern reactions against familial control have utilized the concept of unconditional love in an attempt to do away with control in intimacy. The institution of marriage controlled behavior through roles, idealistic vows, the contractual nature of the institution, and great social pressure to live up to the contract. The phrase "bonds of matrimony" indicates that people expected to be controlled. Now many modern people have a different attitude

---

[12]"The Ambiguity of Parental Authority" in *Control* discusses power and control in the family.

toward relationships and marriage in that they are gun-shy of control and take this stand: "People shouldn't try to control each other, especially if they love each other. To love someone is to accept them as they are." Wanting to be loved for who one is and to love that way in return is understandable, and is another of the great appeals of the idea of unconditional love.

Complete acceptance, either given or received, when occurring creates an emotional bath, the waters of which are compellingly comfortable. But wanting or expecting total acceptance to be totally there all the time is to put futures on an experience that only occurs in the living present. If one was fortunate, infancy had many such moments; but even in infancy, parents begin early to shape children to fit their needs and values. Parents vacillate between giving acceptance and giving messages of their prerogatives to control. As the child ages, acceptance and obedience become more and more interwoven; the child learns that obedience creates a context for acceptance.

Freeing oneself from parental authority and judgments is part of the process of growing up. Though wanting acceptance without control is understandable in an adolescent, should the desire never to be controlled persist in adulthood, this ensures the continuation of adolescence. This is because intimacy in adult relationships contains both the exercise of power and the desire at least sometimes to control the other.

Roles, when accepted, minimize conflict by prescribing behavior and designating spheres of power. But in any long-term relationship where roles are fluid and people value not being role-bound, power struggles around values, what to do, and who gets their way are inevitable. Since intimacy necessarily gives each person some power to control the other, to avoid dealing with the realities of control is to avoid growing up. This is a historically new challenge that evolved as democratic and anti-sexist values infiltrated private life.

Intimacy builds through time as one learns to trust that one's more open boundaries will not be abused too casually. Intimacy can be a context for acceptance but does not guarantee it in every instance. Ironically, the higher one's ideals, in practice the less one may accept the other not meeting them. Absolute values, such as "always being there for each other," bring hurt, disappointment, or resentment, and ultimately more closure.

The ideal of unconditional love also creates more closure. It proclaims that boundaries should remain open no matter what the other does, and that any accommodations made must be done within oneself without trying to control the other. The alternative is thinking one can still love unconditionally with closed boundaries. For instance, people have claimed to love someone unconditionally, even though they do not want to see the person again. What can this mean? One thing it does mean is that they are more involved with their own image of themselves as loving than they are with the other person. The mistake is in looking at both love and control as located only in the individual, instead of seeing that intimacy creates an interdependent relational system that is not totally in the control of either individual.

The ideal of not placing conditions on love can lead people to mistakenly believe power and control need not be factors in relationship. It is common to value openness and intimacy, and also to be anti-control. This idea that one can be open and yet at the same time not subject to being controlled or controlling is a mental framework that is essentially illusory and self-protective. People have a natural desire to maintain some control over how they feel and the direction of their lives. To be open to a person, the world, whatever, is to be affected by it, which means one's feelings are somewhat out of one's control. To be open to one's children is to hurt when they do and to experience joy when they do. So to the degree one's boundaries are open, one is affected by and thus to an extent controlled by what comes in. To the extent one is controlled by external factors one also wants to control how, and how much, this occurs. It is mainly because the lungs' boundaries are permeable to pollutants, which affects health, that people want to control pollution.

Given that being emotionally open to someone gives that

person power to affect how one feels, one has an automatic vested interest in what the person does. At the most obvious level, one would prefer others to act in a way that brings good feelings rather than bad. So to the extent that others can influence one's emotional state, there is an inevitable want to influence and control how they do so. Attempting to curb the effect of others on oneself is done consciously or unconsciously, overtly or covertly, by either controlling them or detaching from them.

One powerful and usually unconscious way control operates in relationships is through the opening and closing of boundaries.[13] Within intimacy, this is not totally—often not even largely—in one's immediate control. It is possible consciously to want to close to someone who is abusive, yet be unable to do so. Or if hurt enough, one's boundaries may close even though one does not want them to. The other may experience this closure as punishment and feel controlled—that is, feel pushed to change. This easily brings resentment, out of which one can either try to make the other person wrong for closing, or become more closed oneself.

Controlling emotions that one does not like to feel is possible to an extent. To do this one can resort to detachment, repression, denial, affirmations, or withdrawal. Emotions are not ultimately controllable, however, in that one cannot close selectively and only eliminate those that feel bad. The accumulation of resentments from either feeling controlled by the other or from controlling one's own so-called negative emotions (by repressing or holding them in) is one of the big reasons relationships that start with people loving each other fail.

The way control is exercised is often unconscious for two main reasons: On the one hand, control is hidden behind

---

[13]The section on boundaries in "East and West: Looking Within and Looking Without" (in *Control*) describes their functions. It also discusses the confusions that arise from not acknowledging the reality of boundaries, and shows that opening and closing are two sides of a dialectical process.

"rights" that come with roles such as parent, spouse, or teacher. On the other hand, people can think they do not have the right to try to control another because of ideologies that make it wrong to do so. With roles, control is masked under rights; those who are anti-control can usually be oblique enough in the way they exercise control to convince themselves they are not doing so—or else justify it by thinking it's being done for the other's good. What is little realized by those who oppose control is that when one person says to another, "Stop trying to control me or I'll withdraw from you," this utterance is likewise an attempt at control. Like it or not, control is an inherent part of intimacy.

Control in the family is legend. Interestingly, the blood family generally has the highest ideals around openness, loyalty, support, and unconditional acceptance. As such, it offers an excellent illustration of what happens when these ideals are institutionalized by turning them into rights, duties, and expectations. To many, blood relationship means, bottom line, "being there for each other no matter what, through thick and thin." What this amounts to is a taboo against closing boundaries. This can result in the family becoming the emotional dumping ground because members are expected to stay open. Consequently, family members are often more inconsiderate, judgmental, demanding, and emotionally abusive with each other than with outsiders who would close their boundaries if so treated. Along with this there is a value that says not to "keep it in the family" is a betrayal.

Here, in private, behind closed doors, the repressed side of the selfless/selfish dichotomy that doesn't look good in public comes out. This is why, contrary to the ideals, families are often pits of pain. It is also why, should one close to a family member, it most usually contains such bitterness that re-opening is very difficult. Although making boundaries taboo offers emotional security, it has a dark side wherein the family is one of the greatest sources of hatred and violence, as well as the overall breeding ground of emotional dysfunction. Not only is taking openness for granted a bane to real care, the taboo against boundaries allows people to both give and take far more abuse than in any other context. The family is also the place where people feel the most emotionally out of control. This is partly due to the buildup of resentments and the ease with which family members push each others' emotional triggers. In our framework, the family becomes the place where the usually repressed, unacceptable parts of oneself come out because other members are expected to take it.[14]

Control is a theme with myriad variations, from the blatant "Do it or I'll kill you" to the veiled "Not tonight dear, I have a headache." Also, attitudes toward control differ from abhorring it to associating it with care. Control operates on so many levels as people try to arrange their lives to get more of what they want (or think they want) and less of what they do not. And if one adopts the idea coming from some Eastern religions that it would be better not to have desires at all, then one becomes busy trying to control the fact that one does. This brings an internal struggle for control between one's desires and the ideal of not wanting them.[15]

Just as trying to control and manipulate the environment for one's own needs and purposes is an innate human trait, attempting to control others is also part of being human. This occurs whether for self-protection or to get one's way, for less-than-benign purposes, or out of the presumption that one actually knows what is best. Since control is inevitable between people, especially in intimacy, the question then becomes, what to do with it? As is the case in all areas that involve strong emotions, there are no formulas applicable to each context where control occurs. This is compounded by the two stances people usually have: One either thinks one has a right to control, or a

---

[14]"Who Is in Control?" elbaorates on how the selfless/selfish dichotomy is a key factor in the unconscious dynamics involved in "loss of control."

[15]"Buddhism and the Abuse of Detachment" in *Control* shows the problems inherent in desiring to be desireless.

right not to be controlled, and often feels each way in different situations. Rights aside, control is obviously and often misused, which has given it a bad reputation. But fortunately, since control is an inevitable component of human interaction, it has positive aspects if used appropriately. Exercising control is one way people can move each other, opening up otherwise unimagined vistas. If control is approached with awareness it can be a source of newness and creativity. Doing what the other wants leads to new experiences that can be transformative for oneself and the relationship, as well as making the other person feel cared for. What keeps an ongoing relationship turned-on and vital over time is the willingness of those involved to be transformed by each other. Transformation comes from the interplay of control and surrender.

Control at whatever level involves setting conditions. The concept of unconditional love means never placing conditions on how open one's boundaries are. This is really another unlivable ideal because no one has absolute control over how open one is at any moment, and also because the future is essentially uncertain. This ideal becomes an authoritarian prescription on how to be that removes one from the living moment where love can flower. Such formulas are a disguised attempt to control love and life itself.

The very construction of the concept of unconditional love as selfless sets it in opposition to some other kind of love that has conditions. Yet it, too, places hidden conditions on love—that it have no conditions and be selfless. People need love to feel fulfilled, and that need, like other needs, is self-centered. That love only comes when one cares about something other than oneself, and that caring for others is self-fulfilling, are both also true. Love cannot be made to fit into unconditional/conditional or selfless/self-centered frameworks. Doing so results in dividing the self into the good part that tries to love selflessly by asking for nothing in return and the selfish part, which can never quite be eliminated, that wants something back.

"Love Addiction"

Two addictions (in the loose way the word is currently being used) are worth examining here because they illustrate the connection between love and control. The first is sometimes referred to as love addiction, meaning being addicted to "loving" someone who is not good for you. Religious addiction is another recent addition to the ever-expanding roster of addictions. This alludes to being addicted to certain kinds of emotional experiences that are part of religious contexts. We deal with these two together because they share a similar dynamic. Actually, if one wanted to classify either under the rubric of addiction, it would be simpler and more correct to call them both an addiction to emotional surrender.[16]

Control and surrender, taking charge and letting go, willing and accepting—these two stances interweave in all of human existence. Janus-like, these two faces of interaction are at the gate of how experience is dealt with. Although seemingly opposite, they have an interdependent relation to each other.[17] When control and surrender are polarized, it is not unusual to become addicted or habituated to the pleasures of one side or the other. The pleasures of control are Promethean, having to do with the exercise of power. Power can be as intoxicating as any drug (perhaps even more so); the power junkie is run by the ongoing need to reaffirm control—usually over others, but often over oneself, too.

The pleasures of surrender are more in line with the passions of abandonment—getting out of oneself through powerful boundary openings. Here people can get hooked into wanting the

---

[16]"The Seductions of Surrender" discusses in depth why surrender itself is seductive. "The Traps of Being a Guru" describes the addictive quality of receiving adulation. When these two symmetrical stances connect, they often produce patterns between two people similar to those of gurus and disciples.

[17]This embedded relationship is described in "Surrender" (Part One) and in "The Abuse of Detachment" (in *Control*).

repetition of feelings they call love or religious ecstasy. These feelings most always occur in special contexts. A usual context for generating religious ecstasy involves being part of a like-minded group whose main focus is surrendering to whatever higher power is mutually believed in. The group acts as a reinforcer and amplifier of the coveted emotions.[18]

The context of so-called love addiction also involves surrendering to a perceived higher power, but here the power resides in the "loved one." This depends on an imbalance of power, with passion being aroused through the other being dominant. The process of breaking someone's will can induce surrender, and with it feelings of passion. Although the dominant person can feed off the other's passion to satisfy a need for power and worship, there can be no real respect for someone so surrendered. When surrender is one-sided, passion and power need to be repeatedly and mechanically induced. Giving abuse which the other takes is a mechanical form of power that can reignite the wanted feelings. (This is the essence of *The Story of O,* a novel of extreme sado-masochism.) Traditionally women were programmed to submit, so surrender is more in line with the female role. Freud thought women to be masochistic because in the Victorian context submission was their main route to passion.

Love addiction occurs in a context of power; the passion it generates, no matter how it feels, is really quite mechanical. "Love addicts" need someone to surrender to, and taking abuse can reinforce their image of being in love. This is often coupled with wanting to save the abuser, believing that if one just loved enough, the other would become more loving, too. Here one is really addicted to a quality of passion that comes through surrendering; submitting to someone dominant is an easy, highly conditioned route to this. People repeat this scenario either with the same person or find themselves attracted to others who create the same context. Of course, the dominant person gets addicted

---

[18]Conversion experiences are covered in "Inducing Surrender" in "Guru Ploys."

to power, which here is having someone so "in love" with you that you are worshipped no matter what. Tellingly, such imbalanced, addictive, modular relationships look like, and from the inside can feel like, unconditional love. This reveals a lot about the nature of the ideal itself, whereby one is supposed to love as if in a vacuum, regardless of how treated.

An aware life involves, among other things, balancing control and surrender, without getting mechanically driven by the pleasures of one to the exclusion of the other. Surrender does open boundaries and is a key to passion. But unless the results are healthy, which from our perspective means enhancing one's sense of self-worth and self-trust, trying to keep one's boundaries open in order to keep the passion going is self-destructive.

The experiencing of unconditional love needs certain conditions, and when the psyche is divided into a good part that tries to be selfless and a part judged bad because it is selfish, the conditions are both mechanical and predictable. Through submission the idealized part of oneself can feel selfless, thus virtuous; and through dominance the other's self-centered part can affirm its power and adequacy. What we are attempting to make clear is that feelings of pure love only occur in living contexts, not in a vacuum. The contexts themselves are never pure, but contain elements of power, control, and more often than is comfortable to acknowledge, dominance and submission. This is especially true between the sexes because historical roles are vested with skewed domains of power. Measuring is essential in breaking out of roles, which means changing the balance of power.

Measuring and Roles

The popular mystique not only has unconditional love always forgiving, but also not measuring. If all is forgiven, why measure? Obviously measuring imposes conditions. Measuring how much one is giving and receiving can appear antithetical to love. By its nature measurement looks to the past for comparison, out of which the quality of the present is judged. Judging the quality or quantity of reciprocity does dampen the ingenuousness of love. When love is fully experienced, encumbrances including measurement are not in play. But does this mean that to experience love, or to experience it more, one should as best one can avoid measuring?

Although love may feel simple, the context in which it occurs rarely remains simple for long. Many previously discussed elements such as power, dominance/submission, conquest, acceptance of roles, the addictive aspects of either control or surrender—all have repetitive, usually unconscious mechanisms that set the stage for the recurrence of the feelings of love. For example, the roles of mother, husband/wife, and disciple all have structured ways to keep boundaries open. Here though, because of dependency, it is difficult if not impossible to separate love from need. Should one buy into and emulate a given role or stance, measuring reciprocity can be kept in the background. This is especially so because most roles are not structured to be reciprocal in the ways giving and getting are played out. In a traditional marriage, the role of husband is to give security and protection, while the wife's role is to nurture and put the husband's needs first. For those who can remain content in this structure, it is possible for love to be an ongoing element in it. The old glue that held couples together was the acceptance of traditional roles, which was made easier by viewing them as God-given, and by surrendering to each other in marriage for life through God. When measuring does occur in such situations, it usually involves measuring how well the roles are being performed.

For those not able to accept and live through traditional roles and structures, the question becomes how to keep love alive in a continuing relationship while moving through uncharted waters. It is here that measuring is not only useful but at times essential for keeping the changing context viable for love. Although people may not be able to fit into traditional roles, this does not mean the roles no longer have any hold over them. It is difficult for marriage not to ignite old archetypal roles and expectations; if children come, this is compounded by the roles of father and mother. Within this ancient framework, traditional expectations of giving and getting are hard not to fall into. To change the patterns and bring about a different kind of balance, measuring is a necessary device. In fact, not to measure just about ensures that old patterns will remain in play.

If a relationship is going well, there is no need to measure. When measuring intrudes, it is because one person rightly or wrongly begins to suspect an imbalance, and so feels the need for some kind of change. Structurally, the one who questions or criticizes the validity of measuring is more content with the status quo. There could be different reasons for this, including fear of change, being more satisfied, or having more power in the relationship. Measuring is a way to justify that change is needed and is an attempt to exercise power. Likewise, belittling measuring and holding up a standard of unconditional love is a way of justifying not changing and is also exercising power. Here one finds the classic argument where one person says, "If you loved me you'd change," with the other replying, "If you loved me you'd accept me the way I am." Anti-control values do not eliminate control, they just give more power to the one who doesn't want to change. This especially happens when both people buy into an unconditional love framework.

Measuring is generally an indication that there is or will be a struggle where both try to get their way. It is here that most relationships fall apart. The image of two autonomous, self-contained individuals who love each other unconditionally and don't change or try to change each other is the *reductio ad absurdum* that the concept of unconditional love leads to. Roles are a way to minimize change and to define spheres of power. If one wants a relationship that is not role-bound, not only is change inevitable, but so is each person changing the other. Therefore, a relationship whose context is change must deal with the realities of power that different wants and needs entail. Not to do so simply means the way power is utilized is less conscious and thus more detrimental.

Once one person changes or even begins to want change, the context has already changed; so the other must change to respond to the new context. Even the one who is resisting really also wants change (usually without realizing it)—namely, to change back to the way things were. Structurally, because of habit, it is more difficult to move a relational system forward than it is to drag it back. It is always easier to repeat the known than to do something different. Consequently, the one who wants to introduce something new into the relationship has a more difficult time because it involves pushing, while the other can just resist. Structurally, the person pushing for change usually looks more controlling and negative than the one resisting it.

Measuring can keep people from falling into old roles and the resentments that come with them. It is a feedback mechanism indicating discontent, and is often a necessary tool for keeping the context for love "clean." Without it the struggles within a relationship polarize, which hardens boundaries, greatly decreasing the likelihood of feeling love. Role-dominated relationships are authoritarian, as prescribed roles define what each should do. The roles, which embody tradition, are the authorities on how to be. They are also static, as no change is condoned that is outside the role. To the extent people value being self-defined rather than role-defined, they must grapple with change, newness, and the power struggle that inevitably occurs when two such people fall in love. When they open their boundaries and experience love, they must be able to grow and evolve in ways that can deal with the other's changing needs. It must be legitimate to say, "I've been going on your track for a while, and now we need to change things." This is measuring.

Love without measure or measuring is a part of the old moral order that denigrates self-centeredness. The ideal is to love selflessly. Once self-centeredness is acknowledged as a reality, the issue becomes how to deal with it intelligently. Love between adults flowers only when there is some balance between self-centeredness and giving, between control and surrender, and if there is conscious care in the way power is exercised. Feedback is the watchdog that helps it stay that way, so neither feels taken advantage of. That is why measuring can help create a context that allows feeling love without measure.

Equating love with total acceptance can be used to test people to see just what they will accept. Love can then be measured by how much one is forgiven. The pay-off is feeling accepted, even at one's worst. Here giving unqualified acceptance reinforces abusive or self-destructive behavior. Testing others is a common dynamic within addictions, with the so-called co-dependent buying into it and forgiving. It is our assumption that the more internally divided and at war with themselves people are, the more they will look for, and need, external acceptance. What this means is that they will want others to accept the parts of themselves they cannot. Being forgiven for one's sins is a large part of Christian morality; but the underbelly of this is one must "sin" to reap the emotional rewards of forgiveness. To have people love even one's "bad" side means that one is really loved.

Forgiving and Letting Go

Loving and forgiving seem inextricably tied together, for how can one truly love someone and not forgive their transgressions? Within any long-term relationship, whether in friendship or sexual intimacy, hurts inevitably come. Forgiveness is often presented as necessary for keeping love or even affection alive. There are moral frameworks that make forgiving a virtue in and of itself. This means it is always worth doing if one can, with a corollary being the more the hurt, the more virtue there is in forgiving. Yet endlessly forgiving offense or abuse does not seem very intelligent, as it rewards the offender, ensuring such behavior will continue.

For many people forgiving is an area of confusion, both intellectually and emotionally. Should one always forgive—and if not always, then when? And even if one wants to forgive or thinks one should, one's emotions do not always cooperate. There is good reason for confusion because the concept itself is confused.

A major source of confusion is the blurring between being hurt and wronged, and also between forgiving and letting go. Surely one is not wronged every time one is hurt; and even if one feels wronged, the other might not agree and feel justified in what was done. What can be the virtue in forgiving hurt if one was not wronged?

Forgiveness that is seen as a moral imperative is part of the framework of unconditional love we have been critical of, and thus contains the same dilemmas. Obviously unconditional love needs ideals of unconditional forgiving as the mechanism that allows it to remain unconditional—that is, forgiving allows one to keep at least somewhat open, no matter what. In order to convince oneself one is loving unconditionally, it is necessary to try continually to let go of anything that stands in the way. When forgiving contains a moral component, there is moral superiority in the act itself that can allow one to feel virtuous. Yet as long as one is judging the other lacking, how much letting go can there be? Where the virtue in "moralistic forgiving" lies is also complicated by the fact that it is often unclear who benefits more from it, the one doing the forgiving or the one forgiven.

When letting go is the product of an ideology that elevates doing so to a virtue, it becomes mechanical and often destructive, masking denial and repression as the disparaged resentments go unconscious. This is a source of depression (which is often repressed anger), addiction, and many physical ailments. Yet carrying resentments, hatreds, or even the accumulation of hurts in one's nervous system is consuming baggage that can also detrimentally impact the quality of one's life.

The problem is that people often have defenses because they may in fact need them. But here too, things are not simple, for defenses, like other activities, become unconscious habits in that one isn't aware of defending in the act of doing it. Unconscious defending because of past hurts puts out a non-selective shield of protection that can deflect too much because the past may no longer be relevant. People and circumstances do change, and holding on to the past can disable one from meeting the present fully. But the idea that it's best not to be defended at all really means that one's boundaries should always be open, which is absurd.

The interesting quandaries within forgiving involve what letting go really means and how it affects one's boundaries. Must letting go be "all or nothing," or can one let go in varying degrees? What does letting go really involve, and when is it appropriate or inappropriate? Does forgiving necessarily mean reopening boundaries; or can one forgive and keep one's boundaries, somewhat at least, closed? A related and basic issue is how to rebuild trust? Trust does not rebuild by forgiving, reopening, and then being hurt again. It only rebuilds through time as one finds that whatever openings occur are not misused.

The easy way of letting go of (or controlling) hurt and anger is to have boundaries so strong that what the other does no longer matters. It might be argued that this is not really forgiving because cutting the other off still involves holding on. This would only be true, however, if forgiving necessarily meant opening boundaries. There are instances where it is actually easier to let go of old hurts if the other can no longer hurt one again, which means one's boundaries are closed. Here the stance could be, "We just don't get along and that's fine." One can let go of past feelings and still consciously choose to keep boundaries closed. Moreover, the more conscious one is of defending (putting up boundaries), the more choice one has in changing how defended one is with changing circumstances. The point is that emotional boundaries do vary and are rarely absolutely either open or closed.

There is an appealing simplicity in having one's boundaries clear-cut and unambiguous; that is why much of holding on is not so much to past hurts, but rather holding on to present boundaries in order to protect against future hurts. Letting go of boundaries (opening them) is different from letting go of hurts and angers. When ideals of forgiveness fail to distinguish between the two, what can result is holding on to hurts out of fear that without them one will lower boundaries and be hurt again. Of course, holding on to hurts generally involves holding on to boundaries, too—but not always. Especially if one is in a dependent position, as children are, it is possible to accumulate hurts and not be able to construct boundaries. This is exacerbated whenever there is a taboo against boundaries, as is often the case in families.

The appropriateness of reopening boundaries depends on the context, so no formula will work. Moreover, letting go is a process that is often not even totally in one's control. One may want to and not be able to, or open up in spite of trying to self-protect. Also a shift in boundaries can occur without conscious effort by reframing one's view of a situation, increasing understanding, or seeing better the total picture. Understanding and empathy are more valuable in softening boundaries than ideals of what one should do. It is helpful to understand the other's point of view and situation, be aware of one's complicity if there is any, and realize that none of us is immune from putting ourselves first—nor is it necessarily wrong to do so. Ideals of unconditional love and acceptance and of forgiving as a virtue do not aid the process of letting go; they merely create unlivable standards that mask defensiveness.

People hurt each other in a variety of ways involving, for example, not living up to expectations, using the other, or putting themselves first in a way that ignores others' feelings, and at times even well-being. When hurt, the solution for many is to put up boundaries and keep them. This is why so often the aging process involves losing friends and even lovers. If one is interested in keeping relations through time, a process is needed that allows boundaries to open or close with changing circumstances. Boundaries really operate in the present and aim at the future. So if one allowed one's boundaries to fluctuate with how one is being treated, one would not have to decide beforehand how open or closed to be. This involves becoming comfortable with ambiguity, which allows more freedom to change. The difficulty is that living with such ambiguity involves being aware of one's changing boundaries and their effects. In contrast, set boundaries need less attention; when they do change, the changes tend to be dramatic. An example is people who are only comfortable with boundaries either totally open or totally closed. When hurt, which happens often because they like to be totally open (and expect this of others), they shut down in a way that usually closes off future possibilities.

When forgiving involves dropping self-protective boundaries it can be used to perpetuate a dysfunctional, violent relationship—wife-beating being one graphic example. Situations of habitual violence and habitual forgiving have cycles of opening and closing that allow one to reignite passion through once more surrendering. Forgiving in this context reinforces abuse. Here to forgive without requiring the other to change is not only self-destructive, but ensures a dysfunctional relationship will remain so by continually rewarding mistreatment. A healthy person does not equate forgiving with having no boundaries, and thus is able to close boundaries for self-protection when abused, and keep them closed if necessary.[19]

Letting go of reliving past emotions that limit one's response to the present is valuable—valuable for one's own well-being, as well as for others, who generally appreciate not being defined by the past. However, letting go of the emotions does not mean that one also lets go of the memory of why one closed one's boundaries, or of the boundaries themselves. The more aware one is of this difference, the easier it is to really forgive, which means not having the emotions of the past cloud the possibilities of the future. This can allow one even to open to love again.

The Religious Foundation of Unconditional Love

Religions that make forgiveness a virtue make it difficult to distinguish feeling virtuous from feeling love. Both Eastern and

---

[19]See "Who Is in Control" on the internal dynamics of seemingly out-of-control violence and of wife-beating as an addiction.

Western religions have generated renunciate moralities where-in one achieves higher rewards through renouncing worldly (self-centered) ones. In both, the ideal of unconditional love is put forth as the way to bridge the gap between the sacred and the secular. But rather than bridging the gap, this ideal actually is part of the artificial separation.[20] Unconditional love is another renunciate ideal of purity that places love and self-centeredness in opposition. Christ is an archetypal figure that proves the extent of his love for humanity through his will-ingness to suffer, sacrifice himself, and forgive. The message is that although one may not be able to be totally Christ-like, the more like him, the better. Christ's love, which is portrayed as pure and unsullied by selfish concerns, is presented as a pre-scription for living. The lofty ideal hides the underlying author-itarian context. Within Christianity, Christ's supposed words are taken as unchallengeable and are set in a larger framework of retribution for disobedience.

As social reformers, Christ and Buddha softened the more rigid ritualistic emphasis of Judaism and Hinduism. They infused a new empathetic spirit into religion through preaching love and compassion. Both disseminated selfless ideals incorporat-ing sacrifice—giving up privilege (caste) and possessions, shar-ing with the poor, loving one's enemies, etc. Both brought a more humanitarian context into a world of much suffering and exploitation. This was achieved by putting forth ideals of self-less purity that humanity was to reach for as best it could. Uncon-ditional love is one such ideal; but what can it really mean, not only for people but for Christ?

"Forgive them, Father, for they know not what they do" is given as an example of how forgiving and encompassing Christ's

---

[20]For more on the nature of the separation between the spiritual and worldly and how it created renunciate religions that control people through ideals of self-sacrifice, see "The Power of Abstraction," "On Channeling Dis-embodied Authorities," "Good and Evil" in "Satanism," and "Dualism and Renunciation" in "Oneness."

love is. Yet this is a strange message if one takes Christianity at all seriously. Not only did Christ's executioners know what they were doing (obeying orders), but so did God, who sent him down to be martyred. Judas, Pilot, everybody concerned was just fulfilling God's plan. Christ was just doing what his father demanded of him. The obedient son was sacrificed to show God's love for humanity. Christ was offered as the sacrificial lamb to be the doorway for a sinful humanity to reach God. How unconditional is God's love? Not very. For if people don't do what they are told, they are shipped to a place of eternal pain. People are made to feel guilty and inadequate (original sin), then rules are given that if obeyed allow them to feel better about themselves.

Christ's unconditional love is part of an overall context. It is usual to focus on the love part of the context, and not on what it is embedded in, which is one of the most authoritarian, thus conditional, structures on the planet. In order to get Christ's love, one has to believe in him; in order to be forgiven, one must not only repent and plead for it, but one must acknowledge the authority that designates what wrong-doing is. This is not condition-free.

Love and self-sacrifice are joined in all renunciate moralities. When unconditional love is made into a prescription of how to be, it is really an authoritarian mechanism of control. If one gives, or loves, or forgives willingly, it isn't a sacrifice. They become sacrifices when done because of an ideal. Here one is not only controlled by the ideal but wants others to be controlled by it, too. Historically control through roles and a morality of sacrifice probably did to some extent mitigate human brutality, although there were always corruptions beneath such ideals. But when the worldview that propped up the roles and offered rewards for sacrifice is no longer believable, the corruptions become blatantly destructive. The ideals then block and distort the natural human capacity to love and bond. Love can only endure in the interface of a relationship that supports both oneself and the other.

Timeless Love through Time

Love, which feels like the simplest, most innocent, most ingenuous experience, becomes complicated because it does not occur as an isolated event free of ramifications nor unobstructed by its social context. The power of love is such that one can be controlled by it, or control others with it. Historically its expression has been structured (controlled) through roles: husband, wife, priest, nun, master, disciple, etc., each offering a particular doorway to opening boundaries. Yet old archetypes are like a master template ensuring repetition, habits, and expectations that eventually tame love's wildness, eroding passion. One may initially embrace given roles as a way of expressing care. When they become duties and routines (as they do) that the other takes for granted, typically one ends by feeling either unappreciated and uninspired if one does one's "job," or guilty if one does not. This is not an erotic context.

As the old social and moral frameworks unravel, so do the roles that made them work. Ideals of love were interwoven into roles, and insofar as the roles necessitated self-sacrifice, so did the ideals. Modern people who wish to be self-defining are struggling with a way to express love from a context that is not role-bound, or at least is less so. The difficulty with pioneering is that, unlike with roles, there are no inbuilt mechanisms for keeping boundaries open, especially after they have closed. The ideal of unconditional love comes from old dualistic, authoritarian systems of morality that divide the pure from the impure, the unconditional from the conditional. Some people who subscribe to this ideal have said such anomalies as: "I love you unconditionally, and therefore what you do does not affect me"; "If you loved me unconditionally you would try to satisfy my needs"; "If you loved me unconditionally you would make no demands on me at all." Where the anomaly lives in the last two examples is that each is self-centered and yet evokes selfless love as justification for it. Such ideas about love have little to do with love because they ignore the living situations that love occurs in. The context includes the self-interest of both parties and also the relationship itself that is a product of, but not reducible to, the parties involved. This means often one cannot divorce one's own self-interest from what's best for the relationship.

Timeless love when experienced feels new and innocent because it is; but in order for it to keep recurring, the context must also foster newness. So for many the most intense feelings occur when the relationship is new, without hurts or disillusionments. The question is, can timeless love flourish through time? Can saying "I love you" represent more than a timeless moment and indicate that there is also an enduring aspect to love? It is the context that moves and changes through time, into which feelings of love come or not. The context always has conditions that can open or close boundaries, that can build or erode trust.

A context is basically the place where the interplay of selflessness and self-centeredness occurs. Roles define the areas where self-centeredness is sanctioned and selflessness is expected. This translates into structuring giving and getting. Roles hide this interplay under the banner of duties, rights, and obligations. Roles can keep boundaries open to an extent, more so if all concerned perform them well. Without roles, it is how giving and getting are played out that most influences trust and the opening or closing of boundaries. The idea that one could or should give endlessly, keeping one's boundaries open unconditionally, with no concern for reciprocity, is unlivable and unhealthy.

In relationships that do not cling to roles, a care-full, aware balancing of giving and getting, of individuating and merging with another, not only keeps the context for love alive, but actually allows it to flourish and grow through time. A context can be protected and nurtured precisely because it has conditions. In general, servants do what their employers do not want to; service usually involves doing this for free. Roles designate areas of service. When service comes freely from the heart, it is a cherished gift; when it is expected or taken for granted, it becomes a duty or chore. A condition that keeps the context for love nurtured is not to expect service in the name of love. This means not expecting another to do things for you that you do not wish to do yourself.

So although in one sense love does not exist in time and expresses itself unconditionally at any given moment, the transformations of a relationship through time create the context for this to keep recurring. Timeless love that has no bounds, that asks for nothing in return, moves through a context of time whose conditions must be taken into account. There are many conditions in which unconditional love is not likely to flower. Large among these are the unaware exercise of power and control. Since power and control are an inevitable aspect of any intimate relationship, they need to be utilized with awareness and care. Social contexts of inequality are detrimental to any aware resolution of the power struggles within intimacy.

Actually, separating an experience from the situation it occurs in is as artificial as the division between unconditional and conditional love. Timeless love, which feels unconditional, can only come out of a context of time which by its nature contains conditions. The conditions may vary from mechanical roles to the interplay of self-defining people. Love is always the same and yet always different. It is the same since it is an energy, a magic unsullied by the encroachments of time. It is different in that its display is uniquely dependent upon an ever-changing relational context. What this means is that there are always conditions underlying unconditional love.

Oneness, Enlightenment, and the Mystical Experience

Many people, through various routes, have experienced what have become known as altered states of consciousness. By "altered" what is meant is that the way experience is both taken in and framed is different from one's ordinary day-to-day experience. The two main routes of alteration (perhaps each as old as humanity) are through substances (chemicals in plants or synthetics) and practices that loosen up the way the mind structures experience. Altered states can also occur through near-death experiences, great stress, or spontaneously without any known cause.

The Mystical Experience

One of the most life-changing of these altered states is what is called the mystical experience, the essence of which is the actual experiencing of an underlying unity within all existence. We call this the Oneness experience. While this experience is occurring, it feels beyond words and concepts, beyond time, beyond all polarities (including life and death), and beyond even the feeling of there being an experiencer who is having the experience.

The infusion of more easily accessed mysticism into Western culture began in the sixties. For still unknown reasons, powerful psychedelic drugs bypass the ordinary ways the human brain integrates, making available experiences that previously could only be read about in esoteric books. Many leaders in the then-budding human potential movement and young aspirants in the arts, humanities, and sciences had their worldviews chemically jolted. Eastern spiritual structures offered routes of explaining and integrating these experiences in a way Western ones simply could not. Some experimenters loudly and publicly extolled their newfound insights, while many others more quietly incorporated them into their viewpoints. Eastern spiritual teachers either came on their own or were brought to the West to plow this fertile ground. The actual mystical experience along with the interpretations of Eastern cosmologies became dual influences on psychology, music, art, and fashion. This even shifted the perspectives of many who were not directly involved in the psychedelic culture. Mysticism was in the air.

Once a person has had a Oneness experience, it is not difficult to make being in that special state more of the time, or all of the time, the meaning and goal of life. This can also be true for those who have not had the experience, but have heard of it and give it credence. Doing this is reinforced by presumed spiritual masters who not only claim to live in this exalted state, but also insinuate that this place of unity is more real and superior to ordinary reality where separation is experienced.

Although all who have had mystical experiences acknowledge they cannot be captured within the frameworks of thought, different traditions do attempt to frame them in their different ways. People having such experiences have been previously conditioned by their culture and time, which affects how the experience is viewed and integrated afterwards. Mystical experiences do not create a *tabula rasa,* a clean slate; but rather, whatever insights occur get interpreted through different lenses. This is why Hindus have Hindu mystical experiences, Christians have Christian ones, etc. Thus Christian mystics can experience God in everything and still keep the transcendent God necessary for dualistic Christianity. The Eastern mystic can experience everything as God, and so not only have an immanent God, but build a framework where ostensible non-duality (Oneness for the Hindu, the Void for the Buddhist) is the ultimate reality. So the way the mystical experience is experienced is not "pure" (nothing is) but is historically and culturally embedded.

The concept of Oneness is an abstraction created by thought as a way of framing and attempting to describe the mystical experience. Insofar as Oneness is placed in a higher realm or plane than the world of separation and multiplicity (the Many), this is done by abstracting out and reifying a presumed quality or essence from life, and making that more important than the individual expressions of life itself. In so doing, the plurality (the many forms) of existence is trivialized. This is representative of the historic pattern followed by all accumulation cultures in which the spiritual was abstracted out from the secular and exalted above it.[1]

In the East, the abstractions derived from mystical experiences of unity have created not only the concept of Oneness, but a religious ideology, ethics, and hierarchy that flow from it. (We define ideology as a worldview containing a program or ideal of how to live—i.e., a morality.) The mystical experience is important, both as a historical factor influencing the perceptions of humanity, and also because of its relevance for individuals. But traditions that made an ideology out of the concept of Oneness created a morality that denigrated or made unreal the individual self with its individual interests. Any worldview that denies either the reality or importance of the individuated self ends up defining virtue as selflessness, which is achieved through self-sacrifice. When renouncing self-interest is the spiritual path, we define the morality as renunciate. Renunciate moralities have neither eliminated nor diminished self-interest, but have often made its expression more hidden and thus corruptible. This chapter will show how the concept of Oneness is used by spiritual

---

[1]"The Power of Abstraction: The Sacred Word and the Evolution of Morality" shows the historical stages of the relation between religion and morality.

authorities to make their pronouncements unchallengeable, and therefore authoritarian.[2]

Those who attempt to communicate the experience of unity usually begin with a caveat on the limitations of words to capture it, and then proceed to describe it in these ways:

1. One experiences being in the eternal, a place that always was and always will be.

2. There can be a great energy that breaks through boundaries to the extent of experiencing one's awareness expanding until it seems to (or could) include everything.

3. The ordinary separations between what's me and not-me either momentarily disappear or become really ambiguous.

4. There are often (though not always) deep feelings of identification—one might even call it love—with the cosmos.

5. One "knows" this place is always there to be tapped into.

6. The place feels foreign and yet familiar at the same time.

7. There is both awe and a feeling of personal insignificance, where the mundane concerns and emotions around self-enhancement and self-protection seem trivial and beside the point.

8. There is no fear, because death feels quite unreal. Or in a slightly different vein, when you cease identifying with yourself and merge with the cosmos, it feels like you've already died, so there's nothing left to fear. This cessation of fear is one of the most marvelously unusual feelings, bringing deep relaxation on levels one didn't even know existed.

9. One feels immune from being affected by the judgments of others, and also free from such petty responses as vengeance and competitiveness. After all, we are all one. Along this line, all so-called negative emotions—anger, jealousy,

---

[2]"Religion, Cults, and the Spiritual Vacuum," "Satanism and the Worship of the Forbidden," and "Symbol Systems and Power" in "The Power of Abstraction" further describe the nature and limitations of renunciate religion.

etc.—can seem not only unnecessary, but silly and based on illusions.

10. There is a recognition that one is (or we all are) an aspect of God.

11. Everything (oneself included), and the way the cosmos is unfolding, is seen as perfect.

Experiencing this underlying unity initially can feel better and more real than normal reality, and afterward it is difficult not to become what we call God- or Oneness-intoxicated. The experience of having no boundaries, feeling eternal, and being at peace with the cosmos can be so powerful that it's hard not to project how wonderful it would be if everyone could only get beyond the ego attachments presumed to be keeping this state away. Being in this state as much as possible can become one's major life goal.

For those who have tasted the above, "ordinary reality" can easily be interpreted as containing opposite characteristics or qualities: fear and ambition, endless preferences, boundaries between self and other, awareness of one's limits, and the march toward death. In everyday life one is affected by the emotions of others and subject to all the unwanted feelings. Instead of feeling at one with the universe, feelings of disconnection and discontent are rife. Perfection is not experienced, but is at best an elusive ideal.

The aspects of ego that separate—pride, envy, selfishness, greed, ambition, competitiveness, etc.—seem not only paltry and pitiful in comparison, but easily can be viewed as entirely negative. The Oneness experience comes to represent all that is positive, true, and real. Separation becomes the bad guy with no inherent value, the enemy that keeps Oneness away, or as in Hinduism, *maya*—the grand illusion. The meaning of life, or the spiritual path, then becomes transcending separation and all the negativities therein.

Dualism and Renunciation

The actual experience of underlying unity is different from thought creating an abstract concept of it, and then making that concept more real than individuated existence. What should not be forgotten is that it takes an individual to experience unity. Oneness is an abstraction that presents itself as beyond dualism, but has within it a hidden duality. Dividing the cosmos into two categories or levels of reality is dualistic by nature. The ideology of Oneness (as opposed to the experience of it) creates an opposition with multiplicity, calling itself "higher" and more real. And although the mystical experience can give a person a deeper connection with the cosmos, by contrast the ideology of Oneness with its camouflaged, hierarchical dualism has separated the spiritual from the worldly and humanity from nature.

Dualism divides everything into two basic categories. In Western religions it is overt—God and God's creation. When existence is so divided, one side of the division—in this instance God—is always valued more than the other. This creates an obvious hierarchy of value between the two categories, as God is superior to its creation. It also creates a hierarchy of value within the lesser category based on the virtues or dictates of the higher one. That is, the more godlike, or at least God-fearing and hence obedient, the better. The same kind of dualistic, either/or framework of conceptualizing is operative in the ideology of Oneness, but is masked by the concept itself, which proclaims the unity of all being and thus seems all-encompassing. But if unity is valued more than diversity, the inevitable result is the attempt to get to unity by negating or in some fashion lessening the value and importance of separation. Thus the way that much of Eastern spirituality has been framed involves identifying with the principle of unity through denying, renouncing, dis-identifying with, or trivializing separation. Becoming more aware, more "spiritual," is then seen as moving one's identity from the personal (and thus the limited) to the totality. "Everything is perfect"; "I am that"; "We are all one"; "Separation is an illusion" are examples of identifying only with unity.

Renunciation requires two sharply defined hierarchical categories—a lower one to renounce in order to achieve the higher one. The higher one is usually made sacred, which justifies sacrificing the lower to it. When unity is considered better or more real than diversity, emulating the values abstracted out of the concept of Oneness is presented as the solution to the problems within individuated life. This results in making people's concerns with their own individual lives the source of all problems. In short, this is the East's way of making self-centeredness the villain. This would include valuing cooperation over competition, altruism over egoism, and giving over getting.[3]

In an article on "spiritual masters" (*Omni*, March 1990), a disciple of an Eastern guru recounted a vignette to illustrate how his master could teach a profound lesson in a few words. The guru was having a temple built in his honor. Disciples from all over the world had come to the cornerstone ceremony with treasures, many of them of considerable value, to be buried in the large hole under the foundation. The narrator had been chosen as the first to deposit his offering in the hole. He describes how in his pride at being selected to be first, he chose a large rock and enthusiastically threw it in. He then looked at his master, who said to him quietly, "Too much 'getting' is going on here." The man concluded by saying that his humbled ego became far wiser as a result of those few words.

For the chastised disciple, the guru's lesson was a statement that his giving was not pure enough. Another entirely different interpretation of the above scenario is possible: To have a temple built in one's honor and then to further waste valuable gifts by burying them to symbolize one's greatness is a sign of a monu-

---

[3]"Love and Control: The Conditions Underlying Unconditional Love" describes the relational conflicts resulting from doing this. The last three sections of "The Power of Abstraction" show how these categories are embedded in each other.

mental ego that has little constraint. One of the cheapest guru ploys is to make people feel inadequate by showing how their behaviors are tainted with self-centeredness—always an easy task. This guru, who was the recipient of all of this "getting," could not even share a little of it with his disciple without making him feel bad about himself. Perhaps the disciple's gift, a mere rock, was not grand enough. But since the guru is viewed by his disciples as a person beyond duality and beyond ego, they could not even entertain the possibility of our interpretation.

Consequently, the disciple entirely missed the real lesson of history: The guru's "getting" and self-enhancement are masked by images of enlightenment and selflessness and thus are made unconscious. Once his purity and hence superiority are taken for granted, it is assumed that he deserves to be "getting" precisely because he is thought enlightened. He can thus reprimand his disciple for the very activity he was involved in on a far grander scale without it seeming hypocritical. Who gets and who gives is never questioned because "spiritual" values mask what is really going on.

The Function of Enlightenment

The major Eastern religions make reference to a state of consciousness of a different order called enlightenment. Its foundation lies in the mystical experience of unity that has been conceptualized as Hindu Oneness or the Buddhist Void. From this came the idea of the "enlightened one" who lives in this exalted place all the time, most of the time, or at least a significantly greater amount of time than ordinary folk—having at the very minimum some control over access to that place. The traditional conception of enlightenment involves two major components:

1. Being at one with the universe to the extent of having no ego or boundaries around the self.

2. A hierarchy of value wherein the more selfless one is, the better, with the highest state being total selflessness.

The way an "enlightened" person is supposed to manifest enlightenment is through being selfless and beyond any need for ego gratification. So the image of the enlightened one is of being totally giving, unconditionally compassionate and loving, and with no taint of greed, envy, lust, or competitiveness. Those who wish to be considered enlightened must present themselves as being "above it all"—beyond all the foibles of ego: beyond preference, beyond negativity, beyond fear and desire, etc. Such individuals paint a seductive picture of a state they can help others get to that is not only eternal but that can solve all the mundane problems of life.

Creating a special category called the "enlightened state" is itself a manifestation of an accumulation mentality, it becoming the ultimate goal to achieve through accumulating merit and partially enlightening experiences. One day or lifetime, one finally crosses the barrier and arrives. Then one is a perfect manifestation of the godhead—a perfect master with nowhere else to go. You work toward the goal of enlightenment and once you get it, you have it. The way the ideal is constructed makes it static and unchanging. The experience of unity feels timeless, but the concept of enlightenment turns a timeless moment into an "all the time" fixed identity that continues over time. Ironically, the identity of being enlightened attempts to crystallize in time what is experienced as timeless.

Once one gives credence to such an identity either in oneself or in another, this creates a dualistic, either/or framework: one is either enlightened or not enlightened—this or that. This is another example of how constructing two separate categories and giving one greater value (it's better to be enlightened) creates a hierarchy of value not only between the two, but also within the less valued (non-enlightened) category. Those viewed as not enlightened are considered better to the degree they emulate the images of enlightenment. This basically amounts to measuring the extent of selflessness.

Once existence is bifurcated into two categories, a bridge is required between the two parts. In both the East and West, religions create the two realms and then become the bridge between them. They design a "spiritual path" from the lower to the higher through defining the proper actions to get one from here (this world) to there (however salvation is defined). In the East via karma/rebirth, the path progresses through levels of spirituality, taking many lifetimes until arriving at the enlightened state—also referred to as *nirvana, moksha,* cosmic consciousness, etc. This conception is linear and hierarchical, as are the religions that produced it. Some schools (Tibetan Buddhism) have even constructed hierarchical levels of enlightenment, so that one enlightened being is held to be more so than another. Among spiritual seekers the burning issue is how far along the path one is.

Asserting a basic unity permeating all existence does not automatically lend itself to hierarchy. Enlightenment is the way hierarchy is brought in by viewing a few individuals as special channels for, and greater manifestations of, this underlying unity. Once it is assumed that some people embody or express the true nature of reality more than others, an authoritarian hierarchy easily flows from that basic assumption. This also lays the foundation for perpetuating the hierarchy, because the one who knows best can decide who is enlightened and thereby transfer the mantle of authority. One person deciding when another is enlightened does seem a bit strange. One would presume that if enlightened, one would know it without being told. Yet this is what occurs within many spiritual frameworks.

The ideal of enlightenment at first blush seems completely innocent of human corruption because it is defined as being totally selfless. Yet it is this sacrosanct concept of perfection that allows authoritarianism to manifest, and indeed flourish. Two mental constructions work in tandem: Enlightenment provides authorities, and karma as a cosmic moral law provides the metaphysical justification for why some rather than others come to be enlightened authorities. These two concepts intertwine and validate each other, creating an impenetrable closed system that perpetuates itself. Superior past lives are used to legitimize special status, while those with special status present the karma/ rebirth ideology as an unchallengeable truth.[4]

Monotheism with one God on top is obviously authoritarian. The authoritarianism embedded within the Eastern ideology of Oneness is less obvious. Believing that God is everywhere and in everything makes a centralized hierarchy more difficult. The concept of enlightenment, however, does bring decentralized hierarchies, each with a master on top. This is what one sees in Eastern religion and in its Western transplants. Whereas monotheism makes the revealed Word of God sacred, Eastern religions make presumed enlightened beings sacred. Thus the concept of enlightenment brings authoritarianism at the personal, charismatic level (gurus, masters, avatars, and buddhas). Here the authority comes from living people, not an institution—although they almost always create an institution around themselves or are already part of one. Not coincidentally, surrendering to and obeying the master is presented as a (usually necessary) step on the path to enlightenment.

The very nature of any structure that makes one person different and superior to others not only breeds authoritarianism, but is authoritarian in its essence. Just as there is no way for humans to question a remote God, there is really no way for a non-enlightened being to question the words or actions of a presumed enlightened one. This is why gurus can get away with anything—they are judged by different standards that make whatever they do perfect by definition. The idea that someone is no longer susceptible to the corruptions of power ensures corruption will occur, promulgating self-delusion in all involved. So the concept of enlightenment, precisely because it is so exalted, almost inevitably lends itself to abuse and corruption. It can be

---

[4]"Do You Create Your Own Reality?" concisely describes how karma works. The section on "Oneness" in "The Power of Abstraction" shows how karma is the moral underpinning of the Eastern Oneness worldview.

used to justify any behavior, privileges, or excesses, creating an insidious double standard for the superior ones.

There are even warnings about the traps of enlightenment within esoteric literature, where it is said that no one who has had truly enlightening experiences ever claims to be enlightened. Perhaps this is because anyone with real wisdom would know that building an identity around enlightenment creates a static, unchanging image of how to be, which is just another cage. Let us leave aside the question of whether there is or ever has been a person of ultimate cosmic wisdom, totally devoid of self-centeredness. The only person who could say "Yes, there is" with certainty would have to be one. And that person would have to be absolutely certain of being free of all self-delusion—not an easy task.[5]

The very idea of enlightenment has hidden assumptions within it that are part of our authoritarian heritage. An example is the presumption that a modern manifestation of enlightenment would say essentially the same things as were said thousands of years ago. This is an odd image of finality within an otherwise evolving cosmos. People do have enlightening experiences and insights, but are they always a repetition of old insights that others had thousands of years ago? Is awareness a path others have trod that leads to a predictable end? The concept of enlightenment needs to be a-historical, unchanging, and infallible to support authoritarian religious hierarchies. This is the East's way of endowing someone with the last word and ultimate authority on cosmic truth.

Buddha initially excluded women from his monasteries. When pressed, he made their entry conditional upon perpetual subservience to the lowliest (newest) male monks. Was this an example of unchanging wisdom? Or were some of his ideas not so enlightened, but rather a function of his place in history? His agenda to end suffering has had millennia to test itself and has

---

[5]"Gurus, Psychotherapy, and the Unconscious" and "The Traps of Being a Guru" show why it is not an easy task.

failed. Are people just not good enough or smart enough? Is there something wrong with people or is something wrong with the agenda? His methodology for ending suffering was tied to the concept of enlightenment, which involves renouncing both the self and self-centeredness. So as an essentially renunciate religion, Buddhism is also essentially authoritarian, with Buddha being the absolute authority on what to renounce and how to go about it. Some modern Buddhists would bristle at calling Buddhism renunciate. They would say that through dis-identifying or detaching from the illusion that there is a self, self-centeredness effortlessly leaves. We view this as their illusion.[6]

Some people may at times see more deeply into the nature of things than others. However, the idea of enlightenment as a state of finality that one reaches once and for all is a viewpoint of wisdom and spirituality that is supposedly true for all people and all times. This static view of enlightenment derives from the a-historic Oneness ideology wherein one transcends the illusion of separateness. Only separate entities can change in relation to each other. Ironically, Buddhists who assert there is nothing but change in the material world hold that spiritual realizations do not change. Denying change in the spiritual realm is basically a fundamentalist stance used to protect the sacred and tradition.[7] But perceiving deeply is a process that is necessarily historically embedded, for each epoch has its particular illusions that must be pierced. Significantly, a less common meaning of an enlightening experience is penetrating the veils of illusion. We see the dis-illusionment necessary for this age as going beyond the polarizations of either/or moral frameworks, which are the source of most distortions and illusions. Any ideology that presents static ideals of perfection and attainment necessarily creates its own illusions. This anti-evolutionary view of awareness and wisdom not only blocks further inquiry, but it limits the possibility of constructing new frameworks that can free people to be truly more aware.

---

[6]The section on Buddhism in *Control* shows in detail why this is so.
[7]See "Fundamentalism and the Need for Certainty."

The One-Sidedness of Oneness

It is through constructing images that idealize unity and self-lessness to the detriment of separateness that spirituality and morality have gone awry. By a sleight of mind which easily passes unnoticed, the experience of an underlying unity is turned into the ideology of Oneness, which contains both unwarranted assumptions about reality and prescriptions on how to be. The commonest ones are:

1. Such experiences are more real than ordinary reality, and so unity is superior to diversity.

2. It is possible to be in the mystical state all the time and, of course, the more you're there the better.

3. The path to unity is through negating individuation. Here descriptions of unity turn into prescriptions for individuals to no longer act like individuals.

4. Following a presumed "arrived" master is the best way to get there.

The experience of being a part of something larger (even the whole cosmos) is very different from declaring the whole more real than its parts. Just as it takes an individual to have this experience, it takes an individual mind to construct the ideology of Oneness—an ideology which quixotically denies the individuated reality of the person constructing it. If, as we see it, diversity (the Many) is just as real as the underlying unity (the One), then attempting to solve the problems of day-to-day life by inappropriately superimposing the values abstracted out of the concept of Oneness will not work.[8] If unity and diversity, the One and the Many, are embedded in each other, then values of moral

---

[8]"A Dialectical Approach to the One and the Many" in "East and West: Looking Within and Looking Without" (in *Control*) describes in greater depth the relationship between unity and diversity.

purity that deny separation and villainize self-centeredness spawn an underbelly of corruption.[9]

We wish to show how elevating one side of a dialectical relationship (unity) over the other (separation) generates an unlivable renunciate morality. If, from the point of view of the One, everything is perfect, then how can one judge this to be better than that, or in fact have any preferences at all? So from this, an ideal of spirituality is built that involves making no judgments and having no preferences. Here the ideal is to love everyone and everything equally, because one is supposed to be free of attachments to any particular expression of this unity—i.e., to any person or object. So problems within individuated life around such issues as power, competition, envy, jealousy, manipulation, sexuality, and self-centeredness in general are wrongly thought to be solvable by adopting the values that come from looking at existence as a seamless web of unity.

But if existence has seams (boundaries), and if individuation is an irreducible aspect of it, then trying to solve the problems within individuated life by superimposing values derived from a different level of abstraction (unity) can only lead to confusion and paradox. An element in opening and closing boundaries involves judgments on the part of an organism as to what to let in or keep out. This serves to protect and to maintain some degree of individual integrity. Judgments are only possible because there are individuals with differences that can be judged. If making judgments and distinctions is necessary when dealing with each other and life, the problems of judgmentalism cannot be unraveled by reactively positing an ideal of being non-judgmental. The fact is, people make judgments about everything all the time. Comparison and judgment are part of the way thought works to sort things out—survival depends on

---

[9] "Buddhism and the Abuse of Detachment" and "What Is Selfless Service Serving?" (in *Control*) describe in detail why ideologies that emphasize unity cannot solve the problems of individuated life.

this. The preference for Oneness is itself highly ironic, as is the judgment that it's better not to judge.

Such ironies abound in mystical writings, where so many of the seeming paradoxes involve a levels shift of identification from the small "I" of individuated life to the big "I" of the totality of being. The mystical experience of unity has an eternal quality. How easy it is to project that quality onto oneself and say, "I, the individual, am eternal." This can then be used to validate any afterlife conception such as karma/rebirth.[10]

Experiencing an underlying unity can alter one's relationship to daily life and also profoundly change the way one approaches death and dying. It can increase compassion and empathy, and bring the capacity to see oneself as a player in an eternal drama. It can also add a poignant dimension to the seeming paradox whereby each of us is less than a speck of awareness in the scheme of existence, and yet each of us is also a center in the universe. To say we are all God is well and good, but not at the cost of denying our humanity with all its seeming foibles.

In spiritual realms, because what is considered proof by science or logic is at times not applicable, the ideology of Oneness has historically remained aloof from serious critique. Challenges coming from overtly dualistic frameworks (monotheism) can be easily dealt with because Oneness is a higher level of abstraction. Similarly, monotheism can incorporate all the wanted attributes of polytheistic gods into one God. A monotheistic God is more remote with more abstract qualities than polytheistic gods. To distinguish polytheistic gods from each other, they must each be given traits and identities, as well as their own realms of power and importance. Monotheism created a

---

[10]"The Assault on Reason" deals more with the nature of paradox. The section on karma/rebirth in *Control* shows that the idea of karma could theoretically operate in many different ways—and that the way chosen by Eastern religions was arbitrary, except that it was the only way to establish a renunciate morality.

new concept of power by subsuming all power traits into one abstract quality—omnipotence. It also did this with knowledge (omniscience) and virtue (perfection). As a higher level of abstraction, monotheism could explain away polytheism, while polytheism could not explain away monotheism. Similarly, as a lower level of abstraction, monotheism has a problem with explaining Oneness.[11]

Pantheism, which simply says everything is God, is an even higher level of abstraction, as it does away with dualism altogether. A straightforward pantheism may be intellectually appealing because of its simplicity and internal consistency, but it has grave moral difficulties. If everything is God, how can the actions of any one part of God be better or worse than any other? How can any trait (love) be better than any other (greed)? The ideology of Oneness contains a hidden dualism precisely to make certain expressions of unity better and higher than others. Still, Oneness is a higher level of abstraction than monotheism because the way it separates spirit from matter is less absolute. It can incorporate monotheism into its framework, while monotheism, by definition, cannot deal with the unity of all being except by denying it. A practical example: Hinduism can call Christ another avatar (pure manifestation of God) and in one fell swoop include Christianity under its banner.

There were Eastern thinkers aware of the hidden dualism in most conceptions of unity. The way they attempted to reconcile this involved using paradoxes that mysteriously evoked the idea that the separate parts are both separate and not separate at the same time: "The One is the Many" (in Hindu terms) and "*Nirvana* is *samsara*" (in Buddhist terms, meaning "The Void is the world of form") are examples of this. We have no problem with constructions that point to different things happening at different levels (the different levels here being unity and diversity). Paradox is useful as an indication that a levels shift

---

[11]"The Power of Abstraction" shows the relation between power and the four main stages of religious abstraction.

is occurring—but not if it is used to cut off inquiry, as is usual. Our problem with such conceptions is that they are embedded in a worldview that acts as if unity were somehow more real. The view of enlightenment that is a part of such constructions still involves shedding ego and identifying with only one side. What these thinkers neglect to mention is that, as with pantheism, if unity is not more real than diversity, the renunciate ethics that are based on giving unity priority come into question.

The ideology of Oneness constructs its hidden dualism by making the whole more sacred or more real than its parts. Sacralizing unity places it in another realm, "the spiritual." Once anything is made sacred, sacrificing to and for it is inevitable. When selflessness is the highest virtue, the spiritual path becomes practices that seemingly promote it. The difficulty of testing this ideology is compounded by making the promised payoffs occur after death. A totally secular ideology that values the parts sacrificing for the whole, like Marxism, does not have that luxury.[12] If within a few generations it does not begin to improve the quality of life, it loses credence and crumbles. Yet not to look at the long-term results of any worldview, no matter how otherworldly, is truly remiss.

One of the longest experiments in history, the approximately 3000-year-old Eastern ideology of Oneness, was first developed in the Upanishads. It does have one component whose results can be examined in this world—the efficacy of its moral system to do what it set out to do: eliminate or even moderate divisiveness and self-centeredness. The failure of its renunciate morality to diminish self-centeredness is a powerful statement that something is amiss. The usual reasons given for this are either that humanity has not tried hard enough or isn't good enough. ("We as a species have more karma to work out.") It is our contention that this morality has failed not because there

---

[12]The chapter on communism in *Control* shows that it was really a secularization of the old renunciate ethics of self-sacrifice—an experiment that was the past disguised as the future.

is something wrong with people, but because the framework constructs ideals that are impossible to achieve, thus setting people up for failure and self-mistrust. That it has been around so long and has not even tempered human divisiveness should not be taken lightly.

The incongruity that the most highly structured and internally divided culture (India) originated and nurtured the Oneness framework is no accident. Caste, with its privileges through the hierarchy it sets up, has proven to be one of the most powerful and lasting ways of dividing people. The moral structure is simple: people do their prescribed duties and strive to eliminate self-centeredness; along the way "good karma" is generated that pays off in increasingly better next lifetimes. The caste one is born in is a function of one's karma. Making separation an illusion is useful to both the "haves" and the "have-nots": the privileged use it to self-protect by removing themselves from the surrounding misery; the miserable use it to cope with a hopeless situation. The message of the privileged to the underprivileged is, "If you accept your lot, which you deserve, next time around you'll be better off." This is the source of the deep resignation one finds there. The category of illusion functions like a cosmic refuse collector into which one can dump whatever one doesn't like or wants to get rid of, by claiming it isn't real.

Holism and Interconnectedness

Concepts of unity are very appealing, since it is increasingly obvious that divisiveness and uncaring self-interest are paramount causes of why the planet is becoming unfit for life. Many who are ecologically-minded and peace-oriented are attracted to the Oneness model because on the surface it seems to fit the planet's need for people to realize that everything is interconnected. The danger in holistic thinking lies in not giving separation an equal place in the scheme of things.

There is a strain within holistic thinking that posits the total interconnectedness of everything (the cosmos) such that every change anywhere affects everything else. In this framework, existence is looked upon as a gigantic mobile wherein a tug anywhere moves everything. This is an example of horizontal thinking (which tends to be holistic). Believing that somehow the shifting grains of sand on a beach either affect or are affected by, say, a fire in the Bronx, let alone a distant star going nova, is necessary if one is to take the above theory seriously. Giving priority to unity over diversity leads to these kinds of assumptions.

Often favoring such holistic horizontal thinking has within it an anti-hierarchical political agenda, sometimes hidden. Hierarchical conceptualizations do involve thinking vertically and creating boundaries of separation. It is also true that the prevalent type of vertical thinking and the justifications therein are at the base of the world's inequities. ("I'm better than you.") So in the quest for justice, it's tempting to try to discard vertical thinking and hierarchies. To us, this is but another example of either/or framing that negates the reality of separation and boundaries. Not to acknowledge boundaries are real and that without them there would be no life (or anything else for that matter) also makes relationships unreal. For without boundaries what is relating to what?[13]

The way systems interrelate is both horizontal and vertical. A human being could be viewed as a hierarchy of interrelating systems, from the sub-atomic through the social. Each system has boundaries that can be crossed by other systems parallel to it (two human beings are parallel systems), as well as those above and below it. A cell is a system with a boundary containing molecules which, because they are part of its composition, are systems on a level below it. The cell itself can be part of

---

[13]"Control and Boundaries" and "Forgiving and Letting Go" in "Love and Control" discuss the problems caused in relationships by unlivable ideals about boundaries. "Looking Within" (in *Control*) shows opening and closing boundaries as two sides of a dialectical process, and describes the confusions caused by denying their reality.

an organ, which is a system above it. Systems in proximity usually have an easier time crossing boundaries and affecting each other.

Within this framework, it is not by any means a given that all occurrences within a system break out of the boundaries of that system to affect anything outside it, let alone everything else. A pebble is dropped in the middle of the lake; ripples expand outward but dissipate before reaching the boundaries of lake and shore. The pebble not only did not affect the shore, but might not have had an effect on any or most fish in the lake.

This is not to say that the movement of a pebble or a grain of sand could not have far-reaching effects; it simply says it doesn't have to. What it does mean is that boundaries are real, and effects can truly be localized and limited. In fact, protecting what's inside from undue or casual outside interference is one of the primary functions of boundaries. Saying that everything is interconnected does not distinguish how it is all interconnected, or whether some things and occurrences have more effect than others, and some perhaps none at all. If the Earth were destroyed by a large meteor, the sun would probably survive. The converse is not true.

If everything were interconnected in the way a mobile exemplifies, it would be difficult to have room for human freedom (or any other kind) since freedom needs some degree of separation to operate.[14] Our perspective views the vertical and horizontal as dialectically embedded (vertical only has meaning in relation to horizontal and vice versa). And although these papers are challenging authoritarian hierarchies (the vertical) and value the concept of human equality (the horizontal), we do not do so by trying to abolish or deny the vertical, or making the horizontal superior. Reframing equality and hierarchy dialectically, instead of treating them as if they were mutually exclusive in an either/or way, is another way of making hierarchy a tool

---

[14]"Am I For Real or Am I On Tape? Free will and Determinism in Karma" in *Control* explains why freedom has no meaning without the existence of separate individuals.

instead of an authoritarian master.[15]

Some modern Buddhist theorists use the concept of inter-connectedness with its seamless web of existence to show that boundaries are really an illusion. It is no accident that seamless-web proponents often use a static noun, interconnectedness, which is constructed from a passive verb (interconnected) that has no subject. This allows them to claim that interconnectedness does not imply two things, that it contains no separate elements or components. Whereas interconnecting and the active verb, connect, raise the question of what elements are actually connecting. This is an unwelcome reminder that individuation and separation are required for things to connect, so that at some level boundaries must be real.

Connecting needs subjects that connect with each other. In order for connecting to occur, there be must distinguishable things or systems with boundaries (however permeable and fluid) that are doing the connecting. Without boundaries and some degree of separation, it is meaningless to speak of connecting. That the universe may consist of hierarchies of interconnecting and overlapping systems whose boundaries are not fixed does not take away from the fact that each system has recognizable boundaries that define it and allow it to connect with other systems. Without this the universe would be one big blob of sameness, perhaps similar to the Buddhist concept of the Void.

The Buddhist Void posits ultimate reality as devoid of differentiation and is structurally identical to the concept of Oneness. Buddhism replaces Hindu *maya* ("All is illusion") with "All is change," making continuity (and thus identity) the illusion. Both change and illusion serve the same function—to deny the reality of normal reality (the world of individuated form). The primary Buddhist agenda of doing away with suffering is geared at doing away with the individual self that suffers through creating "unreal" boundaries. Making interconnectedness the ulti-

---

[15]"Freedom and Equality" in *Control* discusses this more deeply. See also "Authority, Hierarchy, and Power."

mate reality in the world of ever-changing forms is an attempt to do away with subjects that connect (and suffer) as well as with the less emotionally appealing traditional Void. This is none other than the age-old hidden dualism between reality and illusion, however defined.[16]

If the universe is actively involved in joining (coming together) and separating (breaking apart), then separation is just as real as interconnectedness. What this means is that the web of existence has seams, and the way to solve the problems brought about by self-centeredness cannot come through villainizing or declaring unreal the fact of it. One still is faced with these basic realities: that eating, be it carrots or cows, destroys one thing for the good of the other; that people use resources, and too many people will destroy the overall support system for everyone; and that like creation and love, destruction and violence are a part of the web of existence, too.

The old symbol of the serpent eating its tail, Ouroboros, is an image of how unity is a process that assimilates and uses itself. The real question is how this is done—that is, how far the extensions of care go, and where the lines of use are drawn. The idea that an enlightened, or realized, or self-expanded being need no longer draw these lines is absurd, since the questions will always remain: "What will I eat?" and "What will I use for my own survival, benefit, convenience, pleasure, and amusement?" For between cherishing and using (two basic poles of differentiated existence), where are the boundaries of one's consideration to be? How these questions are answered is crucial, at the collective as well as individual level.

Connecting with interconnection can be a powerful and valuable experience that helps alleviate fear and despair. But making it the magical key to the necessary consciousness transformation is but another formula that hopes purity of intention will solve everything. There are those who even state that uncon-

---

[16]The section on Buddhism in *Control* carefully examines the Buddhist worldview and its implications.

ditional love or compassion is the ultimate requisite for survival—the evolutionary leap needed. Here the more unconditional (selfless) the better. This is really a prescription about how people ought to be, which then becomes the measure of one's true humanity. Such standards create a concept of purity and are merely a disguised form of the old renunciate morality that debases self-centeredness. The absolute standards it sets are authoritarian, creating a hierarchy of value—the more loving, forgiving, or compassionate the better. Such one-sided formulas cannot take into account that openness to connect may not always be appropriate; that sometimes boundaries and self-protection are needed and serve a creative function.[17]

Once unity or interconnectedness is made sacred, a category is created that is not sacred—individuals and their individual concerns. Once the sacred was separated off into a special realm, religions became renunciate, with the religions defining both what to renounce and the perceived higher good that doing so brings. The idea of the intrinsic value of sacrifice and self-denial is still a part of many modern moral conceptions, no matter how secularized their veneer has become.

Every morality must deal with self-centeredness. This includes issues of personal and group survival, and the asymmetries of power and privilege which are both genetically and socially constructed. The spirituality embedded in the Oneness worldview creates lofty ideals of selfless moral purity that have worked well with authoritarian hierarchies. Hindu ashrams, Tibetan Buddhist monasteries, and Zen centers are all authoritarian hierarchies. Duty, obedience, and sacrifice are the key authoritarian virtues making such hierarchies work. When unity is valued over diversity, whether it be the One over the Many or the state over the individual, there are always those higher on the hierarchy to define for the lower just what that unity is and what must be sacrificed for it.

---

[17]See "Love and Control" for how "love without measure" becomes a measure of all other love.

Renunciation as Accumulation

That all the major world religions have a renunciate morality seems at first blush a bit odd since these religions all operate within cultures where accumulating wealth, power, and prestige positions people higher on the hierarchy. Accumulating seems to be quite the opposite of renouncing. This seeming enigma is understandable if it is seen as the result of separating the divine from the earthly: Accumulating was the activity that got one ahead in the secular domain; renouncing was the path that got one ahead in the spiritual. Once people's general mode of thought and behavior became based on the accumulation model, this insidiously got applied to everything, including renunciation, whereby one could accumulate spiritual merit through sacrifice.

Renunciation is the mirror image of accumulation, with inverted (opposite) values, but with the same structure (hierarchical) and process (striving), and the same measuring, ambitious mentality. The contents (sacrificing versus acquiring) may seem opposite, but this is only on the surface because the form and underlying structure of each is the same. Accumulation moralities set up standards of purity which serve to measure the quantity of impurity (self-centeredness). They measure how much sin or how much karma has been accumulated (demerits), and then give ways of accumulating merits through sacrifice. So ironically, renunciate religions are all based on accruing and stockpiling spiritual merit and are accumulative to the core. This is but another example of how either/or frameworks create reactive oppositions that, in an unconscious way, bring about the very thing they are trying to do away with. The hierarchical split between the sacred and secular breeds authoritarianism. Actually, authoritarian hierarchies thrive on renunciation, for this can always justify sacrificing the lower to the higher.

The spiritual path embedded in the Oneness worldview involves progress upward toward an enlightened state through becoming more selfless. This state is presented as the same for all people who reach it, no matter where they are historically situated. A path is a place where others have been and is a repetition of the known. Seeing spirituality as a-historical removes it from an evolving universe. Whereas if unity is embedded in its parts, which are changing and evolving, so too would human spirituality change, along with everything else.

The One and the Many, unity and diversity, are opposites only when so framed by either/or thinking. A dialectical framework that is more inclusive sees them as interweaving poles within the process of existence.[18] A view of both spirituality and morality is needed that does not prioritize one pole over the other. Judging as superior the values abstracted out of the mystical experience of Oneness is not only reactive, but itself is just more either/or, dualistic conceptualizing—ironically the very thing the ideology of Oneness claims it has transcended. The mystical experience does not end with unity; it begins there, and then must be integrated into the equal reality of individuated daily life.

---

[18]See "The Power of Abstraction" for more on Oneness and on the authors' dialectical framework.

The Power of Abstraction
The Sacred Word and the Evolution of Morality

" n the beginning was the Word." It is in the spreading of "the Word," or words, that religion gains power. What has given humanity its evolutionary advantage is using its complex brain to think, remember, and project into the future. Thinking is done in symbols (words), which through rules of combination (grammar) bring forth language. The capacity to think in symbols and communicate symbolically with others was the evolutionary watershed that made humans human.

Knowledge is power, but even more basic, language is power. It is through words that culture is created, maintained, and transmitted; so words are what create the mental alignment that defines a culture's perception of reality. But more, words move people, igniting emotion with a vision of possibility. The movement of human history is always preceded by new ideas, which are new constructions within language. Human behavior is not separable from the symbols making up the worldview that is its cultural context. The great diversity of human social systems compared to those of other social animals is made possible only through language.

Abstractions and Power

Deeply interwoven in the power of language is the ability to abstract. Considerations of the mental capacity to abstract could easily appear remote and largely irrelevant. But abstractions not only affect daily life, they are one of the great sources of power. Every worldview contains its unique abstractions that define it and not incidentally are used to control people. Religions have created the planet's most powerful, pervasive, and enduring systems of abstraction—systems still at the foundation of the moral systems of even secularized societies. This chapter shows how the evolution of abstraction enabled religions to increase control through creating more abstract moralities, and then suggests ways of changing the symbol system to foster a non-authoritarian approach to morality.

The common noun "tiger" reigns over all individual tigers by abstracting out what is perceived to be similar and essential, while ignoring whatever is viewed as non-essential (size, coloration, sex, etc.). One philosophical meaning of the verb "to abstract" is to fail to take account of. So in abstracting, one does not take account of anything non-essential to the meaning of the word—that is, all individual differences. By ignoring differences, abstractions can be more inclusive; the word "animal" ignores more differences and is more inclusive than the word "tiger." Tiger, like every other common noun, refers to an abstract class which in this case has concrete individuals as members. To use the word is to be involved in an abstraction, and the ability to do so leverages control and power enormously. One can now ask others to help hunt tigers or protect against them.

The discovery of agriculture brought one of the greatest shifts in human history—the capacity to accumulate and stockpile food. This has had enormous repercussions: It freed people to specialize, that is, to involve themselves in different activities not directly food-related. This in turn made possible a surplus of food and other objects of value that could be accumulated and traded. Whoever "owned," or more properly, controlled the use and distribution of the surplus greatly leveraged the capacity to control others. If I have extra food and you don't have enough, I can "pay" you with food to do what I want—that is, if I'm strong enough to keep you from taking it away from me. But then, I can also "hire" people to protect me. From here it is just a short step to realizing that hierarchies of power enable one person (or a few) to control increasingly larger numbers of people. With accumulation, hierarchical structures of power became the new social organizing principle, with authority located at the top—instead of in the traditions of the group as a whole as in earlier, more egalitarian bands.

Increased levels of abstractions are necessary to make hierarchies work. This is so not only because the concept of hierarchy is itself an abstraction, but also because people had to be objectified in order to be treated modularly—as classes and castes, which are also abstractions. Accumulation brought specialization and with it a major leap in the importance of roles. To think of a person as a role is an abstraction. We strongly suspect that hierarchies that placed authority in the hands of relatively few people were a fast (and perhaps inevitable) track to greatly increasing the overall power of the species. An elaborate division of labor necessarily involves coordinating the different tasks. There also has to be a way to ensure that each specialty, now needed for the workings of the social order, is manned long-term. Authoritarian hierarchy, when coupled with self-justifying belief systems, was probably the easiest and quickest way to bring the necessary cohesion and control of larger, more complex social orders.

Thus accumulation spurred the need for greater abstractions, which not incidentally increased the capacity for greater leveraging of power. First of all, one needed to keep track of what one accumulated. Numbers, and later mathematics, enabled people to manipulate very abstract symbols that could also be used for broader purposes than accumulated goods. A general could say to his king, "To win this war I need 2,000 more soldiers," upon which the king could order up 2,000 able bodies. Einstein through manipulating very abstract symbols could conclude that matter and energy (also abstract symbols) are transformable. The resulting "atomic age" has not only leveraged power but has changed the very way power can be used.

One can look at the history of humankind as utilizing ever greater levels of abstraction. And correspondingly, needing ever more specialized experts to interpret and manipulate them—whether in religion, science, or the stock market. Value is an abstraction. Giving metals, stones, coins, paper money, credit cards, stocks, and bonds symbolic value is using increasing levels of abstraction to allow more complex forms of exchange. This is another way to leverage power. A law of nature is an abstraction, as are ideas around goodness and moral principles that govern large classes of human interaction. Rules, like cultural roles, are abstractions.

The power of abstraction lies in this: the greater the abstraction, the larger the number and kinds of particulars that can be subsumed and included under it. It's not surprising then that religions, too, gained and increased their power by creating sacred symbols—mental constructions of the divine—of greater and greater abstraction. As constructions of the divine became more abstract, they were able to include more of the unknown under their reign, and also to be the foundation for a more abstract morality that could control larger numbers of people. Morality needs some worldview to justify it. The worldview needs to include explanations of why things are this way instead of that, and why people should take the morality seriously. As human interaction became more complex, the worldview correspondingly needed to become more abstract to handle the complexities.

Religions are the oldest, most conservative, and enduring symbol systems on the planet. Their myths, archetypes, and moral codes are deeply embedded in culture. No matter how secular a society appears, its religious heritage still influences its worldview and values. Whenever a predominant religion begins to lose authority, this foreshadows deep changes in human history. What ensues is a struggle between the old and the new for control of the symbol system—between fundamentalists, revisionists, secularists, and differing visionaries. Such struggles commonly were played out over centuries.[1]

This chapter is a broad portrayal of the evolution of abstraction in religion and its effect on social control. It focuses only on what we consider to be the four primary stages in conceptualizing the spiritual: animism, polytheism, Western monotheism, and Eastern Oneness. We are not proposing a neat, straight developmental line in the history of religious abstraction. Speculations about the actual evolution of religious thought are made murky by its antiquity. The point is that higher levels of abstraction needed lower levels to spring from, since they couldn't have come full bloom with the initial evolution of the human brain. Einstein's formulation that placed both matter and energy into the same category is a higher level of abstraction than was previously conceived. In order for him to do this, the abstract ideas of both matter and energy had to have already been constructed. Similarly, before monotheism could have been imagined, polytheistic gods had to have been in place in the human mind. This does not mean the stages delineated always follow an exact progression; lower levels of abstraction need not evolve, and a level can be skipped through contact with a higher one.

A brief definition of each stage:

1. Animism sees individual spirits embedded in nature's forces and objects to where all of nature is in some sense alive and pregnant with intent.[2] The spirits or willful agents are thought actually to be part of the wind, tree, mountain, fire, bear, etc. Tribal or shamanistic "nature religions" even now have an animistic flavor.

---

[1]"Fundamentalism and the Need for Certainty" covers the inherent tension within religion between the old and the new.

[2]The word "animism" is derived from the Latin *anima,* meaning spirit.

331

2. Polytheism posits many spirits or gods that are a higher order of nature. Although they are thought to control or act upon nature from a somewhat separate vantage point (at least compared to animism), they are still deeply linked with nature. Here the budding dualism between spirit and nature is still only partial and ambiguous. (This separation culminated, somewhat differently, in monotheism in the West and Oneness in the East.)

3. Monotheism puts forth the idea that there is one and only one omnipotent, omniscient God who is not only the creator and ruler of nature (and everything else), but essentially different from it. Here the dualism separating spirit from nature becomes absolute.

4. Eastern Oneness looks at spirit as undifferentiated and non-localized. The unity of all existence is seen as the true reality. Here the dualism between spirit and nature is brought about by either viewing nature, matter, and life itself as illusory (*maya*) or by creating levels in which nature is a lower order of reality.

We are not concerned here with the many smaller subsidiary steps, transitions, overlaps, and variations between stages, but rather with depicting the major stages and their respective moralities. Given the ultimate nature of the rewards and punishments promised, religion is one place where people are especially prone to hedge their bets. This makes it the most conservative sphere of culture, so when new forms are taken on, they are often superimposed on preexisting ones. This is one reason why remnants of animism and polytheism can still be found in the current world religions: Judeo-Christianity, Islam, Hinduism, and Buddhism.[3]

---

[3]In this we would include a spectrum of non-material entities with various supernatural powers, including gods, goddesses, angels, demons, devils, spirits, saints, bodhisattvas, etc.

From Animism to Polytheism: The Concrete Abstractions of Idolatry

Humans most probably imbued natural forces with intent very early because of the mind's tendency to seek familiar causes. From there, believing nature's forces and objects (sun, weather, animals, rocks, trees, etc.) contained spirits is not a great leap. When unseen forces or spirits were thought of as immanent everywhere in nature, there was little if any distinction between the natural and supernatural. Tree spirits were part of trees, a wind spirit was within the actual wind, etc.

Animism originated when people had relatively little control over and protection against nature, whose powers largely dictated the rhythms of life. The animistic worldview was a result of a specific balance of power between humans and other elements within nature. The way animism is constructed indicates that people saw themselves as an animal among other animals, a force among other forces that had to be reckoned with. The animistic worldview reflects that people felt totally connected with, part of, and very vulnerable to nature, having awe and reverence for its mysteries and powers. Imputing motive to natural forces allows them to be influenced by human behavior, which opened the doorway to trying to control them through magic and propitiatory acts and rites. The interest in doing so was because these forces (rain, fire, etc.) had great power over people's lives.

It is our supposition that nature as an abstract idea had not yet been conceptualized in early animism, so to call it nature worship would be a projection of the modern mind. Until nature can be contrasted with something else, such as culture or the supernatural, it has no conceptual value. It just is what it is—everything. Worship itself also involves a more conceptualized attitude toward the divine in which the sacred is to some degree abstracted out of nature and made "Other."[4]

Whereas later symbols began to represent qualities abstracted from nature, early animistic symbols seem to have been viewed as extensions of what was depicted, and thus as sharing the same essence or identity as the object itself. For instance, many prehistoric cave paintings of animals were most probably seen as magically connected with the animals, just as names in some sense participated in (rather than merely stood for) their referents' essence and power. We and others think it likely that both types of animistic symbols were considered imbued with sympathetic magical powers triggered by contact. Drawing an arrow through a picture of an animal would aid in killing it; knowing something's name gave some power over it.[5]

The first major step of religious abstraction turned nature's invisible "spirit-forces" into gods by abstracting them out of nature, giving them form, personality—a separate existence. This led to polytheism, the worldview common to all the early civilizations. The idea came that there was a force behind the wind that created all wind; so a wind god was abstracted out that ruled over the wind but was not necessarily in each individual occurrence of wind. The difference between "within" and "behind" could seem like a small distinction, but this shift is the watershed that enabled religion to generate worship and control. There is a seminal difference between trying to placate and control a wind god rather than the wind itself. Once a god is abstracted out, human or superhuman traits (including gender) are invariably projected upon it. Now its motives can be better known. Who knows what the capricious wind cares about? But a male wind god could care about what men care about: sex, virgins, food, wealth, power, adulation. So to gain favor it can be sacrificed to, and through priests its demands can be made known.

---

[4]See "Satanism and the Worship of the Forbidden" on the link between worship and power.

[5]The chapter on animism in *Control* covers it in more detail.

The difference between "behind" and "within" contains the early seeds of the portentous division between the natural and the supernatural, and between matter and spirit. Within early polytheism the seeds were planted that split the sacred from the worldly. This initial mental process of abstracting the sacred from nature was to have enormous ramifications—including eventually placing ultimate meaning outside life itself.

The first religious abstractions creating gods and goddesses were quite concrete. That is, qualities abstracted out of nature were reified into sacred beings, highly anthropomorphized into human form or animals with human traits. These were then literally "embodied" in paintings and sculpture. Once given a particular form, the gods could be localized. Thus early deities were thought to reside in certain sacred locations in nature, and later, also as idols in their own temples. Once so localized, they could be directly approached through offerings, sacrifices, ritual, and worship. Although the gods came to represent a different order of existence, they were still intermixed with nature rather than totally separate from it. They lived in nature (earth, sky, water, the underworld) and manifested themselves in natural events.

Polytheistic gods were thought to act very much like humans, except with far greater power and exaggerated traits. Projecting specific qualities onto the gods involves a level of abstraction whereby the qualities become larger than life (as do the gods). When deities are made human-like, they can display such human qualities as mercy, compassion, pride, anger, vengeance, sexuality, parenthood, etc. Like humans, they were sometimes capricious, protective, or untrustworthy. They were also thought to compete with each other, often in ways that were not particularly scrupulous. These more understandable and approachable deities are easier to worship, praise, appease, cajole, blame, and sacrifice to. And importantly, language can now be used to reach them directly through prayer, hymns, lamentations, covenants, etc. Here special words begin to become sacred.

We focus on the polytheisms of the ancient Near East (Sumer, Mesopotamia, Egypt) where writing originated. Writing accel-

335

erated the abstracting process, as one could refine and build on previous constructions. Also the written word is necessary for controlling larger numbers of people through spreading the deities' orders. Most polytheisms have a vast pantheon of gods (more than 2,000 in ancient Egypt), each with its own powers, responsibilities, and agendas. In the contemporary mind, Near Eastern deities formed a landed nobility whose temples were powerful, independent economic units—great estates with sometimes thousands of workers where food and other commodities were produced and distributed. Humans came to be thought of as having been created for the sole purpose of serving the gods and freeing them from manual labor. A symbiotic master/servant relationship was conceived reflecting the early urban hierarchies. The gods depended on humans to fulfill their very human-like daily needs (to be fed, clothed, bathed, etc.), while humans depended on the gods for their personal welfare, as well as the state's. Nothing could be done without favorable divine intervention. Service became a prerequisite for the gods' favors.

Early polytheistic abstractions had a concreteness that was literal. People worshipped idols (statues) since the deities were believed to be actually present in them. When there are many gods, giving them different traits is the only way of distinguishing them from each other. These traits can be pictured; from there the picture or statue itself easily becomes the vessel for the god. Idolatry is not a hard step to take from the earlier animistic symbols, paintings, and amulets. Both were seen as "real" rather than simply symbolic representations; but while a prehistoric cave painting was thought to have a magical connection with an actual animal (and later, perhaps, its spirit), an idol embodies an abstraction, an idea (a god), making the concept seem to come alive. A serious disadvantage of such concrete abstractions was the necessity of protecting the idol, for if captured or destroyed, divine protection was lost, thus crushing morale.

The abstractions of polytheism greatly increased the rulers' power to control people, for the king as the high priest was the intermediary to the gods, or (as with Egyptian pharaohs) actually held to be divine. Early polytheism began the long process of removing the construction of sacred abstractions from ordinary people. State religions in which official intermediaries became necessary created a privileged class of religious experts, guardians of the Word, who alone could give the right words with which to approach the gods. They also made known the gods' wishes and punishments for disobedience. Writing was an exclusive, elite activity of specialists who deciphered, interpreted (and created) the sacred texts. When the sacred Word was written in stone, literally, it could not be easily challenged except by official revisions, also written in stone. Revisions reorganized the pantheon of gods to reflect shifts in political power. The religious elite, in collusion with the rulers, came to have a monopoly on creating the religious symbol system—the basic worldview that dominated all the other symbol systems of society. So began the symbiotic relation between religious and political power in which religion justifies the ruler's right to rule, and rulers legitimate religion's right to justify.

Hierarchism and expansion of secular power were further aided by new religious notions of morality. In animistic cultures the social code is embedded in the group's ancestral traditions. During the long span of polytheism, morality became increasingly grounded in religion. The gods came to represent abstract moral qualities: goodness, mercy, justice, order, forgiveness, retribution, etc. This was the start of an abstract system of ethics that culminated in the existing major religions, whereby they became the basis of morality.[6]

When a religion becomes more abstract it also becomes more principled. Different principles compete for ascendancy generating a hierarchy of value. Whose words are to be taken the most seriously? Which gods are the most righteous or powerful? Another important step toward greater abstraction was to look for and conceptualize a greater power behind the plethora of gods. In early creation myths a remote power, often female, set

---

[6]The section "The Roots of Authoritarianism" in *Control* describes this progressive ethicizing of religion.

things in motion without further influence. As militarism grew, the gods often came to be seen as created by a more powerful creator god who parceled out powers and spheres of influence. Here, a divine hierarchy of power, not accidentally resembling a king and his court, restructured the polytheistic pantheons.

For millennia, both gods and goddesses had wide-ranging powers that were not limited by gender. Priestesses were often as powerful as priests, commonly heading temples for deities of the opposite sex. As the early states became more entrenched and powerful, however, male gods, along with male priests and scribes, grew correspondingly more dominant. This hierarchical, centralizing movement in religion ran parallel to kings expanding their power and consolidating what many now call patriarchy. Part of this trend involved the replacement of powerful and independent goddesses by newly dominant male gods, who domesticated and demoted them to wives and consorts. This push toward the ascendancy of male power culminated in the Near East in Judaism's monotheistic, covertly male God and exclusively male priesthood.

In early animistic cultures, the mystery of female procreation was most likely greatly valued and even revered, for it was essential to survival. Eventually a life force or general principle of regeneration was abstracted from natural processes and sacralized. In the early agricultural polytheisms, fertility was the central sacred symbol around which nature's cycles, and thus the community's well-being and prosperity, revolved. Since female procreation and sexuality were conceptually associated with fertility and fecundity, worship of the female (in the form of goddesses) was also central to these ancient fertility religions. Regardless of women's actual power, this must have given women some status and respect, which eroded gradually with the rise of militarism.

Religion is inherently conservative owing to the fear of offending unseen powers, and also to the emotional attachment to feeling protected by traditional deities. This conservatism, along with the archetypal abstractions of the female as creator of life,

338

nurturer, and sexual igniter, suffice to explain why female religious symbols, including goddesses, retained popularity while women were increasingly losing secular status and power. In the emerging urban militaristic societies, women were progressively more subordinate; the legal codes eventually reduced them to male property. Inevitably symbols sacralizing the male hierarchy competed with and finally overshadowed the more sexually egalitarian symbols associated with fertility.

The movement into greater abstraction is most graphic in the transformation of creation myths. At first creation, including the creation of the cosmos, was linked with the female principle because the overall capacity to create was literally associated with the actual physical act of procreation, where a new life seems to come out of nothing. The male contribution in paternity was not yet clearly understood, if known at all. Since mysterious fertility emanated from the female, not surprisingly, female deities were the dominant figures in the earliest Near Eastern myths of origin.

When the concept "creativity" was abstracted out of physical processes and made into a separate principle, which of course is a symbolic structure, the act of creation was dramatically changed by making the mental concept both prior to and dominant over the physical expression. This gave more control over creation, making it active instead of passive. This basic shift is reflected in a sentence in the Bible, "In the beginning was the Word." Creativity was relocated within the symbols themselves, making it mental, consciously directed, and broader, instead of a mysterious, uncontrollable physical procreative force. Now a male creator god could bring forth life, or anything, by merely willing it via symbols.

Much has been written about the shifts in the symbols of creativity from the fertile female and earth (both of which physically do the creating) to the male. Some knowledge of paternity was a prerequisite for this shift. Creativity becomes linked to the plow, phallus, seed, semen, etc., stripping the female of significant creative power. The womb and the earth are reduced to passive receptacles for the potent seeds (sperm) that are now considered the sole carriers of the life force, the spirit to be realized. Later, no less a thinker than Aristotle presented this view with certainty, which greatly influenced medieval thought. Examples of this shift in religious mythology abound, a prominent example being in Genesis where Eve is literally made from man (Adam's rib), and considered secondary as man's helpmate. Finally, in the New Testament God is explicitly called "the Father" and made the creator of us all.

Abstracting creativity from the physical was used not only to demote the female, but also to denigrate the body, sexuality, and nature itself. The essence of a person, including the life force, was abstracted out of the human animal and then made into a higher order of existence (the soul). Sexual attraction and the actual act of sex itself (which is, of course, quite animal) become a hindrance to spiritual realization. The idea of woman as the temptress who causes the "fall of man" is thus born.

The removal of creativity from nature and sexuality to an abstract principle occurs in tandem with the split between the sacred and the mundane, which abstracts spirit from nature. Of course, the concept of nature is itself an abstraction that exists only when counterposed to culture, another abstraction. Urbanism exacerbated the conceptual polarization between culture and nature, but this was greatly reinforced by abstracting spirit from nature. Men then came to be associated with spirit and culture, and women with the inferior realm of matter, biology, and nature. This new metaphysical split was made absolute in Hebrew monotheism and perpetuated in Christianity and Islam. Female divinity is entirely absent in the Christian Trinity. Medieval Christians debated whether women had souls, and even today some Islamic sects claim woman don't have souls or go to heaven.

Even though there was a division in polytheism between humans and the gods, between the natural and supernatural, the gods were still held to reside in nature. They were not only conceived as directly operating on nature, but also as being constructed out of its forces. They were portrayed as a higher, separate order of life, but not divorced from earthly life. They could propagate, marry, get hurt, and even sometimes die. And they were thought to continually intervene in nature and in human lives—not only manifesting their powers in nature, but being somewhat dependent on humans themselves. Here the rift between the spiritual and worldly was not yet absolute.

The capacity to abstract is a tool for understanding the general within specific manifestations. This in fact is one meaning of understanding. A basic function of religion is to explain and help control the unknown. As understanding of nature increased through utilizing abstractions, religion had to become even more abstract in order to continue to reign over the natural world. The more one understands the dynamics of, say, thunder or the sun, the less credible a thunder or sun god becomes and the less need there is for them.

Religion's eventual answer to keeping power involved separating the cosmos into two distinct categories, the natural and the supernatural, by abstracting the sacred from daily life. (This is not to imply that this solution was necessarily consciously planned.) From this high level of abstraction, the untouchability of religious concepts is easier to maintain. The higher the level of abstraction, the more removed the concepts are from the concrete vicissitudes of daily life and from challenges to their presumed immaculate nature. Once the split between spiritual and material (and consequently religion and nature) becomes absolute, any challenge to religion can always be deflected by asserting that the sacred is ultimately unreachable by mere mundane knowledge. As the sacred was characterized by increasingly greater abstractions, the separation between divinity and humans grew commensurately larger. In the West, this culminated in an omnipotent monotheistic God that brought an absolute separation between the divine and the world of humans, between God and his creation.

Monotheism:
A Universal Abstraction

The concept of hierarchy (as every general knows) is essential to accumulate and move power. Once the gods themselves were organized in a hierarchy of power, hierarchies of value (levels of virtue and goodness) could flow from that. A more abstract religion could become the foundation of a needed abstract morality that had the power to control the ever larger numbers of people found in the newly forming states produced by accumulation and kingship. Secular hierarchies sacralized the morality that justified caste and class systems through notions of purity and hereditary superiority.

In the West, monotheism became that next level of religious abstraction. The Hebrews, by raising their tribal god from merely the best god to the only God, created a more abstract symbol of universality that became valid for everyone, thus moving into a new conceptual frame. When in the thirteenth century B.C. Moses forbade worship of idols and images, this radical innovation served to prohibit the worship of other deities, thus strengthening the foundation of monotheism. An incorporeal God with no material form or location had the great advantage of establishing powerful bonds between God and its followers that could not be broken through theft or destruction of icons, defeat, or exile.

By making God ineffable and disassociating it from all images, God as a symbol was made yet more abstract and radically different from the more concrete, human-like abstractions of polytheism. This advance in abstraction increased the Hebrews' perception of their God's power, which resulted in greater social control emanating from God's Word. The Ten Commandments contain not only rules for living, but the first five are really demands of submission to God, with punishments for disobedience—particularly idolatry—going "unto the third and fourth generation." Eventually polytheistic practices faded, although throughout the Old Testament a wrathful God is punishing his wayward people for idolatry. The Hebrew God, though "ineffable," still retained such human emotions as anger, vengeance, mercy, and later (in the New Testament) even sired a child with a human, as did polytheistic gods.

A religious framework is a worldview whose power is dependent upon offering a better explanation for the vicissitudes and uncertainties of living, and also offering better beliefs and practices for mitigating against them. Monotheism superseded polytheism for the same reason polytheism emerged from animism. As population grew, contact between groups and beliefs was inevitable, as was competition. Greater abstraction was necessary to deal with more diversity. A quarreling hierarchy of gods initially better explained quarreling hierarchies of people. But its ability to unite diverse peoples was limited.

The strength of monotheism lies in its ability to explain existence better and more simply, and to give a more stable foundation for dealing with the world through its morality. Basically monotheism supplanted polytheism because its God was more powerful and inclusive, as were the more abstract concepts associated with monotheism. Polytheistic creation myths were necessarily vague, as it was uncertain just how the creator god or gods could create anything, even themselves. With monotheism the creation myth is both powerful and simple. God created everything because it had the will and power to do so. For this, the abstract concept of omnipotence was necessary.

Polytheistic gods must each have traits, identities, and their own special realms of power to be distinguishable from each other. Monotheism created a new concept of power by subsuming all power traits into one abstract quality, omnipotence. In order to be truly all-powerful, the God had to also be all-seeing, omniscient. Also, to be the final Word or first cause, it could not have been created by anything else; thus it had to be eternal. Its doings had to be right by definition so it had to be the source of all virtue. It is around the question of whether God, as the source of everything, is also the source of evil that monotheism has its greatest difficulties.[7] All this raised God to a higher level of abstraction, giving it the most inclusive powers.

The ultimate abstraction of spirit to one principle allowed more hierarchical control. This innovation made the Word of God unchallengeable. Competing gods do not have absolute power to punish transgressions. They have competing words, thus obedience can always be hedged by switching allegiance to another god, or worshipping many at once. No one god can demand or enforce total obedience since they all have special powers that need to be taken into account. Omniscience is also a great power for control. It is the ultimate form of "Big Brother is watching you," as it made people believe God knew their every move and thought. The fear of an inescapable and vengeful God is a new foundation for psychological control, that is, mind control. Not coincidentally, great power and authority are vested in those chosen to ensure God's Word be obeyed.

The monotheistic worldview is authoritarian at its core. If one thing is all-powerful, then everything else is not only less powerful, but less in every way. Raising hierarchy to a new level where all power flowed from one source could only be accomplished by making the separation between God and humans absolute. With every new level of abstraction, religion was increasingly characterized by human inferiority and obedience in the face of the divine. Making God the ultimate force to please does not promote self-trust. Once self-trust is undermined, this creates an "authoritarian personality" that seeks to follow those who "know better." Those who know better, of course, are the guardians and interpreters of the sacred Word.[8]

In making the dualistic separation between God and everything else absolute, monotheism set the stage for hardening other polarities that were less firm under polytheism: mind and body, culture and nature, spirit and matter, humans and ani-

---

[7]See "The Problem of Evil" in "Satanism."

[8]Also see "Religion, Cults, and the Spiritual Vacuum" on the relation of religion to social hierarchy.

mals, etc. Monotheism's power and attractiveness lie in its very absoluteness, which created unchallengeable rules to live by, bringing more security, certainty, and social cohesion.

In the West, it is tacitly assumed by many that monotheism was a great advance over polytheism. This may be true in the sense that the abstractions of monotheism led to changes that are linked with some meanings of the word "progress," such as increased power, control over others and nature, improved technology, and more complex social organization. Whether monotheism ultimately brought actual moral progress, however, is being seriously challenged by feminist thinkers who link monotheism to male domination, and also by others who see it as disconnecting humanity from its spiritual relationship with nature and ecological concerns. Certainly monotheism has fueled some of the darkest moments in human history. Examples are rife: the conquest and slavery of indigenous peoples, the Inquisition, and even Nazism.

The judgment as to whether or not one worldview offers a moral advance over another cannot be divorced from the historical context of the competing worldviews. And although comparing differing value systems is fraught with difficulty, we must acknowledge that in at least one important way monotheism offered a real moral advance—for those times. Without getting into the knotty problems involved in justifying any moral claims, simply put, for us a moral advance involves a shift in context whereby people treat each other better. So, for example, a context that does not permit slavery or human sacrifice is a moral advance over one that does, and is thus better.

To call a person principled is generally a compliment. What this really means is that one so considered can be expected to act from a (somewhat) consistent set of values rather than only the shifting sands of self-interest. Such people are usually more predictable, thus trustworthy. Monotheism, because of the very absoluteness of its authority, could set down moral principles that were more likely to be followed than those of its rival polytheism, which did not offer nearly as coherent an ethical system.

In a world of ethical arbitrariness, the Hebrews came to be admired for their strong principles and family and community ideals. The Ten Commandments clearly set forth a strong communal code: Thou shall not lie (bear false witness), steal, kill, commit adultery, covet thy neighbor's wife or property. Until Christianity came to the fore, Judaism was a proselytizing religion spreading its message and morality. With the Hebrew exile in the sixth century B.C., their idea of one God began to spread as they did. One reason so many achieved high positions in the bureaucracies of the lands where they settled is the rulers could trust them. Later this appeal shifted to Christianity, which was grounded in similar moral principles. A personal savior, and eliminating strict Hebrew dietary and circumcision laws made conversion to Christianity much more appealing. The victory of Christianity over other then popular cults and mystery religions was ensured when Constantine made it the official religion of the Roman Empire. A probable reason for this choice was that Christianity offered a reliable set of beliefs and principles that could be used to bind his disintegrating, decadent empire.

Monotheism did put the power of the Word, of religious symbol-making and abstraction, exclusively in male hands. This resulted in desacralizing the feminine. The pastoral Hebrews not being very involved with agriculture, fertility was not centrally sacred to them. Like most pastoralists, their religion before monotheism was dominated by male gods. The Hebrew tribal god that eventually was elevated to the only God retained male characteristics. Though made universal and supposedly ineffable, the God of the Old Testament remains covertly male. This God speaks almost exclusively to Hebrew men; makes covenants only with them (based on circumcision); uses male prophets as intermediaries; and only holds males morally responsible. Later, in the Christian Trinity the female is not only absent, but in naming God "the Father," God was officially declared male.

There is an uncomfortable question as to why women "went for" early monotheism—an obvious patriarchal structure that overtly lessened their symbolic and perceived worth. There are a number of possible historical explanations, including that they were not given much choice. Women under Near Eastern polytheism had not been faring well—in spite of the lip service paid to worshipping the female principle and goddesses. The developing military kingships were hierarchies that used people callously, slavery being an example. When organized killing became the bottom line of power, the status of women gradually was reduced by codes and laws, so that their sexuality and procreative capacity became commodities to use and abuse. A woman could be killed for adultery, and rape was exclusively a crime against the woman's male owner (father or husband).

There is a simple hypothesis as to why women might have felt that patriarchal monotheism was in their self-interest: under its more principled moral codes, women and their children were treated better. Even though they were still male property, the Ten Commandments also promulgated new family values. Hebrew men became renowned and admired for protecting their families. Community standards likewise offered women protection. If beaten, a wife could appeal to the rabbi and community on moral grounds to censure the husband; consequently there was little wife-beating. The community's tightly controlled morality underpinned protecting and taking care of its members. Its strong community values, along with the conviction of being God's "chosen people," gave Judaism a staying power that is still alive after 4,000 years. Later, Christ, continuing this concern for the disempowered, pronounced men and women's souls equal. Even Islam, the most sexually unequal monotheistic religion, at its inception offered women significantly better treatment than they were getting.

Monotheism with its abstract God could put forth abstract unchallengeable principles that were universally applicable. We think it spread in part because it did offer people a vision of a better life, and also because the universal values were a better glue to hold together larger numbers of people. The problem for today is that the very authoritarian morality that was the solution of the past now hinders solutions for the present and future. The simplistic, dualistic worldview that lies under the words of authority is not flexible enough to deal with the different kinds of moral crises that technology and unconscious reproduction have brought.[9]

There are interesting parallels between the two highest levels of religious abstraction, monotheism and Oneness. Both powerful concepts have endured since their inception and are the core of the two oldest continuous religions—Judaism and Hinduism; both Brahmins, the highest Hindu caste, and Hebrews consider themselves the chosen ones; and both Judaic monotheism and Hindu Oneness are a core part of the worldviews of subsequent world religions (religions that have crossed national boundaries). Judaism is the foundation of Christianity (initially a Jewish heresy) and Islam; the Hindu conception of Oneness has greatly influenced other Eastern religions such as Buddhism and Jainism.

Oneness: The Culmination of Religious Abstraction

Oneness, the pinnacle of religious abstraction, is the aspect of Eastern thought the West is currently the most enamored of. The early Vedism of the Aryan invaders that superimposed itself on indigenous forms was a combination of polytheism, ancestor worship, and ritual sacrifice similar to Greek and other Indo-European religions. Later (during the first millennium B.C.) the more sophisticated Upanishads put forth the conception of Oneness, the non-duality of all being *(advaitism)*. In Hinduism, Vedanta is the modern expression of this. This raised the level of abstraction in Hinduism to where Brahman, The One, actually encompasses everything. As with all abstractions, here all dif-

---

[9]"Fundamentalism" shows how protecting God's Word has become a form of "ideological uncaringness" more concerned with maintaining an ideology than with the ideology's effect on people.

ferences are ignored and an all-permeating sameness given ultimate reality. However, differences still must be accounted for, even if they are trivialized by calling them illusion *(maya)*. With the abstract concept of *maya*, which includes all differences under the same umbrella (the multiplicity of existence), diversity is both accounted for and either denied or made lower.[10]

In this way Hinduism, which is both polytheistic and ostensibly monistic, found a way to have its cake and eat it, too. (Monism sees everything as composed of one basic substance.) Underneath the static category of Oneness, a polytheistic pantheon of deities was allowed form at lower levels of abstraction. First The One was split into three personifications: Brahma the Creator, Vishnu the Preserver, and Shiva the Destroyer. Creation, preservation, and destruction became the abstract principles underlying the "dance of life." And from these three flowed different manifestations that could also be depicted anthropomorphically and worshipped. Many of these were the preceding indigenous polytheistic gods. Here the female principle could be brought into an essentially patriarchal religion (another all-male trinity) as goddesses who were derived from it. Hinduism's staying power is that it offers something for everyone: intellectuals and mystics subscribe to the highest level of abstraction, Oneness; others get emotional satisfaction from rituals and devotion to a personal deity—one of its many manifestations, or to a guru.

The more abstract a symbol, the larger the range of events it can include. The word "fruit" is a more abstract symbol than "orange." "Nourishment" could include all food as well as other occurrences that may not have a material referent—love is nourishing. Oneness is an abstraction that reigns over everything by definition, and thus can encompass anything that comes along. Oneness is a higher level of abstraction than monotheism, which has an inherent dualism between creator (God) and created (everything else).

---

[10]See "Oneness, Enlightenment, and the Mystical Experience."

Simply put, monotheism cannot envelop or deal with the concept of the unity of all existence, except by denying it. Its God has to be separate and different. Oneness, however, can incorporate all gods, including a monotheistic one. Hindu Oneness can (and does) look upon Christ as another avatar (living manifestation of the godhead), and in one stroke all of Christianity is subsumed within it. Likewise to many Hindus, Buddha is merely another great avatar; so to them, Buddhism is really another sect of Hinduism. This inclusiveness of Oneness that can absorb anything under its banner contrasts with the inherent exclusiveness of monotheism—"Thou shalt have no other gods before me"; "There is no God but Allah." As the most abstract of all religious concepts, Oneness is therefore the most impervious to direct challenge.

Hindu Oneness and the Buddhist Void are essentially the same abstraction in that both are non-differentiated and all-pervasive. Buddha, a reformer, aimed at changing the moral structure by eliminating the caste system and replacing the endless exclusionary and expensive Vedic rituals of early Hinduism with rules for a social morality. Hindu Oneness accentuates permanence and so acted as a foundation for perpetuating the caste system. In reaction to this, Buddhism emphasizes change ("All is flux"). The concept of the Void initially "emptied" Oneness, so to speak, by stripping away Hinduism's hefty population of deities and related rituals. This simplified the metaphysics and highlighted Buddha's moral reforms. Since a primary tenet of Buddhism was acceptance, and since the Void can be as inclusive an abstraction as Oneness, as Buddhism spread, it too incorporated preexisting local deities and spirits. This was done by retaining the Hindu multi-leveled conceptual structure. (Oneness reigns supreme over a hierarchy of deities that are expressions of it.) In some schools of Buddhism the formless Void, in a similar fashion, came to contain hierarchical levels of form: deities, spirits, demons, and bodhisattvas.

Though Eastern conceptions of cosmic unity appear not to be dualistic, there is a hidden dualism in the Oneness worldview.

It abstracts out sameness, calling it the only reality, and throws all difference (multiplicity) into a lesser category. Buddhism's analogous dualism is between the formless Void and the world of ever-changing forms. The overt monotheistic dualism between God and everything else is replaced by a covert, more sophisticated dualism between unity and diversity. In monotheism, God is higher and therefore must be sacrificed to; in the Oneness ideology, unity is higher and so any individual expression can be likewise sacrificed. Both dualisms justify a morality that allowed more hierarchical control.[11]

There is power in being able to incorporate one symbol into another. When the level of abstraction that people operate in is no longer satisfying or credible, for whatever reason (often because of advances in secular knowledge), the tendency is to look for a still higher level. This is another reason why Eastern religions have gained popularity in the West—they contain a higher level of religious abstraction that can better incorporate scientific abstractions. Because the concept of Oneness is a higher level of abstraction, once it enters one's mind it is not unusual to try to incorporate one's previous beliefs within it. There are those who wish to link Christ's message of love with Oneness. And esoteric Sufi mysticism attempted to bring Oneness into Islam. (Islam being an extremely doctrinaire dualism, the Sufis had to be esoteric to avoid being killed for blasphemy.)

The more abstract a concept is, the more it generalizes; and at the same time, it leaves out particulars, sometimes even the particulars of life itself. By abstracting the sacred from nature, the different religions in their diverse ways made nature low on the hierarchy of importance. Hierarchies are complex organizations

---

[11]See "Oneness, Enlightenment, and the Mystical Experience" on this and on why pantheism, a non-dualistic Western conception that sees God as everything, was not adaptable by renunciate religion, as it does not lend itself to justifying a renunciate morality. "The Hidden Dualism in Oneness" in "Buddhism and the Abuse of Detachment" (in *Control*) also describes Eastern dualism.

with a simple pyramidal form. As religions cut themselves off from nature, they too became both convoluted and simplistic at the same time. Monotheism explains everything simply as the will of God; Oneness goes even further and writes differences off as either merely illusion, or at best as a lesser reality that must be transcended. Each then gives elaborate theories, cosmologies, and theologies to justify why its simplistic explanation should be believed.

Concepts of spirituality became more abstract, moving from individual "spirits" embedded in nature to abstract principles and powers beyond nature. Through manipulating belief in the sacred symbols that represented these new abstractions, greater control over larger areas of human behavior was made possible. When human activities became more specialized, society needed to be more organized, and in turn needed justifications for the way it was organized. The hierarchies within the emerging systems of sacred symbols mirrored and justified the developing hierarchies of secular power.

Complex social hierarchies need some kind of internal control mechanisms, and religions became their source. In the West, it was obeying God's will and promoting the fear of God that kept people in line. The authoritarian nature of the monotheistic worldview is inherent, for revealed writings are necessarily its basis, laying down unchallengeable rules of how to live. Islamic authoritarianism ought to be obvious given the literal meaning of the word "Islam" is submission (to God). What this really means is submission to the presumed words of God, the Koran. Judeo-Christianity also puts forth commandments to obey as the basis of morality.[12]

Unlike monotheism, Oneness does not lend itself to a separate omnipotent authority that dictates how to be, so the authoritarian modes inherent in the religions that institutionalized belief in Oneness are less obvious. Their authoritarianism is not in

---

[12]"Good and Evil" in "Satanism" describes the nature of the renunciate dualistic morality within monotheism.

specific rules, but in a more generalized abstract rule that states the more selfless one is the better, supported by a more abstract force, karma, to ensure that everybody gets what they deserve. The Oneness worldview requires an in-built force that can manipulate fear and desire in order to generate the renunciate moral system necessary to inculcate "voluntary" self-sacrifice. The abstract idea of karma fits this need admirably.[13]

Eastern religions transformed divine retribution and reward into an impersonal universal law. So in the East, karma became the abstract principle underlying all activity that justified the way the social order was organized. Given that virtue and vice do not always display the requisite results in a given life, they had to accumulate on a cosmic ledger across lifetimes, determining future lives. Karma also acted as a bridge to the very abstract goal of escaping the wheel of individuated existence so as to be at One with the cosmos. Its simple formula is: the less one resists one's karma, the less karma one generates, and the better off one will be.

All the surviving major world religions base their ultimate rewards and punishments on some kind of continuity after life. For divine retribution to work it is necessary to abstract something from life that continues after death. Whereas monotheism makes one's earthly life of secondary importance to the afterlife, Eastern religion denies its ultimate reality. The luxury of shifting attention from survival on earth to after-death considerations was made possible by the power of abstraction, which gave humanity more control over life.

Abstractions are products of thought that may or may not refer to something other than thought. Whether the idea of karma refers to an actual objective principle or force underlying the way human existence is structured can be debated. An abstract moral law with intrinsic power to reward and punish can seem more plausible to the modern mind than an anthropomorphic

---

[13]"Do You Create Your Own Reality?" concisely describes some basic elements within karma.

God. It is certainly much harder to question.[14] What is not moot is that the concept of karma became one of the most powerful controllers of human behavior this planet has ever known. The relentless, impersonal law of karma functions like an omniscient God, recording and judging every action. When coupled with ideas of purity and selflessness, both of which are also abstractions, a renunciate moral system of great power was created.[15]

The problems with abstracting unity from diversity come when unity is given more value and more reality than individuated life. Unity and multiplicity (the One and the Many) are two sides of a dialectical process that need each other to be at all—neither has priority.[16] Self-centeredness and selflessness are also embedded in each other. A morality that equates virtue with selfless behavior can have great control over human action, but it cannot eliminate the self-centered. Instead, self-centered behavior merely becomes organized around what is socially acceptable or displays itself unconsciously. The state of the world is a testament to the failure of renunciate values to deal successfully with the core issue of self-centeredness.[17]

---

[14]This is discussed at length in the section on karma in *Control*.

[15]"Religion, Cults, and the Spiritual Vacuum" describes the nature and limitations of renunciate religions. "Satanism" focuses on renunciation within monotheism; the chapter "Oneness" focuses on Eastern renunciate frameworks.

[16]"A Dialectical Approach to the One and the Many" in "East and West: Looking Within and Looking Without" and the section on Buddhism (both in *Control*) further discuss the relation between the One and the Many.

[17]"What Is Selfless Service Serving?" in *Control* shows how a morality that makes selflessness the highest value breeds corruption.

Abstraction, Either/Or Thinking, and Dualism

There is an increasing awareness of the limits of linear thinking. Linear thought goes in a straight line from cause to effect, or from accepted premises to a conclusion at least partially determined by the premises. Two-valued, either/or thinking is an integral part of linear thought. Dualism, the abstraction that stands behind either/or thinking, refers to splitting the cosmos, reality, existence—whatever you want to call it—into two distinct and mutually exclusive categories. Monotheism's division between the creator and creation is an absolute dualism. Other examples are the spiritual and the worldly, reality and illusion, matter and spirit, etc. In dividing reality into separate binary categories, dualism produces more either/or thinking. It is either/or thinking that places the following in opposition: selfishness versus care; need versus love; and on a more abstract level, egotism versus altruism and permanence versus change. Other classical dualistic categories are mind/body, nature/culture, good/evil, insider/outsider, subject/object, higher/lower, reason/emotion, selfless/selfish, masculine/feminine, objective/subjective, etc.

After creating these separate categories, what inevitably follows—owing to the inbuilt nature of preference—is valuing one side of the polarity over the other. This either/or structuring lends itself to a simple morality where good and bad, the selfless and the selfish, are divided in an absolute way. Then comes the mistaken corollary: by suppressing one side of the polarity (the supposed bad, wrong, or less valued side), the other, more desired side is automatically enhanced. This unavoidably leads to trying to get rid of or deny the side that has been villainized.

It may be that the human brain, because of the way it is constructed, has an easier time thinking in either/or categories, or this tendency may be deeply, culturally rooted—or both. Probably when humanity began to realize the power in abstraction through using symbols via writing and numbers, dualistic categories and either/or thinking increased. In manipulating symbols, the more sharply defined a category is, the easier it is to deal with. This is especially true when dealing with numbers. Numbers lend themselves to either/or conceptualizing: I either have three coins or I do not have three coins—I have two or five or none. There is no intermediary or ambiguous state. We also suspect that cultures without writing abstract less, and that whatever categories they make would tend to be less overtly dualistic.

It is important to understand how the clear-cut separations, rigid boundaries, and often artificial polarizations created by two-valued, binary thinking easily fuel and reinforce authoritarianism. Either/or conceptualizing makes it much easier to organize and control people. Authoritarianism depends on such oppositions as: "Do this, not that"; "This is right and that's wrong"; and "I'm here, and you, the authority, are up there." Good and evil as separate, distinct, abstract categories made it still easier to control people. A dualistic morality where the concepts of good and evil, or selfless and selfish, are internalized, coupled with an omniscient God or abstract principle (karma) that "sees" every act, shifts control to internal mechanisms such as fear and guilt.[18]

When one side of a dualism is valued more than the other, or thought of as superior or higher (however defined), this sets up a hierarchy of value. Dualistic thinking lends itself to hierarchy because when the separation between "this person" and "that person" is made absolute, they can be more easily placed on different rungs. Hierarchies of value based upon such constructions as purity (the caste system) or nobility (kingship systems) justified authoritarian hierarchies.

Authoritarian hierarchy was the fast track to using others. Humans themselves became a resource to use, accumulate, and

---

[18]The sections on good and evil in "Satanism" describe this process more fully.

reproduce. Any ruler who did not jump on this bandwagon was swallowed by those who did. The abstract concept of purity in the East became one of hierarchy's most powerful justifications. The idea of purity originally came from cleansing and purification rites done as preparation for rituals. Later only an elite was allowed to perform certain rites; still later, the elite took on the attribute of being more pure by birth. When purity became an abstract quality it could be possessed, rather than only created through concrete purification rites. Purity itself became a hierarchical concept in that a person was considered more or less pure. This served to harden hereditary aristocratic blood lines and class boundaries, keeping the levels of power distinct and also "pure." Either/or thinking lent itself superbly to this: one is either a Brahmin or an Untouchable, free or a slave, a noble or a serf.

There are those today who challenge dualistic thinking. They see how such conceptualizing has been used to justify great inequities by asserting, "I'm this (superior) and you're that (something less)—and these differences between us are natural; thus different status is warranted." Some ecologists rightly link the culture/nature dualism with civilization's alienation from nature and exploitative abuse of it.

In examining the limitations of both either/or thinking and the dualistic categories that underlie it, we are not suggesting they could or should be done away with. Doing so would merely be dualism in another guise. Reactive attempts to do away with either/or thinking by opposing it to "holistic thought," making the latter superior, just create yet another opposition. Dualistic conceptualizing can increase understanding, help clarify, and is appropriate and useful in many domains that lend themselves to thinking in hard categories. An example is computer technology which builds on the binary "on" or "off" of switches. The fact is that either/or thinking makes abstracting easier. The problem is not dualistic abstractions, but how and where they are used. Just as there are areas where either/or thinking works well, there are areas where it creates false or limiting oppositions. Although either/or thinking is not wrong in itself, in some of the most important arenas of life it is inappropriate and even harmful.

When applied to morality, it is this binary or dualistic "either/or" mode that distorts people's perceptions of the world and of themselves. The ensuing attempts to act upon these distortions are at the core of the moral dilemmas now unraveling the social order, worldwide. Without the reactiveness that is a component of either/or thinking, one would be better able to perceive and deal with the reality of self-centeredness in a pragmatic and beneficial way. Instead, the value and even the necessity of self-centeredness are negated. To the extent that this moral conditioning takes hold in us, we spend our lives struggling against that part of ourselves (the "self-ish") that we have been conditioned to believe we and the world would be better off without (or with less of). On the other hand, the positive and necessary aspects of self-centeredness related to creativity and individuation are overlooked by our morality, which leaves people divided and confused in themselves. This is why many who have never even imagined ridding themselves of self-centeredness nevertheless have not found a way to integrate it without guilt—which is one more sign of how deeply conditioned our usually unconscious attitudes toward it are.

The guilt and frustration that result from attempting to rid oneself of self-centeredness (which is impossible) ironically create more self-absorption—which has nothing to do with caring about others—and is itself literally self-centered. This creates a self-absorbing vicious circle, for most guilt can be traced back to guilt about being self-centered. Either/or thinking creates various types of reactions. For example, the "me first" attitudes much in evidence these days (we call it the Ayn Rand syndrome) react against puritanical, selfless values by embracing self-centeredness as the "real truth." This is a way of giving people permission to "go for it" (self-enhancement) without holding back. But being an either/or reaction (which all pendulum swings are), it also mistakes one aspect of the person for the whole. If we were instead to acknowledge the reality of self-centeredness, along with the reality of care and love for others, we would be able to focus more on appropriately balancing the two, both in our own lives and in our social systems.[18]

Eastern spiritual traditions have correctly intuited the serious limitations of linear thought in terms of its being insufficient for other kinds of awareness. But, given this, they have largely concluded that thought itself is the big hindrance to higher realms of consciousness. Their ensuing villainization of thought is, ironically, a revealing example of linear, either/or thinking. The mistake is to assume linear thought represents all thought. The Eastern methodology thus involves negating thought to transcend it, without a recognition of the dangers involved in disarming one's critical faculties. Authoritarianism depends on such "mental disarmament," which reinforces its capacity to control people emotionally through manipulating fear, desire, surrender, etc. This is a grave flaw in Eastern perspectives.

Since thought cannot be eliminated, devaluing it mainly leads to poor and uncritically naive thinking—and ultimately to more unconsciousness, as opposed to greater awareness. What makes us uniquely human is our capacity to use thought not only as a tool for problem-solving, but as a structure-builder that allows us to integrate our experience in creative and self-reflecting ways. "What are the limitations of thought?" can only be asked by a being that thinks. It is altogether possible that the limitations of thought as a tool for insight are very different from what our history has up to this point displayed. The idea that we as a species have already pushed thought to its limit is

---

[18]"Love and Control: The Conditions Underlying Unconditional Love" shows how making selflessness the pinnacle of love is part of an authoritarian moral order. The ideal of unconditional love is the methodology promoted by both Eastern and Western religious worldviews as the way to bridge the gap (a gap they created) between the sacred and the secular. The chapter reveals how the ideal itself is part of renunciate, dualistic frameworks that artificially distort the experience and expression of love.

itself a very limited, and in a sense arrogant, perspective—especially given that humanity's mental capacities have been drastically limited by its authoritarian conditioning.

Since much of history is a product of either/or thinking, what has not been sufficiently realized is that the binary mode is just one mode—albeit the easiest to access. Its predominance is in part due to the dualistic moral structures of renunciate religions. Renunciation is dualistic by nature, for there must be something to renounce, and something to gain from doing so.[20] Binary thought has been further programmed and reinforced in us by our hierarchical institutions that use it to justify privilege. The justification of privilege always has as its foundation "I'm this and you're that."

Symbol Systems and Power

Power within a culture is directly related to who creates and controls its symbol systems. Throughout history abstractions have been consciously or unconsciously used by those who created them to support their self-interest and justify their privileges. Although killing and physical coercion are the base line of power of political hierarchies, their threat is not enough for long-term continuity. Using fear and punishment alone limit the effectiveness and productivity of people, who will work to the level of fear abatement and no more. Also, such systems are susceptible to being taken over. If actual rewards are slim, there must be belief in some future reward. Authoritarian hierarchies that have lasted constructed symbol systems that used religious authority to justify power and give people hope after death. Also, this mollifies those on top who usually prefer not to face, or be reminded, that those below are being used arbitrarily.

Renunciate moralities that glorify spirit make easy the use and abuse of anything merely worldly (including life itself) for the

---

[20]See "Dualism and Renunciation" in "Oneness, Enlightenment, and the Mystical Experience," and "Good and Evil" in "Satanism."

sake of so-called higher concerns. This is done through the creation, elevation, celebration, and sacralization of a key abstraction—sacrifice. Early sacrifice was concrete, involving material objects such as food, animals, and even people. Just as purity was made abstract, so too was sacrifice. It changed from a way of appeasing the gods through offerings to a moral imperative which boiled down to self-sacrifice. This in turn expanded the moral system from obeying specific rules, such as the Ten Commandments, to an overall prioritizing of renunciation, instilling a new mentality. Self-sacrifice is abstract because what is involved is not any specific act of sacrifice, but rather a generalized way to be. Renunciate moralities lend themselves admirably to authoritarian social hierarchies that leverage power by sacrificing those lower on the hierarchy. Whenever possible this is done by getting people to sacrifice themselves voluntarily through inculcating the authoritarian virtues of unquestioning duty, loyalty, and obedience. These virtues are also made abstract, as it is not a specific duty that is lauded, but duty in general.

Our survival as a species now depends on our using what we have (including ourselves and each other) more awarely and care-fully. The symbol systems of the renunciate moralities that hierarchically leveraged human power through turning "difference" into institutionalized dominance and subordination are no longer viable in dealing with a world of limit. The sacrifice of the many to the few that accumulation cultures have required is now counter-productive. This is because the hierarchical, authoritarian moralities that demand sacrifice can do so only by blocking the intelligence, self-trust, and care needed for survival. This is historically new because technology has leveraged human power beyond planetary ecosystems' ability to correct human abuse.

If it is inherent in the scheme of things that human beings need a moral order based on authoritarian beliefs that use fear of retribution as the basic reason for treating others with decency, our chances for survival are slim. If promulgating self-mistrust is necessary to hold the destructive aspects of self-centeredness in check, as authoritarian moralities all do, then we will remain children, unable to handle intelligently the power that our cleverness has given us.

The old symbol systems that are still operative were constructed when humanity moved into its accumulation stage, when unlimited resources were a given. There seemed to be no end to what could be accumulated. Authoritarian hierarchies and the renunciate moralities that propped them up were part of the old control mechanisms that could build pyramids and complex civilizations, and support leaders whose accumulating ambitions were so large that they wanted to rule the world. Hitler was just the most recent example of this.[21]

Technology has brought about a basic shift to where resources are limited, killing at every level is easy, and the symbol systems that held violence somewhat in check are increasingly harder to believe. This is a shift from a planet of abundance to one of limit, which includes the limit of the planet itself to tolerate the pollutions from unchecked accumulation. It is this watershed change that has brought about the necessity of some kind of paradigm shift, which really means a shift in the symbol system and its relation to power. Whatever form the new symbol system takes, it must include a shift from accumulation to preservation, from exploitation to care, and from otherworldly hope to hope in this world.

Transforming the Symbol System: A Dialectical Perspective

There is most probably an aspect of the universe that operates through a tension between poles or oppositions. Some exam-

---

[21]"Renunciation as Accumulation" in "Oneness, Enlightenment, and the Mystical Experience" shows renunciation to be the mirror image and product of the accumulation mentality. That is, renunciation can only operate through a morality based on the concept of accumulating spiritual merit through self-sacrifice.

ples are permanence and change, buildup and breakdown, creation and destruction, living and dying, order and chaos, freedom and fate. On the physical level there are negative and positive charges in sub-atomic particles; in societies there is the tension between equality and different expressions of power; and on the evolutionary level there is the interplay between competition and cooperation. Given this, it's easy to think dualistically, because oppositions are the most apparent aspect of the universe and thus the easiest to perceive. The limits of dualistic thinking lie in excluding other ways of structuring experience. Both the possible unity behind seeming opposition and the dialectical relationship between the two poles are harder to grasp and require more sophisticated abstractions and mental processes than dualistic either/or thinking affords.

Fortunately, human intelligence is capable of other kinds of mental integration, because there are processes especially important in the human arena that linear either/or conceptualizing cannot capture. Either/or thinking is one particular form, which is pragmatically appropriate to those aspects of experience that most conform to it. Trying to squeeze processes that do not fit a binary mode into binary thought must distort them. What has historically been called dialectical thinking is another way thought can operate that better envisions the workings of relational processes.

Whereas binary, either/or thinking is based on each side of an opposition being static and separate, dialectical thinking is process-oriented and sees that within oppositions there is a movement or growth toward more inclusion that can contain both sides. A dialectical perspective can express the dynamic connection of seeming opposites and is needed to perceive two interrelated parts of a whole. Each side is not only totally necessary for the other to exist at all, but is also often embedded in the other. Living and dying are embedded in each other, as are control and surrender. Through surrendering control to an ideology, one can gain control of one's emotions. Attachment and detachment work similarly. By becoming attached to one person or idea, one detaches from others, and so is no longer controlled by them. Even the ideology that glorifies detachment brings hidden attachments to the ideology itself, and to the emotional control that detachment brings. Surrender brings attachment to whatever is surrendered to and to the powerful feelings it arouses.[22]

The dialectical relationship between competition and cooperation serves as an excellent example of our perspective on dialectics. The emotional confusion that many feel around competition comes from treating competition/cooperation as merely opposites instead of as poles of a dialectical interweave. It is easy and common to favor cooperation morally, while at the same time emotionally applauding and being attracted to "winners." Competition can be looked upon as feeding self-centeredness through creating boundaries and separation. It is possible to focus on the aggressive nature of competition, for victory is dependent on the other's defeat. Yet finding examples of pure cooperation not "tainted" by competition is difficult indeed. Good teams cooperate in order to compete better, whether in sports or corporations.

Let's look at an example of an activity that on the surface appears competition-free. A group of people get together for a barn-raising to help a neighbor. The difficulty in seeing where the competition in this lies is an indication of how so many of our actions are seen through "species blinders." The fact is that the barn-building destroys the homes, and often lives, of all the other species that were occupying that space and vicinity. Here human cooperation levers the already great competitive edge we have over other species.

There is a new paradigm in business that values playing win/win instead of win/lose. Among peers this may work well. But it is sadly naive when the haves of the world feel morally righteous because they are playing win/win with each other, without taking into account how their mutual victory is affect-

---

[22]See "The Seductions of Surrender."

ing the world's have-nots. The ability to play win/win is a privilege. You have to have something to offer to enter the game, or else it wouldn't be win/win. This is not to negate the value or progress of the win/win paradigm. It is simply another example of how cooperation at one level most often contains competition at another. If one values cooperation over competition, then it is very easy to remain unconscious of the competitive element.

Competition and cooperation are two interwoven poles of an evolutionary dynamic that brings forth change. Competition is a honing and refining mechanism built into evolution which pushes against limits, accelerating skill, novelty, and beauty. The harmony within cooperation is obvious. There is also a less acknowledged and lauded harmony in the interplay of competition/cooperation that, if seen, creates a broader framework which can eliminate many of our unconscious and reactive attitudes. If what we need to survive is more consciousness, not more unconsciousness (which polarizing reactions create), then we need to see clearly the nature of our competitiveness so that we can utilize it where appropriate, and temper it where it is destructive.

At first glance competition appears to stem from self-centeredness, while cooperation appears more selfless. We say "appears" because if cooperation did not offer any personal benefits, there would be far less of it. Cooperation can increase personal power, wealth, praise, and security. Cooperatively participating in something larger than oneself fills important needs related to being a social animal. Likewise, "Give and ye shall receive tenfold" is a far more appealing message than "Give and you will get nothing back in return."

Ignoring the dialectical interrelationship between the selfless and the self-centered, altruism and egotism, lies at the heart of many moral confusions and dilemmas. This creates what we call the "spiritual paradox," which can be stated as follows: It is self-centeredness that keeps one from higher spiritual realizations, heaven, a better next lifetime (reincarnation), whatever. So by working at ridding oneself of self-centeredness, one's spiritual goals are achieved. The paradox lies in the fact that having one's own spiritual advancement as the focus of one's life is totally self-absorbed, and hence self-centered at a more hidden level. Religion's glorification of spiritual rewards basically presents them as more sublime pleasures. The desire for pleasure, no matter how exalted, is self-centered.

An early school of Buddhism had, in a surface way, seen the above paradox; "the bodhisattva's vow" is an attempt to resolve the incongruity. "Bodhisattva" is the designation that was originally given to a being who was considered to be well along the path toward "enlightenment" (Buddhahood or nirvana). (Nowadays the meaning is looser in that the vow is often taken by people as a sign of giving priority to selfless dedication to others.) The vow takes this form: "I forsake my own enlightenment and will only work for the enlightenment of others until all beings become enlightened."

Here the attempt is to do away with the spiritual paradox by becoming even more selfless—so selfless that one's own enlightenment is sacrificed. This vow does not address the complexity and depth of the issue of self-centeredness, nor solve it. The simple solution given is quantitative—become even more selfless. This, however, creates another paradox: how can you help others work toward something (enlightenment) if you don't know what it is? One must either have images of what this yet unknown state is, or take the word of someone presumed to be enlightened as to what "the work" should be. In either instance, it is an external authority (a teacher or tradition) that defines the proper path. There is also a secret message and agenda in the bodhisattva's vow which is: if one were only able totally to live up to the vow, then one would be enlightened. For living up to the vow, which is presented as the ultimate in selflessness, makes you deserving of enlightenment.[23]

Viewing the selfless and self-centered as dialectically embed-

---

[23]"What Is Selfless Service Serving?" in the section on Buddhism in *Control* discusses this issue.

ded does not do away with moral dilemmas, but it does change the way they are dealt with. Internalizing dualistic renunciate moralities has created an inner conflict between a "good" (selfless) part and a "bad" (self-centered, carnal) part. This is at the root of self-mistrust, for one can never be good enough.[24]

The dialectical perspective offered here is not merely an intellectual romp. It is a way of raising the level of abstraction, enabling one's point of viewing to be more inclusive. It does not separate process from content, and thus takes movement into account rather than reifying abstractions into static, separate entities. Viewing dialectically individuation and merging, the closing and opening of boundaries, the self-centered and the selfless, and multiplicity and unity can bring a deep shift in the human psyche—if this level of discourse does indeed better fit the way things work. One very good reason for thinking things do work this way is that it explains why attempting to eliminate one side of a polarity has never worked.

The seeming oppositions listed above (and others, too), when conceived only within an either/or framework, depict a universe where each side of the polarity struggles with the other for ascendancy. So the more selfless one is, the less self-centered (and vice versa). This has been the basis of all renunciate moralities. The concepts "selfless" and "self-centered" are both abstractions, as they each abstract out only an aspect of a whole living person. They are both abstractions that have meaning only in relation to the other. To use a metaphor from perceptual gestalt theory, they are like figure and ground for each other, and so each needs the other to exist at all.

Perhaps the most basic polarity is between unity and diversity, the One and the Many. The animistic worldview did not have the abstractions to separate them. Polytheism gloried in diversity, populating its world with a multitude of powers. Monotheism constructed a hard dualism between the One (God) and the

---

[24]"Who Is in Control? The Authoritarian Roots of Addiction" covers the dynamics of the inner battle between one's so-called good and bad parts.

Many (God's creation). And finally, the ideology of Oneness conceived the idea of unity by abstracting it from diversity; it then valued only that pole through making it more real. Viewing unity and diversity as dialectically embedded is a more inclusive abstraction that gives as much importance to individuals as it does to their participation in the whole. It can give support to both the selfless and self-centered, seeing them as interdependent poles in the fabric of existence.

Dialectical conceptualizing may appear more difficult, partially because it is different from the usual way the mind is trained to think. It is more demanding, as it involves an alertness to an ever-changing context. The seeming simplicity of the binary mode is a product of artificially slicing reality in two. The ensuing distortions are the legacy that we must begin to unravel. Dualistic thinking simplifies life because it permits the construction of rules for behavior that can be learned by rote and mechanically followed—"This is good, and that's bad." A morality is now needed that can take into account the interplay of the altruistic and the egoistic, without relegating the latter into the shadow of sin. For it is this outmoded either/or morality that is now casting its shadow over the world.

A prerequisite for real change is a vision for the future that is not merely a reshuffling of old forms. This can only occur through alternative constructions of the Word coming from a process that is not authoritarian. For only by reframing the symbol system and the values it generates can the view of possibility also change. The old order does not relinquish control of the symbol system easily, for to do so is to cede control itself. We view the real struggle today as involving who controls the Word. What's at stake is not only the shape of the future, but whether there will be a future for humanity at all.

Epilogue:
Where to Go from Here?

Behind the masks of authoritarian power is the idea that there is some greater intelligence that knows what is best for others. What this always amounts to is that someone either claims to have that intelligence, or to have a direct line into properly interpreting it. This can occur in any realm and in differing degrees. Its most extreme forms occur when moral superiority is linked to infallibility. The image of the guru represents the epitome of this construction, which is the reason for this book's title. Often included in this is the corollary that the authority cares more about your well-being than you do, and can do so because of being selfless. Whether or not a state of ultimate selflessness or infallibility is achievable by anyone can be debated. Then too, there is the question of how anyone could be certain someone else really is in such a state. What is clear, however, is that obeying others because they claim to be morally superior, or to have an inside track to the truth, not only breeds corruption and lies, but removes people from personal responsibility.

We use the development of the individual as a metaphor to help describe our view of humanity's past, where it finds itself to date, and where it needs to go. In this analogy, pre-history is like humanity's infancy where, as with infants, the prime need is survival. During this stage individuals' lives were totally dependent on their immediate small band. With the coming of agriculture, the species moved into its childhood. As with a child, this period was marked by growth and expansion. As the population mushroomed, small group interdependency was replaced by ever larger authoritarian hierarchies. It was here that the still predominant authoritarian forms, including our current moralities, were initiated.

The industrial revolution and tapping into nature's powers through science accelerated development and expansion, moving us into adolescence. Youth is characterized by great self-absorption. Adolescents play with their newly discovered powers without much knowledge or concern for consequences—especially consequences for others. In adolescence there is often rebellion against adult authority, but not against authoritarianism. Teenagers generally look to or construct new gods and idols to follow. Or they develop a misplaced faith in their own point of view, or that of their peers, by ignoring any information that does not fit. This stance of unchallengeability that is directed toward other authorities is itself authoritarian. Adolescence is also marked by feeling and acting as if one were immortal.

A key element of becoming an adult is facing one's mortality. Doing so can bring a shift in the focus of life, which in turn reorganizes basic habits. Upon seeing aging and eventually dying as part of life, the question then becomes how to do so with care and elegance. Adulthood is a time when acting out of longer-term implications becomes necessary instead of insouciant short-term gratifications. The emphasis turns more to care and maintenance, and one must begin to get a handle on excesses that the aging body can no longer ignore. One realizes that although death is inevitable, one can affect not only the length, but also the quality of life by one's actions. Just as the movement from adolescence to adulthood rarely occurs without some struggle, adjusting to the reality of mortality rarely occurs without some denial.

We view humanity as a whole as likewise struggling with the necessity of leaving its adolescence behind, because it too is facing its mortality. That the species will someday vanish, as will our sun go nova, is not the issue. Upon facing the possibility of imminent extinction through self-destructiveness, the real issue is can people shift their habits to prolong both the length and quality of life on this planet? Similar to the individual, this would, in the species, include a shift in values and behavior to greater preservation and care. As in infancy, humans are again collectively confronted with the tenuousness of existence. The difference is that now we are the danger; but we also have the necessary self-awareness to realize that our survival or demise is in our own hands. As with the individual, this confrontation with death is part of the developmental process that forces a reexamination of values and priorities, which must include how our actions today impact future viability. This is essential in order to grow up, as a person and as a species.

Another necessary element in becoming an adult is realizing that ultimately others cannot know what's best for you. Authoritarian power, whether political or ideological, has been the major form of control throughout the history of our species' childhood and youth. This includes looking for a savior to make things right. The very idea of a savior contains the assumption that such a person knows what's better for you than you do, thus making whatever the presumed savior says unchallengeable. The savior approach to problem-solving not only keeps people childish, it is the basic mode of the old paradigm. It has also justified the greatest violence and abuses. The old paradigms all have some authority—be it a leader, wise man, guru, avatar, representative of god, or prophet—telling the rest of us what life is about and how to lead it. How to replace this old methodology that we are outgrowing is a major issue facing humanity.

The past by its nature has a strong pull—a weighty authority and an implicit credibility. It is natural for solutions that worked in the past to be given priority. This is the power of custom, habit, and tradition, for existing paths are easier to take. It is also natural to believe the answer still lies in the old solutions, but that they just need to be done better, or implemented with more forcefulness. This is a reasonable course until it becomes clear that trying to utilize old forms better makes things worse. That point has been reached, and so the past no longer holds the key. When old paths lead to a dead end, the solutions that worked before become part of the problem. This is why the need for a paradigm shift is in the air.

Where to go from here must come from the interacting perspectives of living people exercising their will not only to survive, but to create a world where there is a future. Hope lies in the possibility that our self-destructiveness is not our true nature, but rather that we have the intelligence and courage to change even the deepest patterns, should this be necessary. It is now necessary; and fortunately change is propelled by confronting a dead end. The old systems of belief, morality, and also of the way power has been constructed, protected, and used have served humanity to bring it where it is today, but are no longer serving. They have become self-destructive. If humanity is to grow up and develop its enormous potential for creativity, it must also face the realities of its destructiveness.

In these papers we have painted only a partial picture of how authoritarianism runs deep in the psyches and structures of humanity. The larger work *Control*, of which this book is a part, will examine a greater range of institutions, issues, and beliefs, showing their authoritarian basis. We do so because what precedes and accelerates change is an awareness not only that change is needed, but also why it is needed. This book does not offer programmatic solutions in the form of specific content. It does offer a different way of conceptualizing both problems and solutions. First and foremost, it aims to show that if the process of change is authoritarian, it is not change at all.

What is basically putting humanity at risk is its technologically leveraged capacity for violence toward itself and Earth's ecosystems. This combined with authoritarian hierarchies structurally produces not only corruption, but the likelihood of those on top using those below uncaringly. During humanity's infancy when the group's well-being was linked with caring for every individual, all children were protected and cared for by the group. Now children, the future of the species, get lost in the shuffle, especially if their parents are incapable or unwilling to care for them. This points to one final example of the dead end of our present course.

One of the greatest sources of violence on the planet is unwanted, uncared for, unloved children. Such children as they grow older are not only typically angry and prone to violence, but are potential time-bombs that can capriciously explode and destroy whatever is around them. A world is being created that is full of people without hope, often driven by hatred and envy, who do not care about their own lives, let alone yours. How can such people really care if life on this planet continues or not? The worldwide increase in population coupled with an increasing discrepancy between haves and have-nots creates more and more people without hope. When a large segment of the population lives without hope, it is dangerous for everyone. If we are to survive, what is needed are people who have realistic hope for a better future and who value themselves enough to care about others and the world at large. This would involve forging a viable morality that makes the self-worth and well-being of all children primary. Thus society as a whole must consider itself the parents of all its children, not leaving the responsibility for their care only with legal parents.

The construction of such a morality is the job of all of us. But if its basis is authoritarian, it will necessarily breed the same old self-mistrust and callous use of people in the name of some unchallengeable "higher" principle. It could be argued that it's too utopian to expect ordinary people to look to themselves as the bottom line of what's right, and also to care sufficiently about the state of the world. It is true that this has never occurred in history—but then it never had to. It is not that people need to move toward personal responsibility, mutual respect, and care in order to become or feel morally better. It is rather that we need to do so simply to survive.

Our hypothesis, which this book develops, is that the powerful and pervasive nature of authoritarian programming can explain the mystery of humanity's seeming dual nature, including the capacity to compartmentalize expressions of violence and care. If our perspective is accurate, it is good news in that we are not biologically stuck, and thus at an evolutionary dead end. On the contrary, we are stuck in outmoded beliefs and methods that give us no idea of our potential.

Democracy, which is an idea, has spread throughout the world in a historically short period of time because it ignites people's aspirations to have more control over their own lives. The ideal of democracy has moved much of the world to where it is today. Democracy in itself, however, cannot cope with the extraordinary challenges the world now faces, because at best a democracy can only reflect the values of its members. If, within democracies, authoritarian values and beliefs are conditioned (to varying degrees) in much of the population, this imposes serious limitations on how democratic the democracy can actually be. Yet democracy is an example of the power of an idea. If, as we assert, current problems are a function of outmoded authoritarian beliefs, this is truly a source of hope: Self-perpetuating structures depend totally on beliefs that live in people's minds. Although beliefs tenaciously resist reorganization, should they change, the changes can come swiftly, with extraordinary repercussions. Seeing more clearly the hidden nature and pervasiveness of authoritarian beliefs can itself undermine their power.

For us, hope lies in the possibility of moving beyond our authoritarian past in order to build together a future that values keeping this planet habitable for its interwoven and interdependent forms of life. If the challenge is met, the world will have to be a better place for those living in it, because for the first time since the early small bands of humanity's infancy, everyone's well-being is once again linked with survival.

Index

Boldface numbers indicate definitions or passages of particular relevance.

378